Reparative Therapy of Male Homosexuality

COMMENTARY

"Throughout the book one is impressed by the tragic irony of the male homosexual in that he is valiantly attempting to find his lost masculinity (lost through unfortunate parenting and through no fault of his own) in the bodies of same-sex partners. The author describes the reparative therapeutic measures which will allow such an individual to achieve freedom from the confines of homosexual behavior."

—Charles Socarides, M.D.
author of *Homosexuality: Psychoanalytic Therapy*

"A clearly written, scholarly book that covers the developmental, physiological, social-psychological, familial, interpersonal, and gender-identity aspects of male homosexuality. This book is recommended reading, not only for mental health worker, but its easy style makes it attractive for those outside the profession."

—Irving Bieber, M.D.
author of *Homosexuality: A Psychoanalytic Study*

"This book offers hope to the thousands of men who do not want to feel coerced by either their own internal conflicts or by outside political pressures to live a life inimical to who they are and to who they want to be."

—Althea J. Horner, Ph.D.
author of *Object Relations and the Developing Ego in Therapy*

"Along with the rising tide of homosexual emancipation, there is, both in the U.S. and Europe, an increasing demand from homosexual people troubled over their inner condition, for sympathetic, constructive—and, as far as possible, reconstructive—help. Nicolosi offers a sensible alternative route."

—Gerald J. M. van den Aardweg, Ph.D.

"Nicolosi is to be congratulated for taking up the gauntlet for a much neglected population: the homosexual male who experiences his sexual orientation as ego dystonic and wants to change."

—Elaine Siegel, Ph.D.
author of *Female Homosexuality*

Reparative Therapy of Male Homosexuality

A New Clinical Approach

Joseph Nicolosi, Ph.D.

JASON ARONSON INC.
Northvale, New Jersey
London

Production Editor: Bernard F. Horan
Editorial Director: Muriel Jorgensen

This book was set in 12/15 Goudy
by Lind Graphics
and printed and bound by Haddon Craftsmen.

Library of Congress Cataloging-in-Publication Data
Nicolosi, Joseph.
    Reparative therapy of male homosexuality: a new clinical approach/ by
Joseph Nicolosi.
        p. cm.
    Includes bibliographical references and index.
    ISBN 0-87668-545-9
    1. Gay men—Mental health. 2. Homosexuality, Male. 3. Fathers
and sons. 4. Gender identity disorders. 5. Psychotherapy.
I. Title.
    [DNLM: 1. Father-Child Relations. 2. Gender Identity.
3. Homosexuality—psychology. 4. Men—psychology.
5. Psychotherapy. WM 615 N651r]
RC558.N53 1991
616.85'8340651—dc20
DNLM/DLC
for Library of Congress   91-4534

Manufactured in the United States of America. Jason Aronson Inc. offers books and
cassettes. For information and catalog write to Jason Aronson Inc., 230 Livingston
Street, Northvale, New Jersey 07647.

This book is dedicated to

Father John Harvey

founder of the homosexual ministry, Courage.

Contents

Preface

The psychotherapy of male homosexuals has been explored for many years. What is new in this book is the interweaving of several strands of clinical research: the development of male gender-identity (Abelin 1975, Greenacre 1957, Greenson 1968, Greenspan 1982, Kohlberg 1966, LaTorre 1979, Mahler 1955, Moberly 1983, Money and Ehrhardt 1972, Ross 1979, Stoller 1968), histories of family dynamics (Bell and Weinberg 1978, Bieber et al. 1962, Green 1987, Higham 1976, Money and Russo 1979, Tyson 1985), and the techniques of psychodynamic psychotherapy of male homosexuality (Gershman 1953, Hadden 1966, Hamilton 1939, Hatterer 1970, Horner 1989, Masters and Johnson 1979, Nunberg 1938, Ovesey 1969, Socarides 1978, van den Aardweg 1986, Winnicott 1965).

I would like to thank a number of people, without whose help this book could not have been written. I want to express my appreciation to my office staff—Jennie Gohn, Margaret Guiteras, Edith Joanis, Joan Multerer, and Cindy Anctil, and very special appreciation to my research assistant, Jeanne Armstrong, whose many hours in the library made this book possible.

I would like to thank the advisory board of my counseling center, the Thomas Aquinas Clinic, for their support, and my good friend Jim Johnson of Beyond Rejection Ministries, who has always encouraged me. I also thank Dr. Jason Aronson for recognizing the value of these ideas and having the courage to publish them.

I would especially like to thank my wife Linda, whose advice, suggestions, and writing ability transformed so many fragmented thoughts into a unified and readable manuscript, during the four long years we spent creating it together.

And most of all I want to express my deep affection for the men in treatment who taught me so much by allowing me the privilege of participating in their struggle.

Introduction

There are homosexual men who reject the label of "gay" along with all of the implications that label would bestow upon them. Although "homosexual" may name an undeniable aspect of their psychology, "gay" describes a life-style and values they do not claim. These men experience conflict between their values and their sexual orientation. Experiencing their personal development to be encumbered by homoerotic desires, they seek not to surrender to, but to surmount their homosexual attractions.

In recent years, the psychiatric profession has reversed its opinion that homosexuality is unhealthy. This has resulted in the abandonment of these men, whom I call *non-gay homosexuals*. Although psychology claims to work from a value-free philosophy, in fact it chooses to devalue their struggles and to counsel them instead for what it invariably interprets to be self-hatred due to internalized homophobia.

In reality, the homosexual condition is a developmental problem—and one that often results from early problems between father and son. Heterosexual development necessitates the support and cooperation of both parents as the boy disidentifies from mother and identifies with father. Failure in relationship with father may result in failure to internalize male gender-identity. A large proportion of the men seen in psychotherapy for treatment of homosexuality fit this developmental syndrome.

Failure to fully gender-identify results in an alienation not only from father, but from male peers in childhood. The twin phenomena of nonmasculine behavior in boyhood and problems with male peers are widely acknowledged in the literature as forerunners of homosexuality. This disenfranchisement from males—and from the empowerment of one's gender—leads to an eroticization of maleness. There is often an alienation from the body characterized by either excessive inhibition or exhibitionism. There is also a deficit in sense of personal power. The resultant homosexuality is understood to represent the drive to repair the original gender-identity injury.

A review of the physiological literature demonstrates that genetic and hormonal factors do not seem to play a predetermining role in homosexual development. However some predisposing factors may make some boys more vulnerable to gender-identity injury.

Problems associated with homosexuality include assertion difficulties, the sexualization of dependency and aggression, and defensive detachment from other males. Male homosexuals typically have difficulty with nonerotic male friendships.

Taking a look at gay relationships, we see there are many inherent limitations in same-sex love. Gay couplings are known for their volatility and instability. Research consistently reveals great promiscuity and a strong emphasis on sexuality in gay relationships. Without the stabilizing element of the feminine influence, male couples have a great deal of difficulty maintaining monogamy.

In spite of the gay man's stated valuing of androgyny, there is a contradictory search in the gay world for the masculine archetype, with nonmasculine men perceived to be lower in the status hierarchy. Gay relationships are also inherently troubled by the limitations of sexual sameness, making the sex act characteristically isolated and narcissistic through the necessity of "my turn–your turn" sexual techniques. There is not only an inherent anatonomical unsuitability, but a psychological insufficiency that prevents a man from taking in another in the full and open way of heterosexual couples.

In recent years, gay liberation writers have demanded not only society's tolerance, but its approval of the gay lifestyle and the homosexual condition. Promiscuity is either denied, or it is rationalized as an acceptable part of the new social order which, it is said, the homosexual condition necessitates. Those who do not equally value homosexuality are considered to be homophobic, that is, irrationally fearful. Gay writers do not acknowledge that it is legitimate to place higher worth on heterosexuality within the framework of one's value system.

Reparative therapy for homosexuality is based upon

object relations theory and empirical studies in gender identity. One of the first goals in therapy is to clarify the family dynamics that may have led to a man's homosexual condition. Making peace with father is one early issue. Preliminary treatment goals include growth in self-acceptance and an alleviation of excessive guilt. There is considerable discussion of gender difference, and an acknowledgment of the empowering effects of growing fully into one's gender. Growing out of the false self of the compliant "good little boy" is a goal for many clients. There are many initiatory challenges for ego-strengthening and self-assertion. In group therapy the client is challenged to develop self-assertion through effective verbalization. Male bonding is an especially important goal through the development of mutuality in nonerotic same-sex friendships. For the homosexual, defensive detachment usually creates a resistance to making friends with ordinary, "nonmysterious" males.

The therapeutic relationship is critical in reparative therapy, and particular transference issues must be addressed within it. Many of these are in fact reenactments of the relationship with father. A negative transference can be valuable if it is understood by client and therapist. The female clinician can play a role in reparative therapy, but ultimately she must be prepared to surrender the client to work with a male therapist.

Reparative therapy is not a "cure" in the sense of erasing all homosexual feelings. However it can do much to improve a man's way of relating to other men and to strengthen masculine identification. As a result of treatment, many men have been supported in their desired commitment to celibacy, while others have been able to progress to the goal of heterosexual marriage.

I

Striving for Gender Identity

Masculinity in males is not simply a natural state. . . . rather it is an achievement.

—*Robert Stoller*

I cannot think of any need in childhood as strong as the need for a father's protection.

—*Sigmund Freud*

1

Non-Gay
Homosexuals:
Who Are They?

Much has been written in recent years about embracing the gay life-style and "coming out of the closet." Coming out is said to mean throwing off the burdens of fearfulness and self-deception to embark on the road to freedom and personal integrity.

Yet there is a certain group of homosexual men who do not seek fulfillment through coming out into a gay identity. These men have chosen to grow in another direction. The word *homosexual* names an aspect of such a man's psychological condition. But he is not gay. *Gay* describes a contemporary sociopolitical identity and life-style that such a man does not claim. I call him the *non-gay homosexual*.

The non-gay homosexual is a man who experiences a split between his value system and his sexual orientation. He is fundamentally identified with the heterosexual pattern of life. The non-gay homosexual feels his personal progress to be deeply encumbered by his same-sex attractions.

Before the Gay Liberation Movement, the homosexual was portrayed in psychiatric literature in a one-dimensional manner from the perspective of his "medical condition." Now the gay movement has encouraged new research, often conducted by gay researchers, to shed long overdue light on the personal and relational issues of the gay experience. With the help of these studies, men can now decide whether they want to embrace the gay life-style or to take the road that leads to growth out of homosexuality. It is my hope to help illumine the latter road—the one that leads toward wholeness.

A 16-year-old young man came into my office, concerned that he might be homosexual. I told him that if he was, he could choose Gay Affirmative Therapy, or he could seek to grow out of homosexuality. I then proceeded to tell him about the men in therapy with me. At first he seemed perplexed, and then after some consideration said: "Oh, you mean they're not *yet* out of the closet?"

The young man had been confused by the popular rhetoric that assumes that if you are homosexual, then the only honest response is to live out the gay identity. Believing this, he was surprised to hear that there are men who, out of the fullness of their identities, choose a different struggle.

Those who seek reparative therapy do not blame social stigma for their unhappiness. Many have looked into the gay life-style, have journeyed what became for them a "via negativa," and returned disillusioned by what they saw. Their definition of self is integrally woven into traditional family life. They refuse to relinquish their heterosexual social identity. Rather than wage war against the natural order of society, they instead take up the sword of an interior struggle. As one 23-year-old client explained:

"I've had these feelings and these urgings, but the idea of being a gay person is just ridiculous. . . . it's such a strange lifestyle, on the fringes of society. . . . it's something I could never be a part of."

Another young man said:

"I have never believed I had homosexual tendencies because I was 'born that way.' It is quite an insult to my dignity and a gross disservice to my quest for growth to be told that I have no hope for change."

Said another:

"To me, embracing a homosexual lifestyle has been like living a lie. I have found it to be a painful, confusing and destructive force in my life. Only since I have started to look at what is behind these homosexual feelings have I really begun to find peace and self-acceptance."

Both society and psychology need to understand who the non-gay homosexual is. Society now views this group with a certain derision, and psychology perceives him as self-hating and misguided. His identity is lost between the cracks of popular ideology. The straight world shuns him, and the gay world considers him not their own.

The mental health profession is largely responsible for the neglect of the non-gay homosexual. In its attempt to support the liberation of gays, it has pushed underground the other population. By no longer categorizing homosexuality as a problem, it has cast doubt on the validity of this group's struggle. The non-gay homosexual himself has also contributed to this social neglect. He is not likely to be found at parades or rallies celebrating his identity. He would rather resolve his conflicts quietly and discreetly. How paradoxically conservative are the men who wage this countercultural struggle! Today, even child molesters and prostitutes tell their stories to Oprah or Geraldo.

It is unfortunate that the non-gay must be identified by what he is not. The gay world's assumption is that what keeps him in the closet is fear or ignorance, and that with enough time and education he too will find liberation. Yet *not to be* gay is as much a decision and a conscious choice about one's self-identity as is deciding *to be* gay. For such a man, not coming out can be a dynamic place of growth and self-understanding, a place committed to change. To him, "the closet" is a place of choice, challenge, fellowship, faith, and growth – an interior place that has often opened up into transcendence.

Recently, great progress has been made in acknowledging the gay man in society. Now, the same understanding must be extended to the non-gay homosexual. He has made a valid philosophical and existential choice. He is not a guilt-ridden, intimidated, fearful person. He is someone who, from the fullness of his own identity, seeks not to embrace – but to transcend – the homosexual predicament.

2

The Politics of Diagnosis

All three great pioneers of psychiatry—Freud, Jung, and Adler—saw homosexuality as pathological. Yet today, homosexuality is not to be found in the psychiatric manual of mental disorders (*DSM-III-R*).

Were these three great pioneers just reflecting the ignorance and prejudice of their times about the homosexual condition? Is this radical shift due to our modern-day enlightened, sophisticated attitude? Has there been any new research to account for this shift of opinion? In fact, no new psychological or sociological research justifies this shift. Research did not settle the question. It is politics that has stopped the professional dialogue.

Militant gay advocates working in a small but forceful network have caused apathy and confusion in American society. Gay militants insist that acceptance of the homosexual as a person cannot occur without endorsement of the homosexual condition. Our culture's intelligentsia—which is self-conscious about seeming intolerant—proclaims homosexuality to be normal. However it is still not so for the average person, for whom it "just doesn't seem right."

HISTORY OF DIAGNOSIS

In 1952, the American Psychiatric Association's *Diagnostic and Statistical Manual of Mental Disorders* (*DSM*) listed homosexuality among the sociopathic personality disturbances. In 1968, the *DSM-II* removed homosexuality from the sociopathic list, categorizing it with other sexual deviations. This revised *DSM* classification considered homosexuality a problem only when it was incompatible with the person's sense of self. When the condition was compatible—that is, the man was comfortable with his homosexual thoughts, feelings, and behavior—homosexuality was not considered pathological.

This is a false distinction. The problem lies not in the person's attitude toward his homosexuality, but in the homosexuality itself. Although homosexuality may be compatible with the *conscious* ego, it can never be compatible on the deepest levels of self, for homosexuality is symptomatic of a failure to integrate self-identity. Symptoms will always emerge to indicate its incompatibility with the true self.

In 1973, the *DSM* was further revised, and now homosexuality is not referred to at all: no reference is made to it by name within the diagnostic manual.

Actually, there is an oblique reference in the catchall category of "Other Sexual Disorders Not Otherwise Specified." Here they describe "persistent and marked distress about one's sexual orientation." Reference to homosexual orientation is avoided as if "persistent and marked distress" could also apply to heterosexuality.

Yet in the history of psychiatry, has a heterosexual ever sought treatment for distress about his heterosexuality and wished to become homosexual? When I put that question in correspondence to the chairman of the *DSM* Nomenclature Committee, Robert L. Spitzer, he replied, "The answer, as you suspected, is no."

Why does the profession no longer consider homosexuality a problem?

Political Factors

In his scholarly analysis of the American Psychiatric Association's reversal of the diagnostic classification of homosexuality, Bayer (1981) states: "The result was not a conclusion based upon an approximation of the scientific truth as dictated by reason, but was instead an action demanded by the ideological temper of the times" (pp. 3–4).

The combined effects of the sexual revolution and the "rights" movements—civil rights, minority rights, feminist rights—have resulted in an intimidating effect upon psychology. Some writers have even questioned whether "straights" are capable of doing research on homosexuality

(Suppe 1982). Because there is a fear of offending any vocal minority or of being considered judgmental, there has been little critique of the quality of gay life. Although recent behavioral inventories of homosexual men have revealed more anonymous sex than previously imagined, no one dares acknowledge the obvious.

The removal of homosexuality from the *DSM* had the effect of discouraging treatment and research. The bulk of early psychodynamic research and theory, beginning with Freud, indicated that homosexuality is not a natural, in-born condition. Yet the literature came to an abrupt stop when it became common knowledge that homosexuality was in fact not a problem. This discouraged clinicians from communicating with each other, and from making presentations at professional meetings.

The silence among researchers was not brought about by new scientific evidence showing homosexuality to be a normal and healthy variant of human sexuality; rather it became fashionable not to discuss it any longer. Although analysis of the condition effectively ended, research has continued on a strictly behavioral level—but void of analytic comment.

Other pro-gay researchers fear any inquiry into psychological causes would amount to a concession of pathology; after all, there has been no similar investigation of the causes of heterosexuality (Stein and Cohen 1986). They have encouraged only the search for a genetic or endocrine basis for homosexuality, in the belief that such a discovery would once and for all resolve the issue of homosexuality's normality.

It is possible that there could be some predisposing

genetic factors, but in this regard one might consider a parallel with alcoholism. Although there is now greater recognition of some biological predisposition to alcoholism, it continues to be acknowledged as a problem, it continues to be treated, and the most successful treatments have been found to be socially and spiritually supportive therapies.

Humanitarian Motives

Beyond political pressures, there were two other reasons why the psychiatric profession removed homosexuality from its diagnostic manual. The first is that psychiatry hoped to eliminate social discrimination by removing the stigma of sickness attributed to homosexual people (Barnhouse 1977, Bayer 1981). Most psychotherapists are personally committed to removing emotional distress and diminishing the destructive effects of socially imposed guilt. There was a leap of assumption that continued diagnosis of homosexuality would perpetuate society's prejudice and the homosexual person's pain.

The second reason is that the psychological profession has failed to identify, with certainty, the psychodynamic causes of homosexuality, and consequently to devise a reasonably successful treatment for it. Historically, the cure rate in the treatment of homosexuality has been low. In those few studies that do claim success, the percentage of clients converted to heterosexuality runs from 15 to 30 percent, and there is question whether "cure" was maintained on long-term follow-up. Such results have culminated in an acceptance of the condition.

However, while the humanitarian intent cannot go

unappreciated, failure by the profession to find a successful cure should not be the criterion for determining normalcy. We are resorting to the logic "if we can't fix it, it ain't broke." The psychological profession is responsible for diagnosis — for identifying what is "dis-ease" or loss of ease within the person. It is not for the profession to erase diagnosis for lack of a ready cure.

THE PROBLEM OF REVERSE DISCRIMINATION

Although the intention has been to end discrimination, one result has been discrimination for a different group of people — those men whose social and moral values and sense of self cannot incorporate their homosexuality. In its new outspokenness, the gay movement portrays a false scenario wherein the so-called victim-patient is invariably preyed upon by the "victimizing mental-health profession-al" who trades on such a man's homophobia. Forgotten is the homosexual who, out of a different vision of personal wholeness, legitimately seeks growth and change through the help of psychotherapy. Unfortunately, these men have been labeled victims of psychological oppression rather than the courageous men they are, committed to an authentic vision.

Failure by the psychiatric profession to recognize homosexuality as an unwanted condition for some men serves to discourage members of the mental health profession from offering treatment. Most harmfully, the client himself is disheartened, since the very profession to which he turns for help tells him that it is not a problem and he must accept it. This is extremely demoralizing for the client, and it makes his struggle to overcome homosexuality that much more difficult.

Some people define the whole person by his unwanted sexual behavior, based upon the simplistic phenomenological premise "You are what you do." In contrast, my clients experience their homosexual orientation and behavior as *at odds with who they really are*. For these men, their values, ethics, and traditions carry more weight in defining their personal identity than their sexual feelings. Sexual behavior is just one aspect of a man's identity, an identity that continually deepens, grows—even changes—through his relationship with others.

Is it possible to address the needs of the non-gay homosexual and still propose a model of psychological disorder that will not offend those who do *not* wish to change? The only answer is to "agree to disagree" by allowing the debate to continue, rather than putting an end to the discussion through pressure and intimidation.

We must not lose sight of the fact that the gay man's right to live his life-style is accompanied by psychology's responsibility to discern whether such a life-style and identity are healthy. The psychological profession has a responsibility to continue to explore the cause, nature, and treatment of homosexuality. I do not believe that the gay life-style can ever be healthy, nor that the homosexual identity can ever be completely ego-syntonic.

3

The Failure of the Mental Health Profession

Influenced by the popular assumption that homosexuality is in no way amenable to change, most psychotherapists today proceed to bring about "cure" by encouraging the client to accept his homosexuality. The most effective treatment is considered to be desensitization to feelings of guilt. This is done not because most therapists advocate the gay life-style, but because they see no successful treatment.

Behavioral psychologist Joseph Wolpe (1969) was faced with a religious client who felt guilty about his homosexuality. Wolpe had to decide which behavior to extinguish—the homosexuality or the religious guilt. Rather

than try to change the homosexuality, he chose to amelio-
rate the guilt.[1] This case illustrates both the power of the
therapist and the way that power is used all too often by the
psychological profession. Today psychology claims to work
from a "value-free" philosophy. However, decisions such as
this—to eliminate religious guilt—are in fact being made
from another value hierarchy of the therapist's choosing.

Leahey, quoted by De Angelis (1988), describes how
psychology was first understood to be the practical application of philosophy. This philosophy was based in moralism and religious principles, emphasizing man's need to be
attuned to his spiritual nature. By the end of the nineteenth
century, the newer scientific, rationalistic trend arose in
opposition to this tradition. Psychology sought to break all
ties with its philosophical roots and to be the objective,
empirical, and value-free science of human nature. As
Leahey says, the myth was that we had at last found a
philosophically neutral psychology.

In the 1960s, the humanistic movement then influenced this psychology into a new but disguised version of
moral authority. Its new reliance was on the gauge of
feelings to assess morality (De Angelis 1988). This popular
movement of the sixties and seventies opposed the psychological tradition and preached emotional openness, spontaneity, and loyalty to oneself. Growth was no longer seen
as a product of intelligence and problem-solving, but rather
was viewed solely in emotional terms. " 'Feeling good about
yourself' became the litmus test of good behavior, a sort of

---

[1]Two interesting notes on this case: first, Wolpe said he made his decision based upon
the belief that homosexuality was biologically determined. Second, the client later
discovered heterosexual attraction on his own after undergoing assertion training, and
married. Wolpe considered him to be cured of homosexuality.

bastardized moral sense" (De Angelis, p. 5). This human-istic psychology rejected much of the rationalism of the psychoanalytic tradition. It introduced instead the soft sentiment of full acceptance of the person, as he is, *without expectations.* Following the influence of Carl Rogers' client-centered philosophy, therapists were expected to remain neutral and nondirective, and not to contaminate the therapy through any sort of value system.

In reality, however, effective treatment takes its direction from a shared value system between client and thera-pist. Neither psychology nor any other social science can address the question of "what is" without some perspective on "what ought to be." Because of his day-to-day involve-ment in the human drama, the mental health professional is particularly enmeshed in philosophical issues. He must help people who are struggling for answers, and those answers are not to be found solely in behavioral data. Neither will they emerge in a value-free and nondirective client–therapist interaction. Rather, they unfold through the active interplay between client and therapist within the context of their shared perspective of the homosexual condition. Indeed it is demeaning *not* to provide a treat-ment for those who freely choose growth out of homosex-uality.

HISTORY OF TREATMENT OF HOMOSEXUALITY

In the psychoanalytic literature, male homosexuality has long been understood to be a reflection of gender-identity deficit. Recently, this gender deficit has also been empirically demonstrated. However, no consistently successful treatment has followed from that understanding. This may be due to the fact that traditional psychoanalysis made the error of emphasizing overcoming an assumed "fear of females." Rather, the emphasis should have been on addressing problems in relating to men—that is, resolving defensive detachment (Moberly 1983).

The early work of Stekel (1930) reports a number of cases of complete cure, including one in detail, through Freudian psychoanalysis. The work of Rubenstein (1956) offers some valuable insights about prognostic indicators. Reviewing his ten years of psychoanalytic treatment of homosexuals, Rubenstein warns against extreme optimism, but reports that "a fair number of patients can be helped to a certain extent; some can improve well beyond original expectations" (p. 18).

Following the reparative tradition, Anna Freud (1949, 1952) refers to several cases that show "good results," including four cases that led to heterosexual adjustment. Also from the reparative viewpoint, Ovesey (1969) reports three cases to be successful after a minimum five-year follow-up.

Reporting on Masters and Johnson's short-term, intensive psychotherapy program, Schwartz and Masters (1984) describe encouraging results with only a 28.4 percent failure rate after five years. Mayerson and Lief (1965) also report successful outcomes in a detailed study; they found 47 percent of their patients to be functioning heterosexually after follow-up of a mean of four and a half years.

Bieber (1962) claims a 27 percent cure rate for his patients. Ellis (1956) reports 18 of his 28 male homosexual patients had "distinct" or "considerable" improvement in achieving satisfactory sex–love relations with women. Wallace (1969) describes the successful case treatment of a homosexual through a relatively brief psychoanalysis, as does Eidelberg (1956). Similarly, Poe (1952) details a successful case of a passive homosexual based upon an adaptational view of treatment. Utilizing a group therapy format, Birk (1974) also claims significant improvement in a number of cases.

In a study of thirty homosexual college students, Whitener and Nikelly (1964) report considerable improvement among patients who were highly motivated, had relatively healthy character structures, and had not been acting out homosexually for a long period. Of fifteen college students, Ross and Mendelsohn (1958) report that eleven showed from mild to considerable improvement. Monroe and Enelow (1960) describe significant change in four of seven patients.

In a very detailed analysis of therapeutic results, van den Aardweg (1986) divided 101 homosexual clients into four categories: Radical Change, Satisfactory Change, Improved, and No Change. Among those who continued more than several months in treatment, 65 percent achieved results in the Radical or Satisfactory Change categories.

Wolpe (1969) reports a spontaneous reversal of homosexuality in a client after he had left treatment. Pattison and Pattison (1980) describe eleven men who overcame homosexuality through spiritually based conversion. Cases such as these indicate that change can and does occur outside the realm of psychotherapy.

Within psychotherapy, a broad range of treatment approaches have been used, with results that ranged from promising to clearly discouraging. Not until Moberly's contribution of the concept of defensive detachment was the groundwork set for a treatment that followed from a causal model. Moberly identified defensive detachment as the primary block to healing, thus isolating a basic resistance in treatment.

Some other basic errors stand out in earlier psychoanalytic treatment strategies. The classically trained therapist was emotionally distant. Withholding personal involvement merely frustrates the homosexual client, who particularly needs intimate male connectedness, and whose healing comes primarily through the therapeutic relationship. The emotionally detached therapist reactivates memories of earlier frustration from the cold and critical father. To correct this error, Moberly explains that the therapist must be more emotionally involved and, within therapeutic guidelines, permit dependency. The therapist must be of the same sex as the client to allow him to work through developmental blocks with the same-sex parent. In reparative therapy the therapeutic relationship is the central factor in treatment. Not only is the relationship with the primary therapist important, but also with the members of a like-minded psychotherapy group. Mutual, trusting, and intimate nonerotic relationships with males will further the therapeutic process. There is always an underlying, primal identity—in this case, a latent heterosexuality—on which to build change in the client who seeks it. The naturalistic developmental model is used, which conceptualizes progression toward intimacy as being with a mate of the opposite sex.

In reparative therapy the client looks particularly closely at gender identity and his sense of maleness. Successful treatment is based on the client's choice to grow in male identity. He will come to trust that he possesses all the maleness he needs, and therefore he has no more need to look outside himself toward other males. He commits himself to treatment with the belief that "irrespective of how I feel, I am a latent heterosexual."

Treatment offers a particular way of interpreting one's personal history, and of understanding early childhood events and relationships with parents, especially father. It attempts to diminish homoerotic drives through support and education regarding underlying motivations. The goal is to gain an awareness of the issues and a clarity of direction, which will eventually bring about a transformation of the meaning of what the man feels. As Moberly (1983) explains, "Homoerotic feelings must be reinterpreted as emerging from the legitimate need for same-sex intimacy." But only through nonerotic intimacy will male bonding occur and masculine identity form. One client reports:

> I have heard many theories in my search for understanding, but none have rung so true to my life experience as this one. I must say, this strikes at the core of homosexuality. Because of this understanding of myself I have improved in self-esteem, confidence, maturity, and masculinity. It has also reaffirmed the goodness of my being. I walk as a man wounded but healing . . . but full of hope today and for the future.

Treatment furthers the client's goal of outgrowing homoerotic thoughts, feelings, and behaviors. The direction of some men may be family with wife and children; of others, a commitment to a celibate life-style. Most clients focus first on outgrowing homosexual preoccupation, dependent and unsatisfying relationships, and low self-esteem based upon their gender-identity incompleteness.

Treatment Population

This treatment fits the majority of the homosexual clients in my practice. Some others are inappropriate for reparative therapy because they show no signs of gender-identity deficit and do not match our developmental model. Still other homosexual clients are satisfied with their orientation and have no desire for treatment.

"CURE" VERSUS "CHANGE"

In his final work, "Analysis: Terminable and Interminable," Freud concluded that analysis is essentially a lifetime process. This is true in the treatment of homosexuality, which—like many other therapeutic issues such as alcoholism or self-esteem problems—requires an ongoing growth process. Yet while there are no shortcuts to personal growth, how long it takes to reach a goal is not as important as the choice of direction. A sense of progress toward a committed value is what is important. The nongay homosexual is on the road to unifying his sexuality with his masculine identity. That he can look back over the past months and see a realization of some of the goals to which he has committed—this is what gives hope.

Some readers may decide that this approach is reactionary and antigay, antisexual, antifreedom. Rather, for those men who seek an alternative to the gay life-style, this is progressive treatment. It acknowledges the significance of gender difference, the worth of family and conventional values, and the importance of the prevention of gender confusion in children.

Many men have found these ideas to resonate a truth within themselves, seeing them as helpful in outgrowing the same-sex preoccupation that has troubled their lives.

4

The Importance of the Father–Son Relationship

Homosexuality is a developmental problem that is almost always the result of problems in family relations, particularly between father and son. As a result of failure with father, the boy does not fully internalize male gender-identity, and develops homosexually. This is the most commonly seen clinical model.

THE DEVELOPMENT OF GENDER IDENTITY

As very young infants, both boys and girls are first identified with the mother, who is the first and primary source of nurturance and care. However, whereas the girl *maintains* primary identification with the mother, the boy later has the additional developmental task of shifting identification from the mother to the "second other" (Greenspan 1982). It is through his relationship with father that the boy will change to a masculine identification, which is necessary if he is to develop a normally masculine personality (Sears et al. 1957). This additional developmental task for boys explains why they have more difficulty than girls in developing gender identity (LaTorre 1979) and may also explain the higher ratio of male to female homosexuality (Lynn 1961).

Age of Gender Identification

In the course of the child's life, every significant developmental lesson has its critical periods of receptivity. These periods of heightened awareness appear to have a biological basis. There is a particular period of openness to language, which is best taught during the first three years, after which time it is exceedingly difficult to acquire. Receptivity to gender identity also has a critical period, after which the lesson will not be easily learned. Most researchers agree that the critical period for gender identification occurs before the third year (Greenacre 1957, Kohlberg 1966, LaTorre 1979, Moberly 1983, Money and Ehrhardt 1972, Socarides 1968, Stoller 1968). Within that period, the time of greatest receptivity appears to be the second half of the second year.

The child has some sense of the father from the very early months (Loewald 1951, Mahler et al. 1975), in fact, perhaps as early as 4 months of age (Abelin 1975). By 18 months he can differentiate pictures of boys and girls, men and women (LaTorre 1979). On a social level, he himself is increasingly being treated as a male. During this time, the acquisition of language further reinforces the basic division of people as either male or female.

The boy gradually develops a need to move away from mother. He develops an intense intuition based on a bodily sense that he is not only *separate from* mother—in the way sister experiences her individuation—but also *different from* mother, and this new and exciting difference is somehow like father. He gradually begins to view father as a self-like object. Now open and receptive to maleness, he will "exhibit a special interest in his father; he would like to grow like him and be like him. . . ." (Freud 1921, p. 105). The boy does not yet understand that his emerging interest in father comes from a primal affinity based in their shared masculinity. Nor does he realize that father is the embodiment of what he himself is destined to be. Yet somehow there is a familiarity and a charismatic power.

Now with the boy's emerging sense of being like father, a dependency arises. He desires to be received and accepted by his father, and that fragile emerging masculine identity, receiving its only impetus from instinct, must be reflected in their relationship.

Father needs to mirror and affirm the boy's maleness. As Payne explains, "The masculinity within is called forth and blessed by the masculinity without" (1985, p. 13). This beautiful and mysterious match is the union of an inner need and an outer reality. The boy seeks to take in what is exciting, fun, and energizing about his father. There is a freedom and power to outgrowing mother—and this power is personified by the father.

If father is warm and receptive, the boy will be encouraged to dis-identify from the feminine and enter into the masculine sphere. He will then become masculine-identified and most probably heterosexual. If both parents encourage the boy this way, he will be well on his way to fulfilling his male gender-identification and heterosexuality.

FATHER'S INFLUENCE IN SEPARATION FROM MOTHER

One of father's most significant tasks during this period is to protect the child against mother's impulses to prolong the mother–infant symbiosis (Stoller 1979). This intimacy between mother and son is so primal, complete, and exclusive that the father's presence may have to be almost traumatic to disrupt it (Freud 1910). Through his example, the father demonstrates to the boy that it is possible to maintain an intimate but autonomous relationship with the mother.

This triangular relationship of parents and son helps the boy clarify his separateness and his differentness from his mother. It is in this triangular relationship that the homosexual's family background is commonly faulty. Typically there is an overly close relationship between mother and son, with the father distant from both of them. Ideally, the mother and father should work together to assist the boy in the identification shift from feminine to masculine. However, if a too-close mother discourages this gender-identification shift, a father who conveys dominance and nurturance can counteract her regressive influence.

Perhaps one significant factor is the availability of mother when the boy of 2 or 3 is experiencing problems with the father. A receptive and oversympathetic mother might provide such a haven of emotional security that the boy would find it easy to disengage totally from such a father. If the mother tended to be less emotionally available, the boy might be more inclined to tolerate the frustrations of a difficult father.

Many writers recognize the importance of the father in helping the boy individuate from mother (Abelin 1971, 1975, APA Panel 1978, Greenson 1968, Loewald 1951, Ross 1977, 1979). Mahler (1955) describes the importance of a "renunciation of the mother" and believes that a stable image of the father may be necessary to neutralize the threat of reengulfment by the mother.

It is important that the father commit himself to the development of maleness in his son. For this purpose, it is not necessary for the father himself to be very masculine. An effeminate father apparently has no adverse effects upon the boy's gender identity; in fact, many quite effeminate homosexual men have raised heterosexual sons. Once the boy identifies with maleness, he is open to models in other men.

Renunciation of the Feminine

"The first order of business in being a man is: don't be a woman" (Stoller 1985, p. 183).

In very early childhood, many boys imagine that they need not give up one sex to claim the other. However, reality eventually forces the healthy child to renounce the

feminine and surrender its privileges. Yet many homosexual men still hold onto this infantile wish to be both
male and female, expressing it through androgyny and
occasionally bisexuality. There is sometimes an idealization
of women celebrities—Judy Garland, Barbra Streisand,
Marilyn Monroe, and Bette Midler, for instance—and even
an impersonation of such women in a humorous projection
of a particular man's feminine ideal.

Heterosexual men maintain a vigilance against this
pull to return to symbiosis with the feminine (Stoller and
Herdt 1981). For them, heterosexual pairing is a resolution
to this conflict. Through sexual and emotional intimacy
with his wife, a man is free to merge with the feminine, but
in complementary form—without his masculinity being
engulfed by the feminine.

IDENTIFICATION WITH FATHER

For many years, psychoanalytic child-development literature paid little attention to the role of the father. Recently,
there has been increasing acknowledgment of the emotional intensity of the father–son relationship—and in particular, of father's contribution to the boy's gender-identity
formation (Greenspan 1982, Herzog 1982, Liddicoat 1957,
Miller 1958, Mussen and Distler 1960, Tyson 1985, 1986,
West 1959).

We know that the child attempts to mold his own ego
after the person he has taken as a model, introjecting many
of father's personality traits, values, and behaviors. This
primal need of the boy has been referred to as "father

hunger" (Herzog 1982) and "father thirst" (Abelin 1975). Usually it is the father who is the most significant male figure in the life of the boy during his early development. However, it could be any available male: grandfather, older brother, neighbor, uncle. Usually he is the man who is emotionally involved with mother.

Early psychoanalytic attempts to understand *how* the boy identifies with the father placed the emphasis on the theory of identification with the aggressor. In classic psychoanalytic theory of the oedipal conflict, the boy perceives the father as punitive, threatening, and castrating, and identifies with him out of fear. Later theorists referred to such a process as defensive identification. This concept remains significant to us because it represents the boy's earliest experience of competition with another male for the acquisition of his own masculinity. Indeed, resolution of competition with another male is central to the formation of masculine identity. However, in recent years it has become clear that there is much more to identification development.

Since Freud's time, more recent theorists have expanded our understanding of identification by recognizing the significance not only of punitiveness and limit-setting, but also of positive features of the relationship, such as the father's warmth, affection, and involvement (Brim 1958, Parsons 1955). In fact, paternal qualities of warmth and nurturance seem necessary for male gender-identification (Mowrer 1950, Mussen and Distler 1959–1960, Mussen and Rutherford 1963, Payne and Mussen 1956). Five-year-old boys with warm and affectionate fathers have shown stronger father identification than boys with "cold" fathers (Sears 1953). Similar results have been found with adolescent boys (Payne and Mussen 1956). Mussen and Distler (1958) conclude: "Young boys are more likely to identify strongly with their fathers, and thus to acquire masculine interests, if they perceive their fathers as highly nurturant and rewarding" (p. 353). The same researchers found a connection between high masculinity and a boy's perception of his father as both nurturant *and* punitive.

Failure to gender-identify through relationship with father may be due to many influences, including the following:

1. *More Rewarding Relationship with Mother.* Learning theory shows us how rewards (i.e., nurturance and positive regard) play an important role in the identification process. We can see how the boy would be reluctant to surrender identification with mother, if father was the less rewarding parent.

2. *Lack of a Salient Father.* The father's ability to elicit masculine identification in the son is dependent upon two factors—first, his presence as a strong influence within the household; and second, his warmth, availability, and empathy (Ross 1979). Perhaps the best word to describe this combination of qualities is "salience." In fact the very definition of salience—"something that projects outward or upward from its surroundings"—offers a metaphor for masculinity. Dominance plus nurturance equals father salience.

Dominance refers to the following: in the early psychoanalytic literature, the boy is seen as identifying with the father out of fear. This is known as "identification with the aggressor" (A. Freud 1946). The father upsets the comfortable, nurturing, symbiotic relationship the boy has with the mother. The boy must face this challenge, because the rewards father offers – nurturance, high regard, even material possessions – are dependent upon his responsiveness. The father has to be a strong and attractive-enough parent to induce the son to leave the comfortable relationship and original identification with mother.

Nurturance is defined as: warmth, acceptance, presence and availability, caring and physical display of affection for the boy. The nurturance of the mother is more likely to be unconditional; however, since the father mediates between the boy and reality, his nurturance is more likely to be conditional.

3. *Failure to Encourage Autonomy.* The toddler undertakes two major tasks during the same developmental period: autonomous identity formation (including the development of a sense of personal power) and gender identification. Particularly for the boy, these two tasks are highly interdependent – for personal power reinforces the sense of maleness, and maleness reinforces the sense of personal power.

Some fathers use nurturance of the son as a way of satisfying their own narcissistic needs, loving the child in a way that is controlling and self-centered. Nurturance is not sufficient if the father fails to encourage the boy's own masculine autonomy. When love is used as leverage against the boy's masculine strivings, both personal power and gender development are sabotaged.

Masculine autonomy can be thwarted by both *over-protection* and *overdomination*. Friedberg (1975) made the observation: "Children who become homosexuals are those who have been either pampered or who have found themselves to be in a hopelessly inferior position" (p. 202).

4. *Father Absence.* A number of studies show that father absence in boys may result in dependency, lack of assertion, and/or weaker masculine identity (Apfelberg 1944, Bach 1946, Badaines 1976, Biller 1968, 1969, Hetherington 1966, Santrock 1970). In a study of eighty children of Norwegian sailors away from home for long periods of time, boys showed general immaturity, poorer peer adjustment, and stronger strivings toward father identification (Lynn and Sawrey 1959).

There is clear evidence that boys with absent fathers are capable of heterosexual adjustment if they have not experienced emotional rejection from a significant male figure. Without the impulse to guard against hurt, they can grow up with a trusting and receptive attitude toward masculine figures. For the primary cause of homosexuality is not the absence of a father figure, but the boy's defensive detachment against male rejection. As long as the boy remains open to masculine influence, he will eventually encounter some father-figure who will fulfill his needs. Every male has a healthy need for intimacy with other males. This desire emerges in early childhood and is satisfied first with the father, then later with male peers. When this drive is frustrated, homosexual attraction emerges as a "reparative striving" (Moberly 1983, p. ix).

There are many factors influencing the boy's failure to identify with father. Mother dominance, a more rewarding mother, and the narcissistic needs of either parent are among the contributing influences. Yet the pivotal factor remains the father – and whether he is able to create a relationship sufficiently salient to encourage the development of gender identification.

5

Formation of the Father–Son Bond

FATHER AS THE REALITY PRINCIPLE

The mother's relationship to the infant, as we have described, is usually symbiotic and unconditionally accepting. It is not until he reaches out to the earliest symbol of the outside world—his father—that the boy encounters his first real challenge for acceptance. The father symbolizes strength, independence, and mastery of the environment.

Mastery of the father–son relationship is crucial. Where there is traumatic failure in relationship with father, the boy will be deeply handicapped. Relationship with father represents the lifelong task of balancing internal needs with external expectations and requirements. Relationship with father reinforces the Reality Principle (Freud 1949) for the boy.

PHYSICAL NATURE OF THE FATHER–SON RELATIONSHIP

During their son's infancy, most fathers have felt ill-at-ease handling and caring for a fragile newborn boy. Then as the boy enters the toddler stage of reckless exploration of the environment, his high activity level offers a common ground through which he and his father will be drawn together. Free to venture farther and farther from mother, the boy discovers that Dad has a particular appeal distinct from mother – "Dad does things." There is a physical boldness, a masculine energy about the father that the boy finds exciting.

Father–son relationships have always been based upon the sharing of physical activity. In fact, the boy's "need to be shown how" is characteristic of his relationship with his father during the pre-oedipal period (Herzog 1980). A behavioral, bodily phenomenon of identification seems to result from father and son "doing" together. As one of his son's first play partners, father challenges the boy with his masculine form of interaction. At the same time he is setting reasonable boundaries, the father encourages the boy's youthful energy and optimism. From the father, the boy learns that danger can be fun and exciting.

Not only in toddlerhood but on into adulthood, doing

things together characterizes the way males relate to each other. Men tend to view their bodies in terms of strength, agility, and action, and they need to relate on a physical level. Unlike men, most women can relate in a static manner by sitting and talking face-to-face. Similarly, while men view their bodies in terms of how they function, women are inclined to view their bodies in terms of how they look as static objects (Franzoi 1989). And so the task for the developing boy is to find the normal masculine, action-oriented way of perceiving his own body, and to engage it in his relationships with other males.

Boys with gender-identity confusion are often excited about dressing up and being pretty, while not at all interested (in fact, quite resistant) to doing things with their fathers. While not all prehomosexual boys evidence such effeminate behavior, still they often missed this "doing" dimension of development in the early father–son relationship. Later in life, they are often particularly drawn to the mystique of masculine boldness, strength, and power.

In previous generations, it was the day-to-day labor that unified father and son. Traditionally, they had a functional relationship grounded in shared tasks. The son saw his father confront the challenges of life. He witnessed his father struggle with the soil, with the crops, with tools, and with the weather. Or perhaps father had a small business in which the boy could help. He was able to gain a sense of his father's work, and thus to envision his own place in the male world.

Today's technology and division of labor have eroded the common ground upon which the father–son bond was formed. Today, the boy often doesn't understand his father's work. It is typically away from home and is often technical and beyond the boy's comprehension. Because father's work is detached from home life, men today are detached from their own sons. Today it is the mother who mediates between the father and the son, and consequently the boy now sees father through feminine eyes. The link between the father and the son has become distorted and diluted by this feminine perspective. Mother tells the boy who Dad is, what he is about, and what he is feeling. Today we must often artificially create activities fathers and sons can share, such as Little League, Boy Scouts, and camping trips. Arranged as such activities may be, they are nevertheless an important medium for the male bonding that lays the groundwork for masculine identification.

MASCULINE INITIATION

Throughout world history, the transformation from boy to man has required the challenge of an initiation ritual. These trials have always been an important part of human consciousness for males (Bly 1990, Campbell 1971). The masculine-initiation ritual involves death of the boy's premasculine self and rebirth into manhood. With the elements of danger, vulnerability, and the symbolic threat of annihilation, the boy undergoes a trial to determine whether he is strong enough and wise enough to be worthy of the status of a man.

The first initiatory trial occurs during the separation–individuation phase, when the infant begins to see himself as a separate person and reaches out to the father. As he grows and their relationship develops, he eventually learns that his father – who represents the realities of the outside world – will make demands he must meet. For father's love is not unconditional: the boy must work to come to accord with father.

All rites of initiation into manhood involve some personal trial in which an adult male participates. If the boy is successful, the rite culminates with acknowledgment from that man, who passes on the transforming power of masculine energy. This initiation is played out on a dramatic level in cultures such as the Sambia Tribe of New Guinea (Stoller and Herdt 1981). There is great value placed on masculinity in that culture. Sambian men believe their son's masculinity is threatened by too much intimacy from the mother. During the rite of passage into manhood, boys are taken from their mothers and sisters into the forest. In a ritual that is sometimes brutalizing and frightening, the boy is resocialized into manhood so that he will be brave, manly, a husband and a father.

The Sambian rite of initiation illustrates these points:

1. prolonged identification with mother is a threat to a boy's masculinity;
2. masculinity can only be transmitted by other men; and
3. masculinity is a prized commodity to be achieved, not simply acquired.

Where there is a good fight with the experience of acknowledgment, we have full masculinity and heterosexuality. This is not so with homosexuality. There is no direct struggle, no confrontation or competition. Even where there is hostility with the father, it is never a "fair and square" competition with the possibility of the boy being successful. Rather, we see competition with these father figures as indirect and undermining, particularly in the boy's subversive alignment with mother. The boy conspires with the mother to erode, dismiss, or mock the father.

Homosexuality is an alienation from males—in infancy from father, and in later life from male peers. By eroticizing what he feels disenfranchised from, the homosexual man is still seeking this initiation into manhood through other males.

6

Failure of the Father–Son Relationship

Recent studies of homosexual development have begun to place particular weight on the significance of the father–son relationship (Bene 1965, Biller 1974, Greenson 1968, Moberly 1983, Payne 1981, 1984, 1985, van den Aardweg 1986, Yablonsky 1982). This is in contrast to early psychoanalytic studies of homosexuality, which placed major emphasis on the influence of a possessive, intense, and overdominating mother (Freud 1910, 1921).

RESEARCH SHOWING POOR RELATIONSHIP WITH FATHER

Clinical as well as empirical studies have found homosexuals to be more likely than heterosexuals to have had distant, hostile, or rejecting childhood relationships with father (Allen 1962, Bell et al. 1981, Bene 1965, Bieber et al. 1962, Ferenczi 1914, Freud 1905, Jonas 1944, Milic and Crowne 1986, O'Connor 1964, Schofield 1965, Shearer 1966, Siegelman 1974, Townes et al. 1980, West 1959, Yablonsky 1982).

Some studies have been criticized for using patient populations. In response, Evans (1969) and Apperson and McAdoo (1966) used homosexual subjects who were not in psychotherapy. These subjects, too, were more likely to perceive fathers as critical, cold, impatient, and detached. Evans found fathers had spent less time with their homosexual sons in childhood, and had been less likely to encourage their masculinity. Poor relationship with father and later seeking of male attention and companionship are found in many chronicles of homosexuality: "All through life I never touched my father. I was never allowed to even shake hands with him. Everything was at a distance. Everything was very formal. I found myself wishing to be close to him" (Gottlieb 1977, p. 28).

The masculine qualities conveyed in the healthy father–son relationship are confidence and independence, assertiveness, and a sense of personal power. When homosexual clients report what they are attracted to in other men, the masculine qualities that would have been conveyed in the healthy father–son relationship are mentioned over and over: assertiveness, self-confidence, control of one's life, leadership, decisiveness, and power.

In a study of forty homosexual males, Brown (1963) reports not a single case in which a homosexual had an affectionate relationship with his father. Rosen (1988) says, "For males, the presence of a good loving father during development is probably the best proof against homosexual development. . . . I can think of no case . . . where such a father has been present in the early childhood years of development" (p. 21).

Friedman and Stern (1980) concur, describing "a durable father–son relationship" as "a preventative agent with respect to homosexual development" (p. 437). Socarides (1976) says: "Homosexuals consistently describe the father either as a weak, shadowy and distant figure or an angry, cold and brutalizing one" (p. 145). And Bieber (1962) states: "We have come to the conclusion that a constructive, supportive, warmly related father *precludes* the possibility of a homosexual son" (p. 311).

More recent studies of fathers of homosexuals suggest that conclusions such as Bieber's may have been too extreme. Some homosexuals (particularly those without evidence of gender-identity deficit) have had no particular problems in relationship with father. However, clinical evidence indicates that poor father–son relationships are nevertheless predominant.

QUALITY OF ANGER TOWARD FATHERS

Although heterosexual men may describe their fathers unfavorably, homosexual men are stronger in their *rejection of their father as a model*. This appears to be a particular differentiating trait. With homosexual clients, I have often observed a grudge, an axe to grind. Fathers often report their sons seem to hold an unaccountable antagonism that surfaces unexpectedly when their sons take a swipe at them.

And while heterosexual clients may complain about their fathers, they rarely convey those same qualities of festering resentment, hurt, disappointment, and inability to understand what their father is about.

When heterosexual men express disappointment with their fathers, there is usually less frustration, bitterness, and smouldering sense of victimization. They tend to be much more open and expressive of their anger toward their father. They do not tend to hold onto the grudge as tenaciously; often there may be a simple regret as of one who understands the limitations of a loved one.

I have never heard of a homosexual man having a physical altercation with his father. Typically his hostility is expressed indirectly as a festering resentment, impotent anger, and a sense of inferiority. Except for an occasional brief and probably long-remembered outburst, the homosexual son is unlikely to have a frank, full-fledged expression of anger toward father.

I have worked with many heterosexual young men who still sought their father's acceptance and approval. Some of these men have been counseled in joint sessions with father in an attempt to heal the broken relationship. Here I see less of an imbalance of power between father and son, with sons possessing a more independent self-esteem. The sons are able to communicate with a greater degree of mutuality, and there is less deep hurt and longing for approval. When a heterosexual man is distrustful of others, this distrust is not directed specifically toward males. In the case of homosexuals, discomfort and distrust are primarily directed toward same-sex persons.

These unresolved hostilities toward other men are evident in many ways. Gottlieb (1977) makes reference to the "verbal back-stabbing and bitchiness that mark gay life" (p. 81). Describing the politics of homophile organizations, a gay writer, Barry Dank (1974), portrays this ironic situation:

> Based on my observations of the internal politics of a number of different homophile organizations, I have formulated the hypothesis that individual success is predictive of failure—that is, the more successful the homophile leader, the greater the willingness of others to take actions against the leader. It is only the rare homophile leader who can avoid the pitfalls of being successful. . . . In addition, the homophile leader may suffer from a significant degree of insecurity. In this case . . . [his] own insecurity may motivate him to take actions that tend to downgrade his followers. Such actions often arouse even greater jealousy in the followers and reinforce their desire to take actions against [him]. [p. 193]

Homosexual clients frequently report feeling depressed and out of control after returning from their parents' homes, their newly emerging sense of masculine identity having been shaken. In what seems to be an attempt to recapture this threatened identity, they sometimes follow the visit home with an impulsive sexual encounter.

FATHER AS MYSTERY

I have repeatedly seen the theme of the homosexual holding onto the decision that he does not want to be the kind of man his father is. Yet paradoxically, "who he is" remains a mystery. The son may spend his adult life trying to understand his father, who his father is, what he is about.

These three main themes emerge as clients go through the early phase of trying to understand their fathers. Fathers are usually described as critical, often ineffectual, and always mysterious. One client recalls:

My father was always doing something. . . . raking the leaves, chopping wood, or fixing the car. Although he was physically always there, I didn't know much about him because my mother always controlled everything. I realize now that in reality, he was never really a part of what went on in our family.

Another client explained:

I know my father, but I don't know anything about him. . . . you have to read into things and pick up on clues. Sometimes I wonder, is he really angry or is he acting?

One day in a fit of fury I said to my father, "You are a complete mystery. No one can ever figure you out," and I said I resented having to guess and having to try to "read" him all the time. Finally I realized it's not worth it to try — it's simply too much of a burden.

Other Voices, Other Rooms was gay author Truman Capote's first published novel, and it is considered autobiographical. In it he tells of a shy, dreamy boy in search of the father who abandoned him in infancy. Capote says in the preface to the book that "the central theme . . . was my search for the existence of this essentially imaginary person"

(1948, p. xv). The search for a loving father is also illus-trated by gay writer J. R. Ackerley in his autobiographical *My Father and Myself*. Here we see the intense and painful search for the father he never understood. After his father's death, Ackerley reflects:

> My inclination was to blame myself for the failure in communication . . . except in the matter of health, I never gave him a thought. How should one expect confidence from a person whom one regards more as a useful piece of furniture than as a human being? Yet . . . if I took no interest in him, he did not make himself of much interest in me . . . he could easily have captured me if he wished . . . [but] either he did not realize this, or . . . did not want it. [pp. 175–176]

Some clients realize the connection between homoe-rotic attraction and the drive to repair a failed relationship to father. As one 30-year-old client explains:

> My father was a void in my life, and recently I have come to see that all of the men I've been involved with have looked like him. My first lover, Jack, was tall, older, dark, and had a beard. Although I was 25, I felt like a 15-year-old, and I called him "Daddy." It felt so good, so natural when I was with him.

For the rest of his life, the homosexual tries to figure out his father. For him, both father and masculinity remain elusive and mysterious. If father was hostile and antagonis-tic, then he becomes a *confounding mystery*. If father was emotionally distant and inadequate, then he becomes a *longing mystery*.

FATHERS OF HOMOSEXUALS

A review of the father–son literature suggests that fathers of homosexuals frequently failed to provide a relationship sufficiently salient to propel the boy out of the mother constellation. Father-salience requires strength and benevolence. Some fathers were strong but not benevolent, and others were benevolent but weak. Overall, we see fathers who lack salience, whether they be harsh and critical, or passive and withdrawn. The father's attitude toward the son is rarely consistently hostile; more often, it is deeply ambivalent and contradictory. The father may in fact sincerely express his desire for the son's best interests.

In attempting to outline common traits of fathers, we cannot simply categorize them as "bad" or "inadequate." It must be said that many fathers of homosexuals are no more guilty than anyone who has found himself in an unresolvable conflict with a loved one. For reasons he himself does not understand, he often feels himself to be rejected by his own son, a victim of his son's defensive detachment.

Some such fathers have had a strong degree of concern for their sons. One man, who demonstrated sincere commitment to therapy for his homosexual 15-year-old, recalled: "I remember, when you were just a little baby, holding you in my arms and thinking to myself, I only want the best for you. I want to give you every opportunity to be the best person you can possibly be."

What went wrong? We may only speculate. In his case the father had married in his early twenties, when he found out the boy's mother was pregnant. The marriage was a disaster and a divorce soon followed. The father's own life was in turmoil, and he was unable to attend to the emotional needs of his son.

Many fathers are not by any means characterized by explicit personality deficits. An otherwise sensitive and loving father can become emotionally unavailable through situational influences such as his absence, the financial and emotional burdens of a new family, or a difficult relationship with the boy's mother.

Explicit Personality Deficits

Although it is not always apparent to us why the boy should have experienced rejection from his father during the critical developmental period, in some cases, we see that the father does have explicit personality deficits. These traits are likely to include egocentrism, narcissism, criticalness, and coldness. Sometimes a father who is warm and consciously concerned about his son still fails to accept him in a genuine way. Father might feel threatened by the boy's individuation or even by his presence in the family. He may transfer to the son his unresolved hostility and rivalry with his own father or older brothers. This can all be either conscious or unconscious.

Father must be secure enough in his masculine identity to promote his son's own identity formation. A father who feels threatened may project his insecurities on his son at the critical time of gender-identity formation. A father may behave very adequately with some sons, while displacing neurotic or immature needs on the homosexual son. A negative dynamic, in which both father and son participate, sets in motion early on. For the rest of their lives they unknowingly perpetuate this mutually frustrating relationship. Once male bonding does occur, then future disappointments or rejections from father or other men, while possibly causing emotional hurt, will not affect gender identity. In fact many boys, during the critical period for gender identification, at times may reject the father. A healthy and emotionally resilient father, however, can reach out and reestablish the relationship. The critical variable may be the father's capacity to be genuinely "for" his son rather than requiring the son to meet specific expectations in exchange for acceptance.

One client described his father's narcissistic qualities: "When I came back from South America, some relatives came over and wanted to hear about my vacation. My Dad has this knack for not letting me tell my story. It was his story. I'm fresh off the plane and *he's* telling all the relatives my story."

One oft-repeated criticism of father is his emotional absence from the family. Although he may appear strong, he may have failed to take responsibility for family life. Fathers of homosexuals are often described as detached, helpless, pouting, avoidant, and uninvolved in family affairs except to interject criticism. Homosexual clients often will portray their fathers as being on the outs with the rest of the family, with other family members making fun of "old Dad" behind his back.

Sometimes giving is generally difficult or conflictual for father, and he may place the son in the role of "take care of Mom for me." He is often at odds with the family agenda or involved in his own, being out of synch with what is happening. Mother is busy organizing, the children are

looking for leadership and father is not involved. A client
described his father as follows:

> You get criticism like nobody's business. . . . he's not happy
> unless he can gripe and bitch. He steps back, lets us do the
> work, and just steps in to criticize.
>
> When you are cleaning the kitchen, he'll sit there and
> tell you each move to make, but he'll never lift a finger. He
> won't do it, but he'll make sure you do it his way.
>
> My family gave my father a lot of power he didn't
> deserve. He wasn't the real leader, he wasn't the strong
> person. My mom gave him a lot of power because she
> thought that was the right thing to do. She'd say, "Go ask
> your father." Ask my father? That was a joke.
>
> My father was always in the backseat. If you asked
> him something he'd tell you to ask someone else. He
> couldn't make any decisions at all.

A number of fathers of homosexuals have passive-
dependent relationships with their wives. It is as if they are
threatened by their son, seeing him as one too many males
in the home. I suspect these fathers often had to compete
with their own brothers for mother's attention.

An artistic portrayal of a common type of father of a
homosexual can be seen in gay painter David Hockney's
"Portrait of My Father" (1955). Similarly, in "My Parents"
(1977), we see mother involved while father is tensely
preoccupied and withdrawn.

The cold, detached, narcissistic type of father is described by John Rechy (1963):

> I loathed Christmas.
> Each year, my father put up a Nacimiento. . . . an

elaborate Christmas scene, with houses, the wise men on
their way to the manger, angels on angelhair clouds . . .
Weeks before Christmas my father began constructing it,
and each day, when I came home from school, my father
would have me stand by him while he worked . . . Sometimes hours would pass before he would ask me to help him,
but I had to remain there, not talking. [p. 17]

In such cases, the son is seen as a narcissistic threat by the
father. Ross (1960) refers to this dynamic as "rivalry with
the product."

II

Related Problems

Finally, I submitted my soul to some evaluation. What was going on that kept the homosexual feelings alive? I discovered the unnatural lack of feelings I had toward my father. At closer glance, I became aware of deep feelings of anger and resentment toward him that I had suppressed for years.

— Andy Comiskey

7

Problems Emerging in Childhood

DEFENSIVE DETACHMENT IN BOYHOOD

The prehomosexual boy has typically experienced a hurt and disappointment in his relationship with father. This hurt may be the result of active abuse or simply passive neglect. The boy reacts to this hurt by passing through two phases. If his overtures to the father are ignored or rejected, and he continues to feel frustrated with father's lack of affirmation, the boy may lapse into a strategy natural for all children his age who are frustrated—that of protest (Dallas 1990). This protest period will include crying, demanding, and disruptive behavior.

Within the unhealthy family system these displays of protest are ignored and in some cases punished. This teaches the boy a lesson that direct protest gets him nowhere—in fact, it may make things worse. When parents do not respond to the boy's protest, he eventually lapses into helplessness and surrenders the struggle. The lesson learned from this failed protest is that he has no alternative but to retreat to mother carrying a sense of weakness, failure, depression, and victimization. As protection against future hurt, he defensively detaches from father (Moberly 1983). This final self-protective stance is subjectively experienced as "never again" (Schechter 1978). It says, "I reject you *and what you represent*—namely, your masculinity." Later in childhood he will indirectly express his anger by ignoring father and denying that he has any importance in the family, conspiring with mother in collusion against father.

Defensive detachment becomes particularly apparent when the prehomosexual boy enters the latency period and is about 5 to 12 years old. He is typically fearful and cautious toward other boys his age, staying close to his mother and perhaps grandmother, aunts, or older sisters. He becomes the "kitchen window boy," who looks out at his peers playing aggressively and, what appears to him, dangerously. He is attracted to the other boys at the same time he is frightened by what they are doing. Defensive detachment emotionally isolates him from other males, and from his own masculinity. Females are familiar, while males are mysterious.

Then when sexual needs begin to seek expression in early adolescence, it is understandable that the direction of such a young man's sexual interests will be away from the familiar and toward the unapproachable. We do not sexualize what we are familiar with. We are drawn to the "other-than-me."

A further damaging lesson will be carried over into later life. Having learned that direct assertion—at least in relation to other males—is useless, he will perceive himself as passive and weak in relation to male peers.

CROSS-GENDER BEHAVIOR

A high correlation has been established between homosexuality and nonmasculine behavior in boyhood. In a study of 575 homosexual and 284 heterosexual men, Bell and colleagues (1981) found that the most significant correlate with adult homosexuality was "gender nonconformity" recalled from childhood. Friedman (1988) summarized a recent review of the literature as follows: "Most adult homosexuality is . . . preceded by some type of prepubertal gender disturbance in childhood" (p. 212). In a 1980 study, Friedman and Stern say: "Although we were well aware that prehomosexual youngsters tend to avoid aggressive activities, we were astonished at the universality of this finding" (p. 436). In a 10-year study of sixteen effeminate boys, Zuger (1978) found that 75 percent grew up to be either homosexual, transvestite, or transsexual. Zuger regards early boyhood effeminacy not only as a predictor of homosexuality, but as the first stage of homosexuality itself (1988). Money and Russo (1979) followed eleven boys with gender-identity confusion to young adulthood, and all but two became homosexual.

According to Hockenberry and Billingham (1987), it appears that the five most potent discriminators determining sexual orientation in a boy are:

1. whether he plays with boys or girls,
2. his preference for boys' or girls' games,
3. whether he imagines himself as a sports figure,
4. whether he reads adventure and sports stories,
5. whether or not he is considered a "sissy"

Hockenberry and Billingham found that *an absence of male behaviors in boyhood* is an even stronger predictor of homosexuality than the presence of feminine traits.

In Evans' (1969) replication of Bieber's classic study with the same questionnaire on a nonpatient sample, homosexuals similarly described themselves more often as frail or clumsy as children. They tended to be fearful of injury, avoided physical fights, played more with girls, and described themselves as loners who seldom played boys' competitive games.

In a very large study — 1,400 homosexuals and 200 heterosexuals — Harry (1982) found that significantly more homosexuals recalled being called "sissy," being social loners and wanting to be girls, playing with girls, and cross-dressing.

In a study of eighty-nine homosexual men, Saghir and Robins (1973) also found that 65 percent recalled a "girl-like" syndrome which was characterized by avoidance of play with other boys, aversion to boys' games and activities, and an interest in playing with dolls. Green and colleagues (1987) also found that female role-playing and boyhood doll play were specifically associated with homosexual orientation in adulthood. In a study of 206 male homosexuals and 78 male heterosexuals, Whitam (1977) found significant differences with respect to all of the following childhood traits: (1) interest in dolls, (2) cross-dressing, (3) preference for company of girls in childhood games, (4) preference for company of older women rather than older men, (5) being regarded by other boys as a sissy, and, (6) sexual interest in other boys rather than girls in childhood sex play. Moreover, it was found that the greater the number of childhood indicators, the stronger the homosexual orientation in adulthood.

Homosexuals have been found to score lower in boyhood on the Physical Aggressiveness Scale (Freund and Blanchard 1987) and to have inhibitions in expressing aggression and asserting themselves in social situations (Whitener and Nikelly 1962). Some writers suspect that perhaps on some conscious or unconscious level, the mother communicates an expectation for effeminate behavior (Green 1987, Miller 1958, Wolpe 1969). In some cases of childhood gender confusion, one or both parents have been observed to be in covert collusion with the child (Money and Russo 1979). As Green points out, if the parents do not actively discourage effeminate behavior, their neutrality may be interpreted as condoning (private correspondence). This dynamic is described by a 43-year-old client:

> My friend took a picture of me in drag outside this bar in San Francisco. Later, he showed the picture to my mother. My first feeling was embarrassment, but then I thought, "Well, Mother, isn't this what you wanted?"

The boy who is developing homosexually tends to favor the company of little girls. However, the prehetero-

sexual boy is likely to express a contempt for little girls. There is a need to strongly differentiate himself as masculine in order to solidify his male image. The intense energy invested in rejecting little girls is suggestive of a reaction formation—perhaps against the unacceptable desire to regress to a feminine identification. He is typically involved in "no girls allowed" clubs, team sports, contests, bets, showing off, bluffing, and bragging—the means by which boys compete with each other in order to recognize and reinforce their sameness.

Childhood gender disturbance is associated with "psychopathology and familial pathology" (Friedman 1988, p. 212). Yet there are critics who oppose the treatment of gender disturbance in children. Stein and Cohen (1986) believe that parental disapproval of gender nonconformity should *itself* be confronted, rather than providing treatment for those children.

PROBLEMS WITH BOYHOOD FRIENDS

Most homosexual men report an unease in the company of other males that traces back to problems in early childhood. Research shows a significant correlation between difficulty with male peer relationships during boyhood, and later homosexual orientation. In fact, according to van den Aardweg's (1986) review of the literature, poor peer relations can be identified more often in the background of homosexuals than can poor relationship with father. This is not to dismiss the significance of relationship with father. Often the experience of rejection by father would have occurred at an age too early to be recalled, while problems with boyhood friendships are usually vividly remembered.

Friedman (1988) found male–male bonding relationships to be "frequently painfully distorted during the juvenile phase of childhood in homosexual males" and hypothesized that this phenomenon was "of central etiological significance" (p. 240) in the development of homosexuality. Homosexual clients characteristically describe themselves as feeling frustrated and rejected in boyhood because they felt weak, unmasculine, and unacceptable, and thus were on the outside of their male peers' activities. The male peer group begins to be strongly influential as early as the second half of the second year. The importance of other boys during development is highlighted by Fagot's (1985a,b) studies, which found even nursery school boys to be highly influenced by their male peers—more so than by their teachers.

Through a balance of challenge and support, boys in groups have a unique power to actualize masculine potential in each other. The unique way in which preadolescent boys are capable of alternately putting each other down, then lifting each other up with affection and compassion is captured in the movie *Stand By Me*. Males in groups teach each other a resiliency and trust that the prehomosexual boy—who is on the outside of these activities—misses. Often we hear the vignette of the prehomosexual boy removed and distanced from his male companions, looking out the kitchen window at the other little boys playing actively, even aggressively. The "kitchen window boy" is attracted to yet fearful of them, wishing he could be with them and play freely like them. He envies their boldness but is afraid to join in. Somehow he feels incapable, unprepared, or ill equipped. Instead, he turns back to the company of mother, who is busy in the kitchen. William Aaron describes this sort of situation in his autobiography (1972):

> Contributing to my retreat into homosexuality was that I was one of those sensitive, "artistic" children with neither the talent for nor interest in any of the usual "masculine" pursuits. I hated physical activity—sports and games most of all—and when I would make an effort to be part of the gang I would fail so miserably to perform well that for a long time afterward I would suffer from the shame of ineptitude. . . . I was a classic case in that I (later) felt out of place in a man's world, and comfortable and capable in a more esoteric environment. [pp. 21–22, 29]

The prehomosexual boy's longing may be with him for the rest of his life, along with the window, the symbol of emotional detachment. Malcolm Boyd describes such a quality of detachment in *Take off the Masks* (1984):

> By the time I reached adolescence, I was a frail youngster who read a lot of books, was extraordinarily intense and solitary. My intermittent friendships with a few other boys usually ended abruptly and without explanation. I believed that the fault lay within me, a result of my personal ineptness in sustaining relationships. For the most part I looked at the outside world of boys my own age like a prisoner looking through a barred cell window. I felt locked in the cell of myself, and I ached to get out. [p. 34]

A client often spoke about a relationship with a friend at work to whom he was very attracted. This fellow worker apparently personified many of the male traits that he felt he himself lacked. He reported the following dream:

> I was an adult but I was playing like a little boy, and I was on roller skates, carrying a red toy truck under my arm, on my way to this co-worker's house. There I stood, outside his house, waiting for him to come out to play with me.

This dream symbolized his current predicament. It captured that state of suspension, that passive, receptive waiting for male acceptance. In our interpretation of the dream, the client came to realize the image represented his own unconscious identification as a little boy in a state of waiting. . . . of looking for the masculine to come to him.

A 32-year-old client, wanting to understand and heal his relationship with his two older brothers, reports an insight into his own boyhood detachment:

> The other day we dragged out the old home movies. It was amazing what I could see in myself—the decisions that were already made by 8 or 9 years old. I could see my own defensiveness and awkwardness with my brothers. You couldn't hear the words, but when my mother would ask us to stand together in front of the camera, I could see my separateness from them. When the focus was on one of my brothers doing something silly, you could see my attitude: "Oh knock it off, you're being an ass." I remember feeling apart and different like that a lot of the time with my brothers.

ALIENATION FROM THE BODY

Many studies show the prehomosexual boy to be alienated from his body. Clients often describe an excessive modesty starting in early childhood; and while this is a quality also seen in heterosexually developing boys, the condition frequently continues into adulthood. This shyness may then alternate with exhibitionism, which is an attempt to compensate for the shyness. Both shyness and exhibitionism are forms of alienation from the body. Physical modesty in the presence of other males may begin to show itself before adolescence. Said one client:

> I remember distinctly when I was 11 years old and I was taking a bath, and my mother and aunt were with me in the bathroom. Then there was some sort of commotion because the water wasn't coming out of the faucet, and my uncle was called in to help. When he walked in I remember covering up in front of him. Even then I knew there was something wrong about that.

Other clients have described their disconnectedness from their bodies: "At 13 years old I started to get hair under my arms and like . . . oh, my God! I couldn't come out of the cabana."

Said another:

> When I was an adolescent I was very shy about wearing shorts because I was self-conscious about the hair on my legs. The night before I had to go to our high school picnic I tried to take it off with Nair. Then I tried shaving it, and I was left with all these little cuts and scratches and I was terribly embarrassed for fear the other guys would know what I had done.

Often, family dynamics and father in particular did not acknowledge the boy's maleness. Because his maleness was overlooked, he later will have a deficit—a need to be looked at and admired. This lingering need for male attention has deep emotional consequences. For most homosexual men one's own body is object, not subject. He may be proud of it and anxious to show it off, or he may feel inferior about it and try to hide it. Most typically he will be ambivalent, but either way he lacks a natural acceptance of his body. His body remains an object of continual fascination. We hear another client's confusion between superiority and inferiority:

I hired a photographer to take some nude shots of me. It was a beautiful day and I thought, why not? We went to this secluded spot . . . I just wanted to see myself. Nothing posed, no muscles flexed. Yesterday I got the proofs back and I started to cry. I thought, "I really am so handsome!" People had told me before, but I never really believed them. I was so insecure about my looks that I had always dated older men, father figures who would tell me I was attractive.

Self-integration cannot happen in isolation. Especially in early childhood, we need other people as reflectors to tell us who we are. This is the benevolent function of parents, teachers, friends, and loved ones. Never having united his physical anatomy with his interior identity, the young man quoted above needed the camera to bridge the gap. We cannot reconcile alienated aspects of ourselves without external assistance. To reflect their masculinity, some homosexual men use cameras, some use mirrors, some use the attention of other men.

This search for male attention as an attempt to integrate one's alienated masculinity may explain why some
clients find gratification in getting dressed up and just
sitting at a gay bar, enjoying an evening of male attention.
Another client describes how this need for male attention
gets mixed up with sexual feelings:

> This certain man at work enters the room and suddenly all
> the action revolves around him and I don't exist. I feel like
> it's a significant victory if I can just get him to pay attention
> to me. That's where I get confused by those sexual feelings.
> It's not a question of "Oh, I want him," but it's that need for
> attention . . . I want him to notice what I'm doing. That
> gets all mixed up with sexual feelings, which, objectively, I
> really don't want to have.

Another client describes the disconnectedness with
his physical self:

> I drove by this basketball court on the way home from work
> and there were these guys out there playing and I found
> myself getting turned on by their sweaty bodies. A lot of it
> is that I get turned on by what they're doing, because I've
> never allowed myself to do those things.
>
> My frustration is that when I myself get out there and
> play, I don't get satisfaction from it. I've never really been
> into it. I'll be watching myself and thinking, "How'm I
> doing? Am I good enough? What do they think?" and I
> won't enjoy the game. So instead I end up having sex with
> the guy who was out there playing.

THE EROTIC TRANSITIONAL PHASE

Because needs for affection, affirmation, and identification
remain unmet from the early relationship with father, the

prehomosexual boy feels an intensely painful deprivation. At a certain age, there eventually occurs a transitional phase, when the affectional hunger for male attention transforms into a sexual striving. The exact developmental timing of this transitional phase depends upon the boy's emotional development and sexual experience. For most boys it occurs in early adolescence (13–15 years of age). During this phase these unmet affectional, affirmation, and identification needs take on an intense sexual aspect. These psychological predeterminants have been called "love maps" (Money 1988), which form as developmental templates in the mind, depicting the idealized lover. One client reported this erotic transitional phase as follows:

My problem was always an issue of friendship. It started when I was about 10 or 11. . . . I didn't have friends and I needed them. These friends were hero figures to me and I wanted to get connected and closer because then I felt empowered, and more exciting things happened to me if I could be with them.

I thought, "Why can't I resolve this? Why can't I make these friendships? Why can't I connect? How come these friendships are so frustrated? How come I can't just be there with them?"

It wasn't until I was 12 or 13 that it got to be a sexual kind of thing, where it wasn't just a friend, it was his body and all of that. At the time I thought it was just a function of the fact that I was growing up and issues of sexuality were becoming important. And that sex with guys was just another way of expressing this need. Then in my twenties it started to become more bothersome. Before that, although I had known about this yearning, it wasn't something I was afraid of . . . it was just a problem.

It wasn't until it got more sexual when I thought, "Well, what *is* this, really?" For a long time I didn't even really look at it, because I kept thinking it would work itself out. But I didn't have any tools to really understand it. And then once I did confront it, I realized it wasn't that terrible. I realized what I had wanted all along was not sex with a man. I was really expressing a need for friendship.

During the erotic transitional phase the boy is likely to develop an intense interest in another boy, often older, who seems to possess those qualities he admires. It may be a boy who is particularly good in sports, very friendly and outgoing, or especially handsome and self-confident. He develops an infatuation that at first is nonsexual. Later, there follows a transitional phase in which admiration is eroticized. The testimonies of client after client offer supportive evidence that these unmet affectional needs are the basis for later homosexual attraction. Many clients recall their earliest same-sex physical contact was essentially kissing and hugging, to "fill that empty space inside." In time, the need for romantic-affectional contact is superseded by specifically erotic desires.

HOMOSEXUALITY AS A REPARATIVE DRIVE

In the psychoanalytic literature, homosexuality has long been explained as an attempt to "repair" a deficit in masculine identity. This theory is not new; in fact, it has a long tradition within the psychoanalytic literature. While not all homosexuality can be explained simply as reparative drive, for most homosexual men it is a significant motivation. When the homosexual encounters another man who is what he himself would like to be, he is likely to idealize him and romanticize the relationship.

Reparative-drive theory began with Sigmund Freud (1914), who linked homosexuality to narcissism: "A man can love himself as he is, he can love himself as he was, he can love someone who was once a part of himself, and he can love what he himself would like to be" (p. 90). Elaborating on this last type of love, Freud describes the "impoverished" person who loves someone who possesses excellences he himself never had (p. 101).

Gay researchers Mattison and McWhirter (1984) believe that "homosexuality is not a mental illness but a different expression of erotic-object attraction" (p. 4), yet they too report gay relationships with the need to repair an identity deficit. They interviewed two men who describe their mutual attraction:

> "It was as if we became one person," Joe says, his eyes misting. "It was so peaceful. When I walked down the street wearing Patrick's gold chain, I felt like my English improved and I could stay at the Ritz."
>
> "And when I wore Joe's work boots, I swear my biceps grew two inches," Patrick laughs. "I was him."
>
> "No, I was you!" Joe says. [p. 23]

The authors report that Joe and Patrick experienced each other as mirror images. This has been referred to as "twinning," more accurately described as narcissistic mirroring. Along the same lines, Fenichel (1945) wrote: "In the psychoanalytic formulation, homosexuality is the intermediary stage between love of self and heterosexual love" (p. 428). Nunberg (1938) similarly saw homosexuality as based upon envy and inferiority feelings, as did Miller (1958), who found homosexual behavior used as temporary compensation for inferiority and insecurity. Weiss (1963) understood homosexuality to be the result of an early family environment that alienated the boy from his true identity. In adulthood he seeks a "magic-mirror symbiosis . . . merging with a partner and through this he hopes to become the idealized self" (p. 73). He says, "The partner is often the externalized symbol of the lost, repressed part of his own self, for example, his 'masculinity' " (p. 73). He describes a patient who said, "I don't want to be me; I want to have his balls, I want to be him" (p. 73). Anna Freud saw homosexuality in terms of reparative drive (1949, 1951, 1952), as did Rado (1949). In her clinical observations, she describes homosexual patients who choose "the strong man" as a sexual partner in representation of their own lost masculinity. In her reporting of four successful cases (1952), she was able to lead those patients to heterosexuality by interpreting to them that they sought this masculinity for themselves through identification with their partners.

Refining the psychoanalytic reparative drive tradition, Lionel Ovesey (1969) described homosexuality as an attempt to resolve failures in masculine role-functioning, particularly those involving assertive and dependency needs.

Another writer, Kaplan (1967) views homosexuality as often being rooted in dissatisfaction with self-image. He observes:

> It seems apparent that some homosexuals choose as sexual objects people who have characteristics—physical, personal or both—in which they themselves feel deficient. . . . Dis-

satisfaction with the self, with the way one *is* . . . measured against internalized standards about how one would *like* to be . . . may be one of the major roots of some homosexual feelings and behavior. [p. 356]

Kaplan continues:

Often the homosexual seeks that quality that he feels lacking in himself, but which he sees in the other. Thus, the union gives him the feeling, at least momentarily, that he is now whole, or through identification, now possesses the missing quality. [pp. 152–153]

Kaplan believes that "fusion of the need for a model, a sense of personal inadequacy, and an undifferentiated but powerful sexual drive" (p. 356) are likely to result in homosexuality. He describes the following model:

The person is in some way dissatisfied with his self-image, sees . . . models who more closely resemble his ego ideal, and engages in sexual relationships. . . . The models are chosen as identification objects, and the feeling or fantasy of identification is greatly increased and intensified in the sexual relationship. In a sense, the homosexual has much in common with the narcissist, who has a love affair with himself. The homosexual, however, is unable to love himself as he is. . . . instead he loves his ego ideal. [p. 358]

In her clinical work, Barnhouse (1977) similarly recognizes power and dependency needs as one significant motivator for male homosexuality. She says:

Where dependency needs are prominent, the homosexual adaptation may be resorted to in order to identify with the "masculine" strength of the partner. As one patient of mine expressed it, "It was not so much that I wanted to *love* Peter, I wanted to *be* Peter." Such men feel weak and inadequate, even though they may be in a life situation which looks successful from the outside. [p. 52]

Tripp (1975) understands homosexual behavior as an attempt to "import" admired or desired qualities of the same-sex person for which there is a "felt shortage." Gottlieb (1977) also found examples of this reparative drive in his homosexual clients:

Client: Well, I think this is really a primitive idea, but the physical contact somehow makes you feel more powerful, more attractive, more self-centered. There is a tendency to feed your own narcissism . . . I think the attractiveness of the other person seems to rub off . . . becomes a part of you and enhances you. [p. 39]

Socarides (1968, 1978) offered clinical support to the reparative theory, and in 1962, Bieber's large study gave empirical support to the theory by tracing the deficit to the faulty triadic family constellation. Van den Aardweg (1985, 1986) describes homosexual behavior as an attempt to compensate for feelings of weakness and male gender-inferiority. Moberly (1983) explains same-sex erotic attraction specifically as reparative drive.

An illustration of reparative drive is found in the following transcript of a psychotherapy session with a homosexual man:

I was 3 years old when my father returned from the service; my mother had raised me with all her girlfriends. My father was a drill sergeant and came home to this little kid who wanted to be held all the time and pampered. Since I had been with women, men really did frighten me.

My father was very upset with what his wife, my mother, had raised, and from the time he came home until I was in my teens I remember hearing him say, 'I will make a man out of him, so help me.' If I were to cry or whatever, I used to get a beating that you couldn't imagine. Somewhere along in life, with this very angry man that I had disappointed, I made a vow not to be like my father. For many years that was true. I wasn't like him.

My father and I couldn't say two words to each other. If I said it was black, he said it was white, and vice versa. We would never give each other an inch. If he walked in one door I would go out another just because I couldn't deal with him. He used to go deer hunting and I used to pray that his gun would go off and kill him . . . there was so much peace in my house when he wasn't there.

Later when I started to act out homosexually, I realized I was searching for something that I couldn't get from him and probably at that point wouldn't even take from him. The whole activity became like an addiction.

In a study of prehomosexual boys, Friedman and Stern (1980) also speak of homosexuality in a reparative-drive model. They hypothesize that

the wish to be sexually close to males arose in a setting where there were intense longings for general closeness with male peers at a critical period of development. The erotic desire appears to repair in fantasy feelings of deprivation resulting from inadequate social input. [p. 436]

Carl Jung, an early psychoanalytic pioneer, captures the essence of the reparative drive theory in his description of the homosexual condition as paraphrased by Jacobi (1969):

Homosexuality is a repressed, undifferentiated element of masculinity in the man . . . which instead of being developed . . . from the depths of his own psyche, is sought on a biological plane through "fusion" with another man. [p. 51]

Clinicians have repeatedly observed homosexual behavior to be reparative throughout the psychotherapeutic literature; yet this observation is little known beyond a small scholarly circle. One reason for a lack of consensus on this and other theories of homosexuality is put forth by Ruth Barnhouse (1977):

They [homosexual apologists] claim that because it cannot be demonstrated that 'x' factor *always* causes homosexuality, or because *all* homosexuals do not suffer from 'x' factor, then there can be no relationship between 'x' and homosexuality. [p. 58]

8

Other Factors: Mother and Family Relations

RELATIONSHIP WITH MOTHER

Homosexuals have long been thought to have mothers who are overly close, protective, or domineering. The mother's influence does seem to be a factor that can undermine the father–son relationship and sabotage the boy's autonomy, including his gender autonomy. An abnormally close mother–son relationship has been found in the early childhoods of homosexuals by many writers (Bender and Paster 1941, Fenichel 1945, Freud 1922, Jonas 1944, Jung 1917, Socarides 1968, West 1959). Due to the binding nature of this mother–son bond, the relationship is likely to be not only close, but highly ambivalent (Kronemeyer 1980, Scott 1957).

Studies Placing Emphasis on the Triangular System

So subtle yet profound is both parents' influence on the infant that Winnicott (1965) says, "there is no such thing as an infant." Rather there is "mother, father, and infant, all three living together" (p. 43). The "triangular system" describes the theory that mother, father, and son together bring about homosexual development. It refers to an intensely affectionate, domineering, possessive mother combined with a distant, ineffectual, rejecting father. There are many subtle variations of this basic triangular pattern. It was the prominent body of research by Bieber and colleagues (1962) that statistically established the triangular system in the development of homosexuality. Evidence for the triangular system was later supported by many other writers (Braatan and Darling 1965, Brown 1963, Evans 1969, Shearer 1966, Snortum et al. 1969, Wallace 1969, Whitener and Nikelly 1964).

Marmor (1980) summarizes this research as follows:

> The common denominator in a host of clinical studies appears to be a poor relationship with a father figure which results in a failure to form a satisfactory masculine identification, and a close but ambivalent relationship with a mother figure. [pp. 10–11]

Although he believes that there are additional factors at work in the development of homosexuality, Marmor adds:

That such parental constellations are frequently found in the background of homosexual men has long been known. [p. 11]

Variations of the triangular system are found in this sampling of studies:

Mothers over-affectionate, fathers absent or emotionally distant (Freud 1910, 1922).

Mothers controlling and close-binding, fathers detached and rejecting (Siegelman 1974).

Mothers dominant, fathers passive or absent (Bene 1965, Chang and Black 1960, Gundlach 1969, Stephan 1973, Wolpe 1969).

Mothers overprotective or possessive and relations with father poor or indifferent in approximately half of sample (Westwood 1960).

Mother overprotective, overindulgent, and dominant with an absent or negative father (Bender and Paster 1941, Hamilton 1939, Miller 1958, Whitener and Nikelly 1962). (Bender and Paster found fathers to be absent or abusive in 90 percent of cases.)

Mothers overprotective or possessive and poor relationship with father (Schofield 1965, using nonpatient sample).

Mother overintense with unsatisfying father (West 1959).

Mother demonstrative and affectionate with father unsympathetic, autocratic, or frequently absent (Terman and Miles 1936).

Mother close-binding and intimate and father hostile, detached (Thompson et al. 1973).

Abnormally intense relationship with mother and unsatisfactory relationship with father (Robertson 1972).

It should in fact be noted that a mother who strongly influences and even manipulates her child may not be a dominant personality type. Many mothers of homosexuals were fragile and anxious, which is to say, their personalities were weak, but in fact as a result of their weakness, they imposed a strong manipulative influence on their sons.

The classic triangular pattern is illustrated by William Aaron in his autobiographical book, *Straight* (1972):

My mother was one of those strong, warm, attractive people. . . . She dominated my first five years almost to the exclusion of all other influences. . . . aggressive and single-minded. My father was Mother's opposite in nearly every way. At least during my childhood I thought him weak and indecisive. He never seemed to be involved in any important decision or plan related to us at all. . . . I should add that he wasn't around much of the time. [p. 20]

Studies are less consistent in portrayal of mother as smothering and overprotective, than in portrayal of father as cold, distant, and/or hostile. We believe that mother has an influence, but that the father–son relationship is the more significant factor in the development of homosexuality.

POOR FAMILY RELATIONS

There appears to be a connection between an overall poor quality of family life and the emergence of homosexuality.

"Negative features" in the backgrounds of homosexuals were found in Bieber's 1962 study and replicated in Evans' 1969 nonpatient sample. The subtle communications within the family structure that encourage deviant sexual behavior have been described by Litin and colleagues (1956), with specific application to homosexuality by Kolb and Johnson (1955).

The marital relationship of parents of homosexuals is frequently disruptive or atypical (Jonas 1944, van den Aardweg 1986), often with a struggle for dominance between the parents (Hadden 1966). Homosexuality has been linked with broken homes, unhappy childhoods, and poor relationships with both parents (Ibrahim 1976).

One client said:

> I grew up learning the rules of a dysfunctional family: don't talk, don't feel, and don't trust.
>
> When my younger sister left home my father told her, "You grew up as a stranger and now are leaving as a stranger." That statement could have been applied to any of his children. I have always had a fear of my father, which still afflicts me today. He physically and emotionally abused my mother, sister, my brothers, and myself.
>
> I have been in spiritual direction or therapy for more than 25 years, when I first entered a religious community of brothers. Inappropriate homosexual behavior has been a problem throughout my life in the community. There have been times when I wished I could have told my father, "I have looked for you in the arms of many another man."

EFFECTS OF FAMILY RELATIONSHIPS ON
GENDER IDENTITY

The traditional family structure supports an ongoing and committed father–son relationship, and therefore fosters heterosexual development. We know that "the greatest paternal involvement occurs when . . . adults form enduring monogamous bonds" (Lamb 1981, p. 460).

Since the male requires the cooperation of both parents to assist him in his gender-identification shift, family structure is particularly critical. Both parents should work together to reward the boy's imitation of his father.

Boys who are gender-disturbed have often had less contact with father figures in early childhood due to absence or divorce (Rekers 1987). Those men who report the most cross-gender behavior in childhood are also likely to report the worst relationships with their fathers (Freund and Blanchard 1983, Nash and Hayes 1965). Similarly, boys from father-absent homes are sometimes found to be more feminine (McCord et al. 1962). Boys tend to manifest more conventional masculine behavior when the father is the dominant parent within the home (Hetherington 1966).

A healthy marital relationship satisfies the parents' emotional needs. Satisfied and secure parents will be less likely to use a child to meet those of their emotional needs that should be met by another adult. Besides placing a wedge between mother and son, the father serves to support mother's needs. In an empty marriage, many mothers use their sons to fill the void left by the emotional absence of their husbands. But when there is a loving bond between husband and wife, the father not only provides the boy

with a model of male–female relationships, but also provides the mother with the security she needs to give up any
overintimacy she may have been tempted to maintain with
the child.

Mothers who are continually involved in arguments
with the father are likely to have sons who sympathize and
identify with their hurt, particularly if the boy is close to
them and has had little attachment to the father. What
follows then is a mother and son united against the father.
The boy will see masculinity as brutal and insensitive and
be more inclined to reject his own manifestations of gender.
One client describes such a situation:

> My mother played an important part in what went on
> throughout my childhood. I became her confidante, her
> best friend. Her relationship, I'm sure, was as bad with my
> father as mine was. I know that all played a part in affirming
> my dislike for him, and in vowing not to be like him.

These early family patterns of atypical parent–child
involvement and overall poor family relations are known to
cause many forms of maladjustment. Such studies are
further evidence for our argument that the homosexual
condition cannot be correlated with psychological health.

Issues of Dominance and Aggression

In a home where he feels emotionally vulnerable, the child
may have no other recourse than to identify with whoever
is the stronger parent. Identification often occurs with the
parent who has the most power in mediating rewards and
punishments. "Identification with the aggressor" is particu-

larly likely to occur where there is high stress and relatively little warmth and nurturance from either parent. It is apparently the result of a sense of helplessness on the part of the child.

Parental dominance seems especially important in influencing identification for the boy (Hetherington 1965, Mussen and Distler 1959–1960, Mussen and Rutherford 1963). Where the mother is dominant or relatively masculine, there is a disruption in the formation of the sons' masculine sex-role functioning. Studies show that sons of such mothers acquire more feminine preferences than boys from father-dominant homes. They also tend to identify less strongly with their fathers (Payne and Mussen 1956). It has also been evidenced repeatedly that an aggressive, intimidating older brother can inhibit another sibling's masculine identification.

The Mother's Esteem for Masculinity

The mother's attitude toward father – and men in general – is very significant. If she undermines his role in the family, this diminishes his status as a desirable model. If the mother does not reflect him as a model to strive for, she fails to demonstrate that there is esteem related to being masculine.

Both parents should show visible pride in the son's assumption of gender-appropriate behavior (Tyson 1985). Family harmony and marital cooperation are particularly important in this matter, with neither the mother nor the father undermining the boy's efforts. The history of some homosexuals reveals that the mother degraded masculinity and sexuality, and made the son ashamed to be a male (Wallace 1969).

Higham (1976) emphasizes the influence of "contradictory and confusing gender attitudes within the family [which] prevented these children from acquiring pride and satisfaction in their gender" and adds that "when the mother disparaged her husband, the son rejected masculinity" (p. 55).

9

Physiogenetic Factors

Moving beyond the strictly genetic explanation for homosexuality, it was Freud (1905) who first recognized the importance of family dynamics in homosexual development. Since Freud's time, we have accumulated a great deal of evidence of problems in father–son and sometimes mother–son relations.

Scientific evidence has confirmed that genetic and hormonal factors do not seem to play a determining role in homosexuality (Birke 1981, Perloff 1965, West 1977). However there continue to be attempts to prove that genetics rather than family factors determines homosexuality. These continuing efforts reflect the persistence of gay advocates to formulate a means by which homosexual behavior may be viewed as normal.

The question of a biological basis for homosexuality has also been reopened due to pressure for minority-rights status for homosexuals. Justification for this special civil-rights status would be supported if scientific evidence could be found that homosexuality is inborn. Opponents of this special-rights status, on the other hand, view homosexuality as an acquired behavior. Gays usually strongly believe they were "born this way." The more deeply identified a person is with his sexual orientation, the more he prefers to believe it was prenatally determined.

Physiogenetic research can be divided into two categories—human studies and animal studies. A few of the human studies have reported hormonal differences between homosexual and heterosexual men (Dorner et al. 1975), but little convincing evidence has been found. In addition, these studies are extremely lacking in consistency and replication of findings.

It has been hypothesized by many that a deficit in androgens, such as testosterone, could be responsible for homosexual behavior. West (1977) examined this possibility and concluded: "A deficit of androgens in adult men diminishes the sensitivity and reactivity of the sexual apparatus, reduces lust and eventually produces physical impotence, but does not abolish heterosexual orientation" (p. 65).

Furthermore, West concludes: "Even gross disturbances in hormone levels, sufficient to produce anomalous physical sexual characteristics, do not as a rule alter sexual orientation" (p. 67).

Although manipulations of hormonal levels in rats

have consistently produced homosexual behavior (West 1977), the implications for humans are very limited. To generalize from the behavior of rodents would be to reduce the human sexual experience to a level much lower than what we know that experience to be. As West (1977) explains: "In higher animals, and particularly in human beings, sexual behavior ceases to be . . . directly and immediately dependent upon the hormone concentration at any given moment" (pp. 64–65). A critical look at the hormonal basis of sexual behavior by Ross and colleagues (1978) concludes: "[It] plays no part in determination of sexual activity or sexual preference in any of its forms, including homosexuality and transsexualism" (p. 315). Perloff (1965) states: "Homosexuality is purely a psychological phenomenon, neither dependent on a hormonal pattern for its production nor amenable to change by endocrine substances" (p. 68).

Contrary to many claims of evidence of homosexuality in the animal kingdom, Gadpaille (1980) explains: "Preferential homosexuality is not found naturally in any infrahuman mammalian species. Masculine/feminine differences and heterosexual preferences are quite consistent up through the phylogenetic scale" (p. 355). In his investigation of this "nature versus nurture" debate, Gundlach (1969) argues: "In the light of evidence of cultural determination of gender role and sexual practices, the possibility of an innate physical/personality characteristic determining homosexuality seems quite remote" (p. 139).

A summary of Ehrhardt and Meyer-Bahlburg's (1981) review of the literature states: "Gender identity depends largely on postnatal environmental influences. . . . A role of the prenatal endocrine milieu in the development of erotic partner preference . . . has not been conclusively demonstrated" (p. 1312). Money (1987) states: "Sexual orientation is not under the direct governance of chromosomes and genes. . . . [but] . . . it is influenced thereby, and is also strongly dependent on postnatal socialization" (p. 384). As Masters, Johnson, and Kolodny (1985) tell us: "The genetic theory of homosexuality has been generally discarded today" (p. 411). In his classic work, Karlen (1971) concludes: "The evidence is overwhelming that the genes do not cause homosexuality" (p. 337).

These findings call for a redirection of efforts to the psychological arena. Hoult (1984) expresses this well:

Claims for the biological model are questionable since the evidence for that model either derives from animal studies (and is thus not generally applicable to human behavior), or is inconclusive, contradictory, or methodologically deficient. It is concluded, therefore, that behavioral scientists are at present, on firm ground in using a social learning in preference to a biological model to interpret most aspects of human sexual behavior. [p. 137]

After a review of the literature, it is necessary to consider why it has been so difficult to find a significant biological influence on homosexual behavior in humans. The answer is that physiology has no significant influence. While there remains the possibility of some genetic contribution to gender identity and thus sexual orientation, our emphasis should return to psychological and environmental causes (Meyer-Bahlburg 1977).

Serious consequences can result from unjustifiably attributing homosexuality to biological causes. The most troubling of these is the implication that one had better not hope for change. Believing homosexuality to be biologically determined discourages any attempts at growth beyond it.

We may consider the possibility of some biological predisposition, but not in terms of the mythical "homosexual gene." There could possibly be some physiological factor that *predisposes* a man toward gender deficit and consequent homosexuality, but not one that *predetermines* homosexuality. An analogy with alcoholism is fitting here. Although there is conclusive evidence that some people are born more prone to alcoholism than others, one is not inevitably fated to it because of his heritage.

10

Associated Features of the Homosexual Personality

MALE GENDER-DEFICIT

The very early psychological writings of Krafft-Ebing in 1894 describe the male homosexual as tending to be more feminine than the heterosexual, and this view was furthered by one of the first champions of gay rights, Hirschfeld (1920), who saw the homosexual as an intermediate type or "intersex" with feminine characteristics, who was attracted to masculine men.

Since that time, other writers have linked male homosexuality with either effeminacy or a sense of the self as inadequately masculine (K. Adler 1967, Anomaly

1948, Beecher and Beecher 1972, Bergler 1971, Bieber 1962, Evans 1969, Friedberg 1975, Hatterer 1970, Jung 1922, 1934, 1954, Marmor 1965, Money and Ehrhardt 1972, Saghir and Robins 1973, Whitam 1977). Socarides (1968, 1978) proposes that homosexuals suffer from "gender-disturbed self-identity." Bieber (1965) notes that homosexuals generally do not have a concept of themselves as "real men," nor do they view other homosexuals as completely masculine (p. 257). In fact the founder of the modern gay rights movement, Harry Hay, called members of his group "androgynes" (Timmons 1990). Robert Stoller (1978) sums up the research as follows: "The relationship between femininity and male homosexuality has been known for thousands of years, so those of us working on this subject are probably only tightening the fit on this observation" (p. 543).

Gender identity, as defined by Stoller (1965), is that part of identity concerned with masculinity and femininity. Male gender-identity is a man's awareness—both conscious and unconscious—that he is masculine or manly. We see the homosexual as having a deficit in male gender-identity.

This is not to be confused with *core* gender-identity, the basic awareness that one is a male. Confusion in core gender-identity may result in transsexualism. For most homosexuals, core gender-identity is intact, but there remains a private and subjective sense of simply not feeling fully male-identified.

Male gender-identity deficit does not mean simply that this man fails to fit into his culture's image of masculinity. The heterosexual may have an artistic nature and enjoy theater, art, and cooking; on the other hand the homosexual may be a rodeo rider or professional football player. Rather, it refers to an inadequacy in the inner sense of maleness or femaleness. Gender-identity deficit is the internal, private sense of incompleteness or inadequacy about one's maleness, and this is not always evident in explicit effeminate traits. Some outwardly masculine homosexual men have carefully cultivated their outer images as an armor against inner anxieties of masculine inadequacy. This kind of overcompensation is sometimes seen in "leather" bars, where the charade of masculinity includes men dressed in motorcycle jackets, cowboy outfits, military police uniforms, and other caricatures of maleness.

Some clients are very clear in understanding their sense of masculine deficit. As one client explained it: "Even before I came here, I realized that I did not want another man—I wanted a manly me." The gender-deficit syndrome of homosexuality fits a majority of the clinical population I have seen. Another group of homosexual men—a minority in the clinical population of my experience—do not fit the gender-identity deficit syndrome.

Measurement of Gender Deficit

Numerous attempts have been made to measure objectively the internal sense of masculine deficit that has long been thought to be correlated with homosexuality.

In 1936, Terman and Miles reported greater femininity in male homosexuals. Similar findings were reported by Manosevitz (1971), using the Minnesota Multiphasic Personality Inventory (MMPI) masculinity–femininity scale; Thompson and colleagues (1973), using a variety of tests; Bernard and Epstein (1978), using the Bem Sex-Role Inventory; and Evans (1971), using the Adjective Check

List and Heilbrun's Masculinity–Feminity Scale. With a revised version of the Bem Sex-Role Inventory, Kurdek (1987) found homosexuals to be less gender-specific in their self-descriptions. Overall, homosexuals were more likely than heterosexuals to describe themselves in terms of feminine characteristics. Using six major scales, Hawkins and colleagues (1988) found the most consistent difference between male homosexuals and heterosexuals was the former's greater femininity. Significant association has been found between feminine gender identity and homosexual feelings (Buhrich et al. 1982, McConaghy et al. 1979).

Measurement of gender identity has posed a difficult problem. A number of studies question exactly what is being measured by the available tests (Bernard 1981, Lunneborg 1972). Many scales have been criticized for confusing gender-role and gender-identity. Indeed, it is difficult to sort out culturally stereotypic notions of male and female from the inner experience of gender-identity.

Freund and colleagues (1974) attempted to correct this problem in the design of the Feminine Gender-Identity Scale (FGI), and it proved to be one of the most discriminating instruments available for this purpose. Freund was looking for a correlation between homosexuality and feminine gender-identity. One-third of homosexuals were indistinguishable from heterosexuals. However, two-thirds did show a greater degree of feminine gender-identity. A revised version of this test (FGI-R, 1977) showed similarly high feminine gender-identity among male homosexuals. Other researchers using different methods of scoring the test (Sanders et al. 1985) found homosexuals to be not so much feminine-identified as less masculine-identified than heterosexuals. A corroborative finding in Bell and colleagues' large 1981 study is that the majority of homosexual men feel "neither especially masculine nor feminine" (p. 80).

PROBLEMS WITH ASSERTION

Many homosexual clients complain of difficulty in assertion; associated with this is particular difficulty with competition with other men. Numerous researchers have observed assertion difficulties (Brown 1963, Ellis 1956, Jung (1951), Kronemeyer 1980, Mintz 1966, Ovesey 1969, van den Aardweg 1985, 1986, Weiss 1963, Wolpe 1969). Dallas (1990) identifies marked passivity in about 70 percent of his homosexual clients and defines it as "accommodation at the expense of integrity."

According to Toby Bieber (1967): "The life history of homosexuals almost always reveals a serious defect in readiness to cope aggressively with threat, which is associated with lack of identification with a hostile or detached father. . . ." (p. 60).

When the boy reaches out to father and experiences rejection, there is an initial stage of protest. In the unhealthy family system, this protest is ignored, punished, or distracted, and the prehomosexual boy eventually surrenders the protest. In later confrontation with male authority figures he may adopt a style of passivity or passive-aggression. This failure in relationship with father occurred during the critical separation–individuation phase. It was Socarides (1973, 1978) who first specifically placed homosexual causation during this period; it is during this phase that the boy acquires intrinsic power. Father reinforces the Reality Principle, and failure with father during this critical period may therefore lead to a general sense of failure in meeting the demands of the world.

If the prehomosexual boy remains identified with mother, he will be assured safety and nurturance but will feel stifled, confined, and weak. And he will be left with two deficits—the first in male gender-identity, the second in personal power. If he leaves mother and goes to father, he will experience autonomy and individuation. However, father is a dimension of reality that does not anticipate and accommodate his wishes in the way that mother does. With father, the boy risks rejection. Many prehomosexual boys simply straddle the fence between mother and father, only one foot in the outside world.

A deficit in assertion and sense of personal power almost invariably lead to difficulty in making major life and career decisions. Clients describe many problems of assertion in the workplace, complaining that an inordinate need for male appreciation compromises their healthy need to speak up for themselves. Although women's opinions are of minor consequence, any slight or criticism from another man can be very upsetting and may lead to anger or depression. One client described this hypersensitivity to other mens' opinions:

Yesterday I was doing great, I was feeling good, and then my friend Jack called up. The purpose of the call was to say that he couldn't play golf on Wednesday. He was being very casual about it, like it didn't matter, like no big deal, we just can't play. When he hung up the phone I was feeling terrible. I thought, "How is this possible I can be feeling great and three minutes later I can be feeling terrible?" I decided this guy was no friend. I should get him out of my life if he has that effect on me.

Then today I had to go out to rent a tux for a wedding. The salesman asked the big burly guy who was being measured ahead of me, "Hey, do you work out?" Then he fitted me next, and it was just kind of man-to-man; he didn't make any comments about me being kind of skinny, and by the time I left there I felt good again. I asked myself, "What is it that happened?"

I think Jack took away my sense of adulthood, masculinity, and then later here's this sales guy. . . . He never said, oh God, this guy's so skinny, he's going to be hard to fit for a tux. . . . He measured me, said it was okay, and smiled. . . . It was just kind of two guys, man-to-man, and it made me feel good.

Problems with assertion occur most often in relationships with male authority. The homosexual is likely to find himself caught up in a style of either covert sabotage, aligning himself with women against the male authority as he may have done with mother against father; or direct expression of anger in a particularly hostile, reactionary and consequently self-defeating manner. The dialogue with powerful authority figures is not typically on an equal basis of man-to-man. For the man with a homosexual condition, honest verbal exchange with a powerful male authority figure poses a particular problem. His task is to surrender old patterns of verbal back-stabbing or impotent rage in order to establish and maintain man-to-man dialogue on an equal basis.

Problems in assertion often extend to an overvigilance against hurting other peoples' feelings. Clients describe a common pattern of failure to speak up for their true feelings or convictions and allowing themselves to be manipulated for fear others will be hurt or angered. There is difficulty expressing appropriate anger, which results in a general sense of helplessness and frustration. Problems with assertion can show themselves in the form of peculiar phobias. These troublesome fears seem more common to homosexual than heterosexual men. One young man reported a fear of merging on the freeway. He felt anxious about not going fast enough for the driver he saw behind him in his rearview mirror, especially if that driver was male. Another said:

> I've got this fear of tall bridges or tall freeway overpasses. I get worried I might pass out. I was late to my appointment today because I was afraid to go over the ramp, and I drove way out of my way to avoid it. I was so ashamed and angry at myself that I was crying. All the other cars were going over the bridges with no problem. . . .

Another client said:

> I have this phobia with the phone. Somehow placing the phone call feels like being the aggressor. Will they listen to me or not, and when I ask a question, will they laugh at me? I can't see their faces, so I don't know what they're thinking about me. Yet I know if I don't make phone calls it'll become more and more of a problem.

One frequently found fear of assertion is what gay men call "pee shy," that is, having difficulty urinating in public restrooms, especially when other men are present. This

phenomenon has been equated with anxiety about competition with other men and concerns about homosexual
feelings (Myers 1989). Of seven men I have seen who
reported this problem, six were homosexual. The one
heterosexual client had difficulty with assertion and unresolved anger toward his father. The problem is often related
to the commonly expressed fear of having too small a penis,
but there are other implications. Said one client:

> I've always had difficulty just being able to stand there and
> piss. I'd give anything to do that simple act—it's one more
> thing I can't do. The problem existed long before bath-
> rooms became a place of erotic stimulation for me, you
> know, when guys check out other guys. It's not that, I just
> can't relax.

Psychodynamically, urination is a form of assertion, of
symbolically letting go with other men. The above client
made the insightful connection between not being able to
"flow" in conversation and having difficulty "flowing" (urinating) with other men.

THE SEXUALIZATION OF DEPENDENCY AND AGGRESSION

The psychoanalytic literature has a rich history in its
understanding of homosexuality as the sexualizing of dependency and aggression (Horney 1937, Thompson 1947).

Researchers have found an antagonism toward colleagues of the same sex (Barnhouse 1977), manifested by
"injustice-collecting, fault-finding and accumulation of re-

sentments" (Bergler 1971) or authority problems (Fenichel 1945, Ovesey 1969). There is a tendency to express hostility indirectly, covertly, and backhandedly—keeping it in and smouldering, or blowing up inappropriately to the situation. Of course, behind this hostility is fear.

Sexualizing aggression is a defense, a way of submitting yet conquering. These unresolved dependent and assertive drives in homosexuals are described by Thompson (1947), Scott (1957), Brown (1963), Shearer (1966), and Fenichel (1945), who speaks of sexualizing or "loving" a feared or hated male as a way of evading competition. Similarly, Tripp (1975) describes how the adolescent boy may cultivate a sexual relationship with a peer group leader, using sex to "master a feared male."

It was Ovesey (1969) who most clearly developed this connection between homosexuality and power and dependency needs. His concept of the dynamic relationship between homosexuality, power, and dependency explains ways in which men not sufficiently masculine-identified seek masculine power through homosexual behavior. Ovesey distinguishes three separate motivations for homosexual behavior: sexual, dependency, and power needs. Only the first seeks sexual satisfaction as the ultimate goal, while "the dependency and power components . . . seek completely different, non-sexual goals, but make use of the genital organs to achieve them" (pp. 32–33). The homosexual motivation, according to Ovesey and Woods, "does not exist in isolation, but in association with the pseudo-homosexual motivations of dependency and power" (1980 p. 331). He adds, "It is clinically observable that the three motivations interact with each other and are mutually reinforcing" (p. 334).

As a consequence of his early sense of rejection by father and resulting defensive detachment from masculinity, the homosexual carries a sense of weakness and incompetence with regard to those attributes associated with masculinity, that is, power, assertion, and strength. He is attracted to masculine strength out of an unconscious striving toward his own masculinity. At the same time, because of his hurtful experience with father, he is suspicious of men in power. Homosexual contact is used as an erotic bridge to gain entry into the special male world. It is a way of finding masculine acceptance—not through personal strength, but vicariously through erotic power. Since the homosexual is particularly inclined to see relationships with men in terms of power, there is sometimes an overcompensation in power drive. He may work particularly hard in business to compensate for a private sense of inadequacy, or from a fear of dependency or exploitation by other men. He may carry out this need for success "with a vengeance," as if undoing some former injustice.

Conversely, there may be a masochistic satisfaction in submission (Thompson 1947), which gives rise to same-sex clinging behavior. In almost every case, homosexual men report dependency problems, and their relationships often take on an addictive character. Boundary and power issues are very common, as is merging of identities. These issues are often cause for the breakup of the relationship.

Almost without exception, homosexual clients report an increase in preoccupying sexual fantasies when they have experienced a disappointment. They feel most out of control and likely to act out sexually when they are feeling weak, lonely, and generally down about themselves. Similarly, the opposite is true—when they are feeling more adult, more masculine, more successful, more personally empowered, the attractive men in their environment may be appreciated, but they are less likely to be sexually compelling.

Clients often describe becoming angry at themselves, feeling depressed, and attempting to get out of the depression by acting out sexually. The sexual behavior is an anxiety reducer and an attempt at reassertion of self. The emotional energy that could have been appropriately directed toward self-assertion is repressed, turned against the self in the form of depression, then released sexually. This self-defeating cycle further reinforces a nonmasculine self-image and the feeling of being out of control.

Nonhomosexual men who experience defeat and failure may also experience homosexual fantasies or dreams. It is not unusual for transient homosexual manifestations to emerge in "straight" men from feelings of being out of control and overwhelmed by business, marital, and family responsibilities. However these drives spontaneously resolve themselves when their life situations change for the better.

DETACHMENT FROM MEN

Defensive detachment has long been recognized in the literature as an infantile, self-protective maneuver against emotional hurt. Moberly (1983) made a significant contribution to the treatment of homosexuality by recognizing that the homosexual's hurtful relationship with father results in defensive detachment, which is carried over to

relationships with other men. Moberly discovered her first
clue to the dynamic of defensive detachment while in
conversation with a gay-activist friend. He said he sometimes suspected their meetings were "jinxed," since divisive
arguments would almost always break out among members. It was from this, that she first began to suspect an
unconscious negative dynamic (Moberly, private correspondence).

Just when he was developing his sense of masculinity
and was especially receptive to the father's influence, the
prehomosexual boy experienced a hurt or disappointment
in his relationship with father. To protect himself against
future hurt, the boy developed a defensive posture characterized by emotional distancing. Not only does he fail to
identify with father, but because of this hurt, he rejects
father and the masculinity he represents. Trauma is central
to this drama. In order for the boy to turn away from so
powerful and attractive a figure as his father, there must
have been some painful traumatic experience. Trauma
creates fear, which is the basis of alienation. When we are
imprisoned by fear, we remain alienated from others and
our own authentic natures. This alienation is the essence of
homosexuality.

Defensive detachment is only one side of the ambivalent nature of same-sex attraction. The other side is hostility and distrust. Together they form what Moberly (1983)
calls same-sex ambivalence. Same-sex ambivalent feelings
of love and hostility toward other men function as lifelong
blocks against full male identification. Although the homosexual may eroticize relationships with men, defensive detachment blocks his ability to fully identify with maleness.
Although he may love other men, he is also hostile and

distrusting of them. This frustrating ambivalent attitude toward men is one explanation for the great promiscuity in male relationships.

Defensive detachment also prevents the homosexual from internalizing the missing masculinity that would allow him to grow in heterosexual identity. It is his healthy desire to *take in* the masculine—which is *blocked* by defensive detachment—that binds him into a frustrating predicament. Then with the introduction of the sexual possibility, what could have been a healing same-sex relationship takes on the quality of a game, with an undercurrent and unspoken agenda.

Defensive detachment explains the quality of loneliness and alienation so often associated with the homosexual experience. John Rechy (1963) recalls his boyhood:

> I liked to sit inside the house and look out the hall-window—beyond the cactus garden in the vacant lot next door. I would sit by that window looking at the people that passed. I felt miraculously separated from the people outside; separated by the pane, the screen, through which, nevertheless—uninvolved—I could see that world.
>
> I read many books, I saw many, many movies. I watched other lives, only through a window. [p. 20]

Many clients report a sense of detachment in meeting the demands of relationships. If problems appear to be overwhelming, they are inclined to disengage from the other person, pretending he is of no importance or does not exist, in a reactivation of defensive detachment. Other clients, who are seemingly very popular and outgoing on the surface, having many friends, are often really lonely, with no one really knowing them. This deep-seated isolation is usually accompanied by low self-esteem, depression, and the sense of being out of touch with themselves. Clients often report this sense of isolation and frustration leads them to the impulsive pursuit of anonymous sex, which brings the sense of an infusion of masculinity and of connectedness with themselves.

In *Take Off the Masks* (1984), Malcolm Boyd not only captures the quality of defensive detachment from other men, but intuitively senses he missed a rite of male initiation. Needless to say, Boyd had felt neglected by his father:

> I felt at that time in my life [adolescence] a particular attachment to, but also fear of, men and masculinity. On one occasion I visited in a house where I saw two men, wearing only their shorts, seated in a bedroom. Their easy camaraderie, with a sense of male secrets shared and easy body contact between them, made me feel like an outsider. Had I missed an initiation into maleness? If I had been with them in that room, I would have remained rigid and aloof. The full impact of what I understood to be maleness was ambiguous and confusing. [p. 35]

Defensive detachment means more than the personal rejection of father. It says, "I reject you and what you represent—your masculinity." More than the little boy could ever imagine, his maneuver to reject father's masculinity would have a lifetime of personal and interpersonal consequences.

11

Homosexual Love Relationships

THE LIMITATIONS OF HOMOSEXUAL LOVE

Each one of us, man and woman alike, is driven by the power of romantic love. These infatuations gain their power from the unconscious drive to become a complete human being. In heterosexuals, it is the drive to bring together the male–female polarity through the longing for the other-than-me. But in homosexuals, it is the attempt to fulfill a deficit in wholeness of one's original gender.

Two men can never take in each other, in the full and open way. Not only is there a natural anatomical unsuitability, but an inherent psychological insufficiency as well. Both partners are coming together with the same deficit. Each is symbolically and sexually attempting to find fulfillment of gender in the other person. But the other person is not whole in that way either, so the relationship ends in disillusionment.

The inherent unsuitability of same-sex relationships is seen in the form of fault-finding, irritability, feeling smothered; power struggles, possessiveness, and dominance; boredom, disillusionment, emotional withdrawal, and unfaithfulness. Although he desires men, the homosexual is afraid of them. As a result of this binding ambivalence, his same-sex relationships lack authentic intimacy.

Gay couplings are characteristically brief and very volatile, with much fighting, arguing, making-up again, and continual disappointments. They may take the form of intense romances, where the attraction remains primarily sexual, characterized by infatuation and never evolving into mature love; or else they settle into long-term friendships while maintaining outside affairs. Research, however, reveals that they almost never possess the mature elements of quiet consistency, trust, mutual dependency, and sexual fidelity characteristic of highly functioning heterosexual marriages.

This is not to dismiss same-sex friendships. To the extent that there is friendship, there is love; but it is love limited to friendship.

A LOOK AT MALE COUPLES

Most people, regardless of sexual orientation, hope for a permanent relationship. Lifelong relationships offer most people a higher level of self-esteem, emotional security, health, and happiness.

Homosexuals, too, report the desire to share their lives with a partner (Saghir and Robins 1973, Weinberg and Williams 1974). They see stable relationships as the solution to many personal problems (Hoffman 1968). When in a relationship, the gay man is less worried about public intolerance, and he feels less depressed and guilty (Weinberg and Williams 1974).

With the exception of the pioneering work of Warren (1974), little attention was given until recently to long-term same-sex relationships. Then in 1984, McWhirter and Mattison published *The Male Couple*, an in-depth study designed to evaluate the quality and stability of long-term homosexual couplings. Their study was undertaken to disprove the reputation that gay male relationships do not last. The authors themselves are a homosexual couple, one a psychiatrist, the other a psychologist. After much searching they were able to locate 156 male couples in relationships that had lasted from 1 to 37 years. Two-thirds of the respondents had entered the relationship with either the implicit or the explicit expectation of sexual fidelity.

The results show that of those 156 couples, only seven had been able to maintain sexual fidelity. Furthermore, of those seven couples, none had been together more than five years. In other words, the researchers were unable to find *a single male couple that was able to maintain sexual fidelity for more than five years*. They reported:

> The expectation for outside sexual activity was the rule for male couples and the exception for heterosexuals. Heterosexual couples lived with some expectation that their rela-

tionships were to last "until death do us part," whereas gay
couples wondered if their relationships could survive. [p. 3]

McWhirter and Mattison admit that sexual activity
outside the relationship often raises issues of trust, self-
esteem, and dependency. However, they believe that

the single most important factor that keeps couples together past the ten-year mark is the lack of possessiveness
they feel. Many couples learn very early in their relationship that ownership of each other sexually can become the
greatest internal threat to their staying together. [p. 256]

Other researchers also see sexual freedom as beneficial to
gay relationships (Harry 1978, Peplau 1982).

A host of studies have found infidelity to be characteristic of prolonged male relationships (Bergler 1951,
Dailey 1979, Saghir and Robins 1973). In a study of thirty
couples, Hooker (1965, p. 46) found that all but three
expressed "an intense longing for relationships with stability, sexual continuity, intimacy, love and affection"—but
only one couple had been able to maintain a 10-year
monogamous relationship. Hooker concluded, "For many
homosexuals, one-night stands or short-term relationships
are typical" (p. 49).

The desire for sexual fidelity in relationship and the
benefits of such a commitment are universal. In the long
history of man, infidelity has never been associated with
maturity. Even in cultures where it is relatively common, it
is no more than discreetly tolerated.

Faced with the undeniable fact that gay relationships

are promiscuous, gay literature has no choice but to promote the message that faithful relationships are unrealistic. McWhirter and Mattison go further to say that we must redefine fidelity to mean "emotional dependability." That is to say, while it is understood that they will have outside sexual relations, there is an agreement that the partners will nevertheless manage to be faithful to each other emotionally.

Yet how can a relationship without sexual fidelity remain emotionally faithful? Fidelity as such is only an abstraction, divorced from the body. In fact, the agreement to have outside affairs precludes the possibility of trust and intimacy.

Disillusionment and the Choice to Love

The homosexual relationship is doubly burdened with both defensive detachment and the motivation to compensate for personal deficit. Therefore it will usually take the form of an unrealistic idealization of the person as an "image." The pursuit of this image often means developing a self-denigrating dependency on the other man. This unrealistic perspective is based on the superficial aspects of the other person and leads to disappointment. Because of these unrealistic projections, the homosexual couple has difficulty moving beyond this "disillusionment" stage in a relationship.

As he did with his father, the homosexual fails to fully and accurately perceive his lover. His same-sex ambivalence and defensive detachment mitigate against trust and

intimacy. Easily disillusioned in relationship, he often re-
news his hope by seeking another partner. Yet it is this
disillusionment stage that offers the opening into a mature
relationship. Here we are required to make a realistic,
honest perception of the other person, including his faults.
Based on that honest perception, we may then choose to
love. It is this choice to love that marks the beginning of a
mature relationship.

In seeking out and sexualizing relationships with other
males, the homosexual is attempting to integrate a lost part
of himself. Because this attraction emerges out of deficit, he
is not completely free to love. He often perceives other men
in terms of what they can do for him. Thus a giving of the
self may seem like more of a diminishment than a self-
enhancement. The person who brings into a relationship a
deep sense of deficit may fail to weather the disillusionment
stage because by choosing one person, he cannot have it all.
To commit to one person is to give up future options. There
is the fear—actual anxiety—at the possibility of doing without. Thus the homosexual person is inclined to place his
hope in possible future relations.

Choosing to love is having to accept the limits of the
relationship. It may never have this, or that, or the other
thing. The loved one will never be such and such, and so
on. Yet maturity means to accept these limitations and
create out of them. The creativity to see new options in the
relationship comes from a flexibility found within. For in
reality, there will always be options—perhaps not externally, but in our expanded repertoire of response.

The moral of this story is: do not expect a monogamous homosexual relationship, for recreational affairs are a
part of the gay life-style.

THE SEARCH FOR THE MASCULINE IDEAL

In spite of gay rhetoric about androgyny, masculinity remains the gay ideal. It is one's own deficient masculinity that is sought out in sexual partners. Hooker (1965) observes the particular valuing of masculinity; Hoffman (1968) describes masculinity as "the single most desirable feature" (p. 17) and says that "effeminate men are held in much lower esteem than are masculine-looking homosexuals" (p. 145). The following was observed by Barry Dank (1974):

In the gay world masculinity is a valued commodity, an asset in the sexual marketplace. . . . If there is a consensus on any subject in the gay world, it is that masculinity is better than femininity. The norm in the gay world is that one should be masculine. One should "be a man" and not "a sissy." Statements such as, "Those nellie queens make me sick" are typical. This preference for the masculine involves not only the area of sexual attraction. . . . in the friendship groupings and homophile organizations I have studied . . . status differentiation . . . is highly related to masculinity –femininity, with the most masculine being nearest the top of the status heirarchy. [p. 191]

In their landmark study, Bell and Weinberg (1978) similarly noted:

A chief interest which many of our respondents had in a prospective sexual partner was the degree to which he conformed to a stereotypically "masculine" image. [p. 92]

As one client explained:

This week I made a list of all the guys I've ever had sex with. I wondered, what was I attracted to? I realized it had to do with exterior traits of masculinity and an appearance of self-assuredness. Some of the guys had this hypermasculinity—they were bodybuilders and so on. Looking back, I realize this attraction to masculinity had to do with my not being confident in myself. I also realize now that most of them were actually as insecure as I was.

Anna Freud (1949) describes cases in which the search for the "strong man" as a sexual partner represented a striving toward one's own lost masculinity. Secondary masculine sex attributes (hair, strength, roughness) were used as determinants of sexual object-choice because they represented what the patient himself lacked. Nunberg (1938) also describes a type of homosexual client whose "sympathetic magic" leads him to believe that "through mere contact with a man of strength, or through an embrace, or through a kiss, he would absorb this strength and become himself as strong as the man he desired" (p. 5).

The heterosexual, on the other hand, is not as psychologically dependent upon finding the feminine ideal for gratification, since he has no unconscious need to fulfill a deficit in original gender.

A client describes this drive toward another man's maleness and its roots in his own sense of deficit:

I was born a man. It is my identity. I have always liked the idea of being a man, but I've always felt insecure about it. I was not born insecure. Insecurity was given to me by people and situations the same way that confidence is given. All my life, I've received messages that told me I was not good enough as a man. My father taught me that men worked hard, then continually criticized and belittled me.

I was born with an orthopedic condition which kept me away from rigorous exercise and competitive sports. I spent a lot of years watching my peers express their exuberant maleness through these activities, clearly enjoying themselves and feeling accomplished. However I, trying to do the same, was left in physical pain and in fear of collapse, and it was another message that I was failing at being a male.

I felt intimidated trying to mix with guys who were accomplishing things that I could not. They saw me as second best; I stood back and got left out of the club of men. I felt not only insecure, but disenfranchised from all of maleness. I was supposed to be a guy, but didn't feel it because of what was happening to me. And then society said this craving I had for masculinity was because I was "born that way"! During my two and a half years of therapy, I have seen that my homosexual tendencies were not a cry to have another man, but a manly self. I wasn't born this way. It was a wound inflicted upon me. It was a sin of pride that made me believe that brokenness is shameful. I have forgiven the men that failed me, as I have forgiven myself for the years of running away. And I have been blessed by freedom and empowerment.

THE MISSING FEMININE ELEMENT

Women bring stability and complementarity into a love relationship. Without the stabilizing element of the feminine, and the stimulation of her complementary physical and emotional makeup, men are generally unable to sustain sexual intimacy and closeness. When romantic passions wane and same-sex familiarity sets in, one person will usually fall out of love. Typically, an event or situation will serve as a catalyst—something unexpected or uncharacteristic that disappoints one partner. Suddenly the other is seen as failing to live up to the ideal he was originally thought to be. There is deep hurt and a mutual sense of betrayal. There may follow an increasing number of petty quarrels, after which one or both partners decides that they are not as compatible as they first believed, or there may be a single violent and destructive showdown.

With the first experience of boredom in the relationship, male couples often resort to narcissistic maneuvers to regenerate interest. And so there is cheating, teasing, a show of disinterest, and fights, followed by romantic makeup gestures. Homosexual relationships are "often bedeviled from the start by dramas, anguish and infidelities" (Pollak 1985, p. 51), with a particular intensity of dependency, jealousy, and rage. The most volatile domestic relationships I have worked with have been those of male couples. There are typically complaints of intense ambivalence, violent conflicts, and sometimes physical injuries. Because the relationship is forced to bear the burden of unmet childhood dependency needs, there is a great deal of jealousy and suspicion. The homosexual partner is often preoccupied with such questions as "Where is he now?" "Who is he with?" "If he is masturbating, who is he thinking about?" There may be sexual impotence or a deliberate sexual frustration of the other person as a form of control. The partners frequently become demanding or envious and complain that personal boundaries have been intruded upon. When the couple splits up, they often become cynical about relationships.

Later, a new romance will often bring romantic love with another twinning stage, characterized by excitement with the discovery of each shared trait. However, because these discoveries are often projections of nonexistent similarities, the stage is set for disillusionment. Soon again such a man feels smothered and overwhelmed, and restlessness and disappointment spark the desire for yet another lover.

Carol Lynn Pearson's description of her gay husband's relationships in *Goodbye, I Love You* gives a sensitive portrayal of this cycle of infatuation and disillusionment. Pearson describes how her husband left her and their four children to pursue life in the San Francisco gay community, falling into step to the drumbeat of the "unseen sergeant of Castro Street." (He later died of AIDS.)

Pearson's husband came home periodically to tell her about his lovers, believing each time that he had found the right man for a lifetime. Yet after a brief period of infatuation, he invariably became disillusioned. His affairs were characterized by emotional swings from elation and optimism to deep disappointment and hurt. He complained that his lovers were overly dependent, demanding, and immature, and bemoaned the fact that he could not find a man like his wife. William Aaron describes how he resigned himself to a similar problem:

> I had accepted the facts of life of the gay world and was able to enjoy sexual contacts for what they were: transitory, immature, but often pleasant adventures. . . . of the gay men I've known, the ones who are happiest are the ones

who have made a good-humored adjustment to the facts of homosexual life and don't expect much. [1972, p. 138]

The tendency toward repeated disillusionment in relationships is often interpreted by gay affirmative therapists as the result of internalized homophobia. We disagree. Rather it is evidence of both defensive detachment and the fundamental incompatibility inherent in any same-sex coupling. Men tend to much more readily separate sex and love than do women. Without the feminine influence in a love relationship, an essential grounding force will always be missing.

THE CHALLENGE OF RELATIONSHIPS

We come to know ourselves best in a committed relationship, and the more intimate the relationship, the greater the opportunity for personal growth. We learn about ourselves by the way we affect our partners, and the way they affect us, on the deepest levels. Very often, however, homosexual clients report that when they begin to know another man intimately, their sexual interest in him diminishes. It is always, they report, the distant person who is sexually attractive. We see here the frustrating cycle of distant attraction and then close disinterest, a cycle of continual, and for so many, lifelong, frustrated desire for intimacy.

The Problem of Boundary Setting

Every couple committed to a relationship is challenged to surrender to the partner, yet paradoxically, to establish boundaries for their intimacy. The relationship can simultaneously enhance and threaten individual identity. Consequently, in all relationships there is an unavoidable approach–avoidance conflict. This approach–avoidance conflict is particularly evident in homosexual relationships. Many clients who have been in long-term relationships describe them as possessive, controlling, and smothering. When threatened by what seems to be a fusion of identity into someone else, a person usually attempts to establish new boundaries, and in the gay world, this typically involves an outside affair.

Having an outside sexual experience can be a devastating way to recoup the weak sense of boundary. Contrary to the popular gay dictum about its recreational nature, sexual relations remain a profound interpersonal exchange. An outside affair violates trust and creates a new separateness between the partners. To move from one person to another and from one relationship to another is like wandering about in a hall of mirrors. Everywhere a man turns, he comes face-to-face with himself. When he stops and looks at his life, he is faced with the pattern of his disappointments: while each of his partners looked like the problem, he in fact remains the constant.

12

Gay Sexuality

RESEARCH FINDINGS

The compulsive, addictive elements of the gay life-style
have been documented by many writers. In 1948, Kinsey
observed that long-term homosexual relationships are
notably few. More recent findings have told a similar
story. Hoffman (1968) states: "Sexual promiscuity is one
of the most striking, distinguishing features of gay life in
America" (p. 45). In *The Joy of Gay Sex* (1977), Silverstein
and White say that gays today represent hedonism in its
most extreme form, with one-night stands and brief
flings offering constant variety and excitement.

In 1978, the Kinsey Institute published a study by Bell and Weinberg, described as the most ambitious study of homosexuality ever attempted. It showed 28 percent of homosexual males having had sexual encounters with *one thousand* or more partners. Furthermore, 79 percent said more than half of their sex partners were strangers. In that survey, only 1 percent of sexually active men had had fewer than five lifetime partners. The authors concede: "Little credence can be given to the supposition that homosexual men's 'promiscuity' has been overestimated" (p. 82). "Almost half of the white homosexual males . . . said that they had had at least 500 different sexual partners during the course of their homosexual careers" (p. 85).

A client describes this type of promiscuous life-style:

> I was into totally anonymous sex, and never into relationships with people. And now I look back on it as a huge, huge waste of time and energy. What in the hell was I doing? If I focused my energy in more productive ways I think I'd be in a different place right now. I think I probably would be more productive, maybe more successful, happier. It took a lot of energy. When the time came to do it, it was exciting and impulsive. I just went and did it. Whatever the consequences at the moment, I figured I'd deal with them later. When I was involved in such an experience, I never thought about anybody else but me. I was just totally, totally engrossed in what was going on at the moment for myself.

Pollak (1985) reports that homosexual relationships seldom last more than two years. He describes sexual behavior among gays as "an average several dozen partners a year" and "some hundreds in a lifetime" with "tremendous promiscuity" (p. 44). He says:

> The homosexual pick-up system is the product of a search for efficiency and economy in attaining the maximization of "yield" (in numbers of partners and orgasms) and the minimization of "cost" (waste of time and risk of one's advances being rejected). Certain places are known for a particular clientele and immediate consummation: such as "leather" bars, which often have a back room specially reserved for the purpose, saunas and public parks. [p. 44]

William Aaron's autobiographical book *Straight* draws similar conclusions:

> In the gay life, fidelity is almost impossible. Since part of the compulsion of homosexuality seems to be a need on the part of the homophile to "absorb" masculinity from his sexual partners, he must be constantly on the lookout for [new partners]. Constantly the most successful homophile "marriages" are those where there is an agreement between the two to have affairs on the side while maintaining the semblance of permanence in their living arrangement. [p. 208]

He concludes:

> Gay life is most typical and works best when sexual contacts are impersonal and even anonymous. As a group the homosexuals I have known seem far more preoccupied with sex than heterosexuals are, and far more likely to think of a good sex life as many partners under many exciting circumstances. [p. 209]

In the face of these repeated findings on infidelity, some counselors advise the homosexual to develop a monogamous relationship. However, a true understanding of the cause of homosexuality—the symbolic seeking of one's own maleness—explains the naivete of such counsel.

Because they have witnessed the promiscuous character of the gay life-style and its consequent frustration and demoralization, a number of clients enter reparative therapy to outgrow homosexuality. They are aware that their need for a life-long, monogamous relationship is almost certain to remain unsatisfied in the gay world.

FACTORS CONTRIBUTING TO PROMISCUITY

The addictive aspect of cruising has been recognized by many researchers, including Masters and Johnson (1979). A man who is depressed may gain a temporary sense of mastery through anonymous sex because of its excitement, intensity, even danger—followed by orgasmic release and an immediate reduction of tension. Later he is likely to feel disgusted, remorseful, and out of control. Through repentance he regains control and is all right again. But when there is nothing to feed that healthy state, it is a matter of time until he gets depressed, feels powerless and out of touch with himself, and seeks anonymous sex as a short-term solution to getting back in touch and feeling in control again.

Often a homosexual client will report seeking anonymous sex following an incident in which he felt ignored or slighted by another male. Feeling victimized, he acts out sexually as a way of reasserting himself and getting something back he feels was taken from him. Once again, he feels guilty and has to repent or make amends. Many gay men become addicted not just to the sexual release, but to the entire compulsive cycle. Sexual compulsivity tends to dominate the person's life, if not by behavior, then by preoccupation and fantasy.

In these repetitive, compulsive, and impersonal sexual behaviors so often found in the gay life-style, we see the qualities that are generally associated with perversion, namely, a focused engagement with the object, with a desire for an intense relationship, but at the same time, a resistance toward intimacy. Men living such a life-style naturally tend to separate sexuality and affection. Hoffman (1968) describes the "sex fetishization" found in gay life (p. 168), and Gottlieb (1977) points out the strong element of sexual fantasy that has become institutionalized in gay culture. Masters and Johnson (1979) found those fantasies tend to be more violent than those of heterosexuals.

Homosexual attraction is often characterized by a primitive response to body parts or aspects of the person, and when interest in these traits diminishes through familiarity, there follows a loss of interest in the rest of the person. These attractions are often characterized by compulsivity, suggestive of the unconscious, symbolic attempt to satisfy a deficit. In comparison, heterosexual men seem less trait-fixated. While some may envision their ideal woman as tall, blond, blue-eyed, or possessing certain ideal body parts, we hardly see the distinct disinterest in women without these traits.

The Problem of Sexual Sameness

The sex act between two people of the same gender is characteristically isolated and narcissistic. It is "individually enjoyed rather than mutually experienced" (p. 214) by a technique of "my turn – your turn" (p. 214) and "you do me, I do you" (Masters and Johnson 1979). Orgasmic episodes are experienced separately, and more discussion is required for their negotiation. Sexual sameness diminishes interest and creates the need for greater variety, including other partners (Masters and Johnson 1979). Gay writers Mc-Whirter and Mattison (1984) corroborate this viewpoint, saying, "The equality and similarities found in male couples are formidable obstacles to continuing high sexual vitality in their lasting relationships" (p. 134).

Emphasis on Sexuality

One writer – who, it should be mentioned, believes society is responsible for the unhealthy conditions in the gay world – observes these conditions as follows:

> It must be remembered that in the gay world the only real criterion of value is physical attractiveness. . . . The young homosexual will find that his homosexual brothers usually only care for him as a sexual object. Although they may invite him out to dinner and give him a place to stay, when they have satisfied their sexual interest in him, they will likely forget about his existence and his own personal needs. . . . Since the sole criterion of value in the homosexual world is physical attractiveness, being young and handsome in gay life is like being a millionaire in a community where wealth is the only criterion of value. [Hoffman 1968, pp. 58, 153, 155]

Aging is viewed particularly negatively in the homosexual culture, with high value placed on youth and physical attractiveness (Bell and Weinberg 1978, Kelly and Worell 1977). In his psychoanalytic study of ten couples, six of whom were homosexual, Gershman (1981) observed that in homosexual coupling, "sexuality is of greater importance and plays a larger role." He further makes the observation that those homosexuals with whom he has worked have "shown a good deal of loneliness, common narcissism, possessiveness, insecurity and inferiority" and that "sexuality fulfills their needs more effectively and becomes more important to them" (p. 154).

In his investigation, Gershman found that the majority of male couples he studied had agreed upon promiscuity, as long as it was kept discreet. He found that while the male couples studied were capable of high compatibility in many respects, there was great difficulty in maintaining sexual interest.

The gay identity is built around sexuality, and indeed sex is a central theme throughout gay life. This is a strong contributing factor to the inability to maintain monogamy.

13

The Refusal to Acknowledge Pathological Elements

THE GAY LIBERATION ARGUMENT

The Gay Liberation Movement began in 1969 with protests at The Stonewall Club in New York City. Now into its third decade, this movement makes two distinct demands:

Tolerance. Gay leaders have spoken up for social, economic, and political equality. There has been a call for civil rights in every aspect of society and an end to the long history of discrimination against homosexuals.

Approval. This second aspect of the gay-lib position goes a step further, attempting to persuade society that homosexuality is normal—sort of like being left-handed, an admittedly less common, but nonetheless healthy and natural condition. Any disadvantages to the condition are attributed to the bias of a right-handed society.

These two arguments are frequently blurred and presented synonymously. For there is a faulty assumption that if society is tolerant and respects an individual's right to pursue the gay life-style, it must go one step further to equally *value* that life-style, as well as the homosexual condition. Although we must respect individual rights, we as a society still have a responsibility to inquire: "What is healthy?" For the past twenty years, the Gay Liberation Movement has been demanding not only the right to political and social equality, but an endorsement of normalcy.

The logic of the following assumption has always eluded me: because perhaps 4 percent of all people are homosexual, then homosexuality *must be a normal variation* of human sexuality. The fact that it occurs in other cultures and in subhuman species, under certain conditions (Ford and Beach 1951) is also seen to prove its normalcy. Such logic would be equivalent to concluding that since a given percentage of people will break a leg skiing each winter, then a broken leg is a natural condition and one should not attempt to avoid it.

For many people, homosexual desires indeed feel natural. However, what feels "normal," we believe, is the unconscious striving to heal oneself through sexual intimacy. What feels "natural" is the symbolic search for wholeness of gender. The homosexual condition, if understood properly, is always a barrier to developmental completion.

Out of fear of intolerance, we as a society have not been ready to separate rhetoric from reality and to evaluate the condition honestly.

THE DENIAL APPROACH

In reviewing recent studies of gay relationships, a reader cannot help but be struck by the persistent absence of reflective comment. Gay researchers remain tenaciously descriptive, but rarely evaluative. While the sexual behavior within the relationship is quantified and discussed in greatest detail, there is a void of qualitative comment on psychological or emotional issues. These studies are typically approached sociologically, and consequently any pathology is assumed to be socially caused.

Findings Regarding Promiscuity

The promiscuity of the gay world is sometimes vehemently denied by gay apologists. Then again, others concede to it and label it normal. While not every homosexual has multiple anonymous partners, the undeniable reality remains that the gay world is, in fact, characteristically promiscuous.

Gay apologists who do acknowledge the research evidence of promiscuity tend to rationalize it as part of the gay condition. This argument is justified by (1) blaming heterosexual oppression for causing promiscuity, (2) diluting the worth of intimacy in sexual relations, or (3) denying that promiscuity plays any role in the avoidance of intimacy. In minimizing the significance of promiscuity, homosexual apologists speak of "the person temperamentally suited to impersonal sex" (Fisher 1975, p. 241) as if this were merely a matter of personal taste unworthy of serious psychological inquiry.

The characteristic promiscuity of the gay life-style places it in unavoidable conflict with the values of conventional society. To gain acceptance from the culture at large, gay leaders must underplay these antisocial practices. Because sexual liberation has always been a fundamental demand of the gay movement, gay leaders have been unwilling to call for monogamy and relational responsibility. A recent maneuver around this obstacle to mainstream acceptance is the promotion of a national media campaign that will convey a respectable image of the gay life-style. In attempting to educate straight society about homosexuality, these leaders propose playing down the sexual aspects of gay life in the hope of gaining civil rights and broader approval (*Time* magazine, July 10, 1989).

A Question Not to Be Asked

Gay researchers prefer to present the etiology of homosexuality as a nonissue, an a priori fact beyond inquiry. Just as one would not investigate the cause of heterosexuality, one is not to ask the cause of homosexuality (Stein and Cohn 1986). Gay apologists propose that homosexuality is nothing other than sexual preference (Stuppe 1982), as one has preference for vanilla or chocolate. Disagreeing, Money (1988) says "preference" has nothing to do with it. Similarly, Friedman (1988) says "sexual preference" is as meaningless as "gender-identity preference."

Those committed to the "homosexuality as natural" ideology minimize repeated research observations of unhealthy family patterns in the backgrounds of homosexuals. They dismiss the preponderance of research evidence on the grounds that there have been some inconsistent findings. They have discouraged research into the origins of homosexuality for fear of readdressing the question of pathology. Gay apologists offhandedly dismiss earlier research and theory on homosexuality as outdated or old as if it is an established fact that such research has been disproved. In fact there is no scientific data to controvert 75 years of clinical and empirical research on homosexuality. In what other public forum has it ever been generally concluded that 75 years of professional observations have been simply "disproved"? The debate must in fact go on.

Cross-cultural Considerations

In an effort to demonstrate that disapproval of homosexuality is simply a Western bias, gay researchers often point to research into other cultures. In fact a review of cross-cultural studies reveals a wide variety of homosexual behavior patterns.

The first modern and extensive cross-cultural investigation of homosexuality was Ford and Beach's *Patterns of Sexual Behavior* (1951), which analyzed 76 societies worldwide. The authors concluded that all known cultures are strongly biased in favor of heterosexuality. Carrier (1980) says that even in societies where males are free to participate in homosexual activities, exclusive homosexuality is not sanctioned.

However, ritualized homosexual behavior is sometimes a part of the masculine-initiation process in primitive
tribes. The Sambia Tribe of New Guinea has often been
used as an illustration of culturally accepted homosexual
behavior. A fuller understanding of that culture reveals
that the homosexual behavior of young boys and men is in
fact a symbolic preparation for that society's more highly
valued heterosexuality (Stoller and Herdt 1985). The so-
called institutionalized homoeroticism for all boys is only
preparation for eventual heterosexual marriage. "In that
tribe, both men and women are not defined as full persons
without children" (p. 400). "Homosexuality is negatively
sanctioned and the man who insistently indulges [in homo-
sexuality] would risk being despised as 'rubbish man'" (p.
401). In another culture, the Kimam people of Irian Jaya,
we again see ritualized homosexual behavior used with the
aim of strengthening the boy's subjective sense of maleness
(Gray 1986).

Among some American Indian cultures, the moon
was believed to appear to a boy and offer him either a bow
and arrow, or a squaw's pack strap. If the boy hesitated, the
moon handed him the woman's pack strap—and his fate
would be sealed as a homosexual (*Indians* 1973, p. 129).

The Mentor–Student Relationship

Throughout history, mentors have played a part in a boy's
maturation and the development of his masculinity. As a
coach, godfather, rabbi, or sponsor, a mentor is charged
with imparting his knowledge about the male view of life.
Fenichel (1945) describes the young man's search for the

secrets of masculinity through "apprentice love." In ancient Greece, where boys were educated by older mentors, homosexual behavior was often a part of the relationship with the mentor. In many cultures and traditions, homosexual behavior is used as a ritualized attempt toward the goal of attaining masculinity and heterosexuality. In fact, it could be said that all homosexuality is the *sexualization of the natural need for a mentor.*

THE BLAME APPROACH

Gay writers often blame the problems inherent in homosexuality on the poor self-image of gay people resulting from an internalization of our cultural bias against homosexuality. Their solution to this problem is social, claiming that with the resolution of this heterosexist bias, problems associated with homosexuality will be resolved.

Homophobia

Although a phobia is actually defined as an exaggerated, irrational fear, homophobia has recently become a one-dimensional, catchall term to explain any and every negative response to homosexuality. Every painful developmental stage of the homosexual is blamed on either social or internalized homophobia. The poor father–son relationship is said to be caused by the father's homophobia—his feeling "threatened" by the boy's effeminacy. The boy's alienation from his childhood peers is said to be caused by his internalized homophobia. The homosexual adult's alienation from family and society is attributed to homophobia.

In adolescence, his depression, loneliness, low self-esteem, and any drug and alcohol abuse are often blamed upon social or internalized homophobia. Even narcissism has been attributed to introjected homophobia. Similarly, passivity and lack of assertion are viewed as a reaction to a hostile environment. Interpersonal problems, such as failure to establish and maintain long-term relationships, are blamed on homophobia. Intrapsychic conflicts that become manifest in the course of treatment are attributed to homophobia (Malyon 1982). Cruising is attributed to self-punishment induced by internalized homophobia. There is a disavowal of the idea that there could be any deficits inherent to the homosexual condition.

Weinberg (1972), who coined the term *homophobia*, has five defining criteria for it. The most frequently cited characteristic is "the threat to values" (pp. 16–17). Homophobia has actually been extended beyond Weinberg's earliest definition, to be "any belief system that values heterosexuality as superior to and/or 'more natural' than homosexuality" (Morin 1977). By this definition, probably every religious tradition and every culture in world history could be considered homophobic. If we were to survey parents and ask if they would want their children to grow up homosexual, nearly every parent would be homophobic. The term has been extended ad nauseam.

Yet many who use the term neglect to acknowledge that without being "phobic" about it, it is quite possible to reject the gay life-style within the framework of one's own values. This does not mean that one is threatened that such a life-style will erode his values; it is simply a nonacceptance of the life-style as a viable and natural alternative.

Restrictions on Treatment

Fear of being labeled homophobic can prevent psychologists from offering treatment that clients themselves report to be beneficial. Psychologists have been pressured not to treat children with gender-identity disturbance. This sometimes makes it very difficult for parents to find help for their children. Some consider it unethical to treat *adults* who seek therapy, since homosexuality per se is not categorized as an illness. The argument is that conversion therapists are agents of social control (Marmor 1980). In spite of this criticism, a number of clinicians continue to believe homosexual clients deserve the opportunity to undertake the treatment available.

Lack of Support from Society

One often repeated sociological explanation for gay promiscuity is the lack of cultural support from society. There are few successful role models for gay couples to learn from, particularly since their heterosexual parents could not serve as examples. It is said that as the gay life-style gains visibility and social acceptance, homosexual couples will stay together longer. It is said: "[The] lack of social and material cement that tends to make heterosexual relationships last" is largely responsible for the "great divide between affectivity and sexuality" in the gay world (Pollak 1985, pp. 50–51).

There are other explanations for gay promiscuity. Many researchers believe that the more closeted a gay man, the more likely he is to engage in anonymous sexual activity. Some researchers blame gay promiscuity on the lack of the restraining influence of woman. It has been also been suggested that the cause of infidelity is due in part to the gay culture, with its built-in sexual opportunity structure.

Although homosexuals do lack cultural supports and institutional guidelines, we contend that the central cause of gay promiscuity is to be found in the *inherently unfulfilling character of the homosexual condition*.

THE "NEW ORDER" APPROACH

Some researchers attribute the gay world's negative reputation for promiscuity to "cultural labeling" and propose a different set of expectations for homosexual couples (Warren 1974). Many writers propose that homosexual behavior should not be judged by heterosexual norms, and they conclude that fidelity is impractical in natural homosexual relationships (McWhirter and Mattison 1984, Warren 1974).

This "new order" approach is part of a general cynicism among gay writers toward heterosexual values and a contention that human nature is inherently promiscuous. Some researchers say the strength of heterosexual marriage is primarily due to institutional pressure. One says that "many straight men and women would give a great deal for the chance to be a bit more promiscuous" (Fisher 1975, p. 241).

Another such author, Churchill, reveals a hopeless-ness about enduring relationships:

> It may be reasonably supposed that there never was nor ever will be any person who can fulfill all of the spiritual and physical needs of another person. Hence, husbands and wives alike must spend a good deal of time and effort in artful deception and flattery. . . . They must sustain the illusion upon which their marriage is based and upon which their sexual relationship is justified. [1967, p. 301]

Churchill describes the "dreary" picture brought to mind by the term *family man:*

> It is difficult . . . to imagine any person who is engaged with the world at large as a family man or a homebody. It is almost an impossibility for any man or woman who is laden with the cares and preoccupations particular to family life to be very deeply concerned with others. [p. 305]

Of the traditional Judeo-Christian family, he says:

> Far from being the source of each and every good, it is one source of a great many social and moral evils. If all the homely virtues are learned in the bosom of the family. . . . It should not be forgotten that many of the more contempt-ible vices are also learned in the bosom of the family: complacency, jealousy, bigotry, narrow-mindedness, envy, selfishness, rivalry, avarice, prejudice, vanity, and greed. [p. 304]

Yet where else can the child learn about love and sharing, giving and intimacy, if not in his early home environment among his immediate family members? Receiving love in childhood is a prerequisite for future altruistic attitudes. This cynical portrayal of family life often encountered in gay writings may reflect the authors' attitudes about their own families; indeed, one could say many gay men were betrayed by their own family systems.

GAY AFFIRMATIVE THERAPY

In recent years, Gay Affirmative Therapy (GAT) has emerged to facilitate the homosexual's acceptance of his orientation.

GAT is motivated to lessen the burdens imposed upon the homosexual by society. However, when promoted as the only acceptable form of treatment, it imposes burdens of its own—through the guilt it places on those non-gay homosexuals who seek reparative therapy.

GAT makes the arbitrary assumption that the coming-out process is the answer to every homosexual client's problems, presupposing a hierarchy of personal growth from "in" to "out." The implication is that one's development is arrested when he addresses his problems in the closet.

When a client reports the desire to pursue reparative therapy, GAT presumes that he is only reflecting prejudices of society, which he has unconsciously internalized. Many gay-affirmative counselors believe that reparative therapy will only serve to heighten a man's sense of guilt and low self-esteem.

William Aaron, in his autobiographical book, *Straight,*

has a different perspective: "To persuade someone that he will make a workable adjustment to society and himself by lowering his sights and settling for something that he inwardly despises (homosexuality) is *not* the answer" (p. 13).

Philosophy of Gay Affirmative Therapy

While support of the gay man in adjustment to his life challenges is a worthy GAT goal, we take issue with GAT's assumptions.

At the foundation of those assumptions is the intractable conviction that homosexuality is a natural and healthy sexual variation. With this a priori assumption, GAT then proceeds to attribute every personal and interpersonal problem the gay person develops to social or internalized homophobia. GAT's theoretical model frames the life experiences of the client in the context of victimization, inevitably setting him against conventional society and disenfranchising him from family and even ethnic identity. Yet mature identity always requires more than blaming the influence of others—either "out there" or internalized—for one's deepest personality development problems.

GAT reports that their clients experience significant growth in self-esteem, and they attribute this growth to the resolution of internalized homophobia. Yet, how would GAT explain the fact that we report the same benefits in reparative therapy—which *does not* integrate homosexuality, but holds that nonacceptance of homosexuality is valid and pursuit of change is valid?

Ironically, GAT and reparative therapy agree on what

the homosexual man needs and desires: to give himself permission to love other men. However, GAT works within the gay ideology of eroticization of these relationships. We believe this sabotages the mutuality that will lead to bonding.

Gay Affirmative therapists disclose their homosexuality to the group members and hope to serve as positive gay models. Their therapy carries with it the heavy baggage of a countercultural life-style and ideology. Reparative therapists offer a positive heterosexual model, while working within the framework of traditional values.

If and when GAT works, then it works for the wrong reasons. When clients experience benefits from GAT, they do so not because of its ideology, but in spite of it—through the same-sex bonding that may occur serendipitously within the treatment environment.

THE PROBLEM OF REACCULTURATION

The process of coming out has been repeatedly referred to in gay literature as essential to the gay man's growth and happiness.

What was first thought to be a one-time event is now often seen in the gay literature as a lifetime process. It is a multistage and apparently nonlinear process that sometimes requires readdressing old issues, due to the persistence of negative social forces (McDonald 1982). The coming-out process includes abandoning the hope for a "straight" identity and marriage and family.

Coming out means not just admitting one's homosexuality to oneself and others, but taking leave of the dominant heterosexual culture. Reacculturation into the gay subculture is an often-found theme in gay literature; it is seen as a fundamental second step of the coming-out process. This means alienation from the culture-at-large, as well as separation from family, friends, and loved ones with whom the homosexual man formerly identified. Many of the values and norms of society, such as marriage and monogamy, are surrendered during the reacculturation process. Gay writers have increasingly resorted to the contention that homosexuality requires its own set of principles and standards "radically at odds with heterosexual culture" (Suppe 1981, p. 76) in which

> one must . . . learn to accept sex as primarily a recreational activity wherein going home with a partner can be as casual and uncommitting as picking up a partner at the tennis court for a few sets. [p. 77]

This need for reacculturation and new identity reflects an alienation, not from society but from *the deepest and most genuine self*. Reacculturation merely reinforces the original childhood response of defensive detachment, in which the prehomosexual boy's solution was to split his identity from a rejecting father. In reacculturation, this intrapsychic split is projected onto society—for reacculturation is actually defensive detachment on a social scale.

How can wholeness be found by embracing a gay identity? Indeed, it seems tragic to build a new identity—worse yet an entire culture—around one's gender-identity incompleteness.

III

Psychotherapy

Every homosexual is a latent heterosexual.

—Irving Bieber

Our heterosexuality is buried under a thousand fears.

—Colin Cook

14

The Treatment

A man may consciously believe he accepts his same-sex desires and even celebrate them, but on the deepest levels of self, he will always be at conflict. Nature made man complementary to woman, and to cling to the sameness of one's own sex is to look at the world with one eye. I do not believe that any man can ever be truly at peace in living out a homosexual orientation.

The binding predicament of the homosexual is that he unconsciously seeks to fulfill his masculine identification through relationships with other men—but at the same time defensive detachment leaves him fearful of the masculine, and therefore, he never allows himself to take it in.

In relationship with a same-sex therapist, a client can find some of what he missed in the failed father–son bond. This is the way that a man absorbs the masculine—through answering the challenge of nonsexual male friendships characterized by mutuality, intimacy, affirmation, and fellowship. When he eroticizes a male relationship, a man is perpetually frustrated in absorbing the masculine.

BEGINNING OF TREATMENT

In the first session the client often reveals an optimism, even an excitement. He has finally found a therapist who is willing to help him overcome his homosexuality. There is also a happy anticipation about his new relationship with the therapist, a man who he hopes will, perhaps for the first time in his life, intimately understand and accept him.

Although he has hopes, yet he still has doubts. A part of him will resist change. He may have the common anxiety of being made over or undone. Yet his hope is stronger than his skepticism. As one client expressed it: "I have a right to *be* that man and all those male things that I've spent a lifetime admiring in others. I have a right to my own masculinity."

Treatment will help to put the issues into clear focus and create clarity out of the maze of confusion. Developing healthy male relationships will be one of the first orders of business, as will growth in a general sense of success in meeting life's challenges. Surprisingly, the original issue of sexuality usually falls to the background as issues of personal power, assertion, and male relationships come to the forefront.

In the early phase of treatment, when there are strong feelings of hope and a sense of mastery, a new and powerful dimension of awareness temporarily supersedes the old sexual patterns. There may be a reduction in homosexual interests and even overall sexual arousal. This is due to the power of hope, whose worth should never be underestimated.

However, this dramatic change in behavior may also be symptomatic of a transference cure, a temporary abatement of symptoms caused not by resolution of conflict, but by a sublimation of the client's feelings in his desire to please the therapist. A transference cure traces back to the client's self-fulfilling fantasy that the therapist holds the power to heal him. On some level, it results from the unconscious collusion of both client and therapist. The impulse to assume the false role of the "good little boy" and to please the therapist by being the "cured" client must be interpreted. Once this dynamic is understood, both therapist and client can go forward in deeper honesty.

Soon after the initial surge of hope, the return of the old sexual feelings brings into perspective the long struggle that lies ahead. But the return of these feelings and patterns should not be cause for despair. The client should be reminded that this is only the first of many natural developmental cycles of hope and disillusionment.

Over time, the sexual intensity will subside once more. As he continues to develop closer mutual relationships with significant men in his life, the client begins to see his sexual attractions from a different perspective. The more he gets to know his male acquaintances on a personal level, the more unlikely it is they will remain objects of his sexual fantasies. The erotic power of their traits moves to the background as the whole person comes into focus.

SELF-ACCEPTANCE

According to popular gay rhetoric, if a man attempts to resolve his homosexuality, he must be unable to accept himself as he is. Even popular psychotherapies promote this false dichotomy.

Critics of reparative therapy suspect that it is primarily guilt that keeps clients coming to treatment. Although guilt may have been a strong motivator that originally propelled the client into therapy, it is never the foundation for successful treatment. In fact, after some months in therapy, the client typically reports a diminishment of guilt. What has diminished here is not actually valid guilt, but the excessive guilt he has felt so long that it feels natural.

While a welcome relief, this diminishment seems too good to be true; some men then feel guilty about not feeling guilty. They may even blame the therapist for reducing the guilt they felt they needed to keep them from falling back into unwanted habits. Gradually, however, the client will come to realize that with his deepening commitment to healing will come a new support structure to take the place of that oppressive mind-set that earlier "kept him in place."

The best part of surrendering excessive guilt is that it frees the mind to see clearly the natural dissatisfaction that results when one's behavior is at odds with one's sense of self. This dissatisfaction emphasizes, simply, what valid guilt is—disappointment with oneself for doing something discordant with what one desires to be. This subtle but deeply felt displeasure with oneself is more effective than excessive guilt in fostering lasting change.

Excessive guilt locks a man into the old, self-defeating thought patterns that reinforce a sense of weakness and self-pity. Excessive guilt erodes self-esteem, which is essential to meet the initiatory challenges of reparative therapy. Self-acceptance and a sincere desire for wholeness open the way to growth. It is through self-acceptance that the man gains the ability to stay in the pain in the faith that he will get better.

One client describes how the way to his own growth was opened:

I used to feel overwhelmed and preoccupied by my homosexuality. Homosexuality took my power away. It depressed me. I used to be alarmed, upset; I felt trapped by it. I used to believe that since I'm homosexual and I don't act out my sexuality, then I'm not being true to myself.

Now, it feels familiar; I get hungry, I get crabby, I get the homosexual feelings. I no longer deny them or act out, but understand them. My homosexual feelings are just a "snapshot" of who I am right now. They tell me something about where I am.

Acceptance of my homosexuality does not mean approval, but a familiarity; "Yeah, this is me, that's weird, but it's me." It does not need to mean loneliness and despair. I don't feel trapped by it, but rather I say to myself, "Oh, here I go again, this is what I do."

Homosexual feelings loom larger when I feel the need for deep friendship. I try to act on the knowledge, not the feeling. There's a power in the option of redirecting the energy; of giving new meaning to the feeling. I've gained the personal knowledge of understanding that my homosexuality is an urge toward male intimacy.

Instead of getting all worked up, I ask myself where I am lacking in personal contact. Then I see that the sexual energy will disappear or significantly diminish.

In computer language, you have "default," which is where the program goes if you fail to give a new command. Our default is homosexuality . . . and our new command is male intimacy.

THE POWER OF GENDER

Gender identity structures every man's and woman's way of being and defines each person's participation in society. Gender identity is the grounding for all personal identity. We are all much more than simply "persons." Yet gay liberation groups, along with radical factions of the women's movement, have exerted pressure on the social sciences to deny inherent gender differences and condemn sex-role concepts. There has been a substitution of "nonsexist" language, which denies even basic human differences. Little by little, modern consciousness has lost its image of healthy masculinity and femininity.

In freeing himself from his bond with mother, the boy needs help in becoming fully male. He needs to know who he is, and only another man can tell him. Mother, by her grounding in human nature, has told him *what* he is. But father—through his grounding in the outside world—can tell him *who* he is. By bestowing upon the boy a personal identity, he defines his unique relationship to the world.

To be able to identify oneself to oneself is so fundamental a need that we would rather call ourselves anything than have to call ourselves nothing. We can see how a young man who grew up without father's support might look for personal identity through a homosexual relationship. He has eroticized the need for his own masculine identity. As one 32-year-old client said during his first session: "I've always suspected my problem is not about homosexuality, but about masculinity."

Androgyny

In the absence of an appreciation for healthy masculinity and femininity, androgyny is now unchallenged in our culture. In popular usage this term has become synonymous with genderlessness, describing a diluted or neutered version of both genders. Yet true androgyny—in its correct sense—implies a complete integration of both the masculine and the feminine within the personality.

Before one can develop aspects of the other sex, one must claim one's primary gender. The young woman who fully identifies with the feminine gender will possess the qualities of gentleness and nurturance; later, she may also grow into assertion and independence. She will develop those masculine traits out of the foundation of her femininity. The same is true for the male. In his fullest masculine identity, he may not only be aggressive and risk-taking, but also empathic and sensitive.

The gay-identified man often attempts to minimize the

significance of gender difference as a justification for his own supposedly more highly evolved androgynous style. Yet androgyny in the gay culture is not so much the true assimilation of femininity, as a mockery of it in the form of effeminacy.

The true integration of femininity—if it is ever to be accomplished in a man's lifetime—occurs later in life after full assimilation of his primary masculinity, and evolves through intimacy with the opposite sex. Through integrating aspects of the opposite sex, we grow into full humanity. Full humanity is not acquired by distilling, compromising, or denying characteristics of our original gender.

Gender Empowerment as Treatment

Successful treatment of homosexuality is undermined in a culture where androgyny is upheld as the ideal. There must be acknowledgment by society of the existence of sex-linked traits, behaviors, and perceptions, and a respect for their value. As clients progress in reparative therapy, they develop a deep appreciation of gender difference and how it enhances the individual.

Men in treatment typically report that when they are feeling more masculine, mature, strong, or "adult" (each client describes this gender empowerment in his own way), then same-sex attractions are less distracting, less compelling. When they are feeling good about themselves, feeling up, and feeling strong, their homosexual preoccupations markedly diminish.

These clients also report the opposite: if they have

experienced a setback or rejection, then spontaneous homosexual fantasies will increase to a level of preoccupation. Such feelings of disappointment, discouragement, or failure often lead to anonymous sexual encounters.

This clinically observed relationship between negative feelings about oneself and same-sex fantasies and behavior tells us something about the deficit nature of homosexuality. Can we imagine a married man who would say, "When I'm feeling weak and unmasculine, I'm preoccupied with the need to make love to my wife"? And even more bizarre—"When I'm feeling good and strong about myself, I lose most of my desire to make love to my wife"? There is a motivation in the homosexual drive that has nothing to do with the sexual behavior per se, but all to do with a man's sense of himself.

Client testimonies offer strong evidence that in many homosexual men, same-sex eroticism is used as symbolic reparation of a deficit in masculine strength. Several clients have described what they found attractive in other men:

Client #1: Certain guys have a sense of freedom about them—that they could do whatever they want and get away with it. Like they don't even care, it's just so natural to them. That's what I'm attracted to—that inner freedom and power. Like my straight roommate, Bill, who used to say, "You can do just anything if you want to," and sometimes he did. I feel so constricted, like "Oh, I could never do that." I admired that, I wanted to have that power.

Client #2: I'm attracted to a guy having a lot of control. That power and control—I've always wanted to draw off of that, to be so together.

Client #3: The issue for me is disconnectedness from my masculine identity. I feel like an outsider when I'm with men. I don't feel accepted by them, and I have difficulty living out or expressing anything that I see as a masculine trait. Risk-taking is a masculine trait, and goal-setting requires a masculine energy that I feel very intimidated by. I've always had a tremendous craving for the masculine, whether it's a male friend or some activity that is masculine, some kind of sports.

Searching for different ways to reach that masculinity I feel detached from, I realize I don't really want to sexually pursue other men. I see that I'm trying to bond with them so that I can feel a part of them, connected with them, equal to them, and not to feel that I'm less and the other man's more.

Client #4: What is it that defines a man? What is it that is essential to men? Right away I blurt it out—power. A sense of power whether it's physical strength, power over others, or a power over oneself in the form of leadership.

I just know what I *really* want and it's not him or his power, it's me—*what I want me to be.* I want to have all the assuredness I need—I don't want to be frightened of anything. I want to have the ability to deal with whatever comes my way and not want to just go into a room and close the door. I want to have the confidence to go ahead and pursue the kinds of friends that I have always wanted.

IDENTIFYING MASCULINITY

One of the earliest questions that must be addressed in psychotherapy is: exactly what is the client's perception of masculinity? And in what ways is he, and is he not, in possession of that masculinity?

Many men beginning treatment report the sense they have somehow never completely grown up. They may have the sense of themselves as children, as boys. For many of these men, masculinity feels similar to, even synonymous with, adulthood. To feel masculine is to feel adult, and vice versa.

Essential for success in treatment is that the client learn to identify when he is feeling more or less masculine. With practice, he discovers that this is a subjective feeling experienced at different times with varying intensity.

Taking stock of his deficits in masculine identity is important because it tells him what he seeks in other men. He may be quite surprised to realize that what he typically seeks in others, he himself feels deficient in. Sometimes he seeks father figures to lean on, or mirror images to bolster his sense of self. There may be a fascination with particular body types, mannerisms, or styles. A number of male clients report that it is a certain style of male strength that is attractive, particularly a confident, outgoing, energetic personal style. Repeatedly, homosexual clients express an admiration for the basic qualities inherent to masculinity: independence, control of one's life, assertion, self-assuredness, and, they will often say, a "physicalness." Within the first few sessions, the client can identify those particular traits he is attracted to, thus beginning the process of de-mystifying these men.

Growth involves not just a behavioral change of giving up homoerotic behavior, but a deeper transformation of personal identification. It will enable him to feel different about himself, relate differently, to see the world from the perspective of a fully male-identified man. When one is in possession of his gender identity, he inherits along with it a vitalizing power.

MAKING PEACE WITH FATHER

I am often amazed to see how adult men can become so upset by the briefest contact with their fathers. A weekend home or a telephone conversation can enrage or depress an otherwise rational 30-year-old man. These painful paternal encounters are often followed by a regressive phase that may impel the man back into anonymous sexual encounters.

There is a particular quality of anger that usually characterizes the homosexual man's relationship to his father. While heterosexual men also report hostile relations with fathers, there is a qualitative difference. The heterosexual man's anger is usually accompanied by a resigned acceptance. But the homosexual man holds a profound grievance, a grudge, and a deep-seated antipathy that blocks acceptance.

A frequent misunderstanding of many a client is that to accomplish resolution with father, he must gain his father's acceptance in the present. This misunderstanding is based upon the unconscious assumption that father has something he needs in order to outgrow his homosexuality. This idea is rooted in the client's early experience of father as having the power to share or withhold his masculinity.

A significant step in the client's treatment is the realization that it is now *he himself* who holds the power of transformation. Central to the attainment of that power is forgiveness of his father. The realization that healing comes from an attitudinal shift on his own part is particularly important in cases where father will not or cannot change. As one client said: "A lot of us know that our fathers aren't going to change. We will get as close as we can to our fathers and that's going to be it. We can't really change them because they'll always be the same way."

Then, too, the client may also need to be reminded that the true damage was done not by father, *but by his own defensive detachment from him.* Now he is called to give up this defensive attitude toward all men, beginning with his father.

Forgiveness of father is not an easy task because it often means accepting father for who he is, with his limitations, including his limited ability to demonstrate love, affection, and acceptance. It often feels like a death experience for a young man when he realizes that he must bury once and for all the fantasy of receiving his father's love. To understand and forgive and love his father is, paradoxically, to be father to his father—to give him what he, the son, would have desired. Compassion for father is the final step of forgiveness. Often compassion grows out of an understanding of his father's father, and how he treated his own son.

Almost all of my clients report that their fathers have very little to say about their own fathers. Sometimes this "shadow father" can be traced back for two generations. Thus the problem of homosexuality may have had its foundation laid in an earlier generation.

As he grows in the resolution of his homosexuality, the client simultaneously begins to appreciate his father as a person and as a man. During this stage—to his initial annoyance – he discovers how much like his father he really is. Those same traits of explosive temper, rigid opinion, easy blame, and difficulty in directly expressing feelings may equally belong to him.

It is interesting to note that gay ideology continues to deny the important common denominator of these problems with father. This results in the ignoring of a key piece of evidence that homosexuality is a developmental failure. In fact there is a deep-seated tendency to refuse to concede any importance whatever to the father. Long ago, many gay men made the decision that father would play no role whatsoever in their lives. This defensive disregard for the importance of the father may in fact have contributed to psychoanalysis's early emphasis on mother, as analysts may have been misled by patients who preferred to spend time and money talking about mother.

FACTORS AFFECTING PROGNOSIS

Motivation to change has repeatedly been found to be a primary predictor of success in treatment (Hatterer 1970, Mayerson and Lief 1965, Monroe and Enelow 1960, Ovesey 1969, Schwartz and Masters 1984, Stekel 1930, van den Aardweg 1985, 1986). Motivation means the client is unambivalent in rejecting a homosexual identity and is striving toward heterosexuality. Other indicators of favorable prognosis are lack of indulgence in self-pity, a positive sense of self, and the ego-strength to tolerate stress and frustration. Heterosexual fantasies and dreams are also strongly favorable. Also the stronger family relationships the client has, the better his prognosis.

Traditional values and the sense of oneself as a member of heterosexual society are also strongly supportive in providing a framework from which to reflect on the homosexual experience. Clients who enter reparative therapy are strong in the conviction that psychological development does not come from a surrendering of identity into the gay subculture. Other factors in treatment success are the ability to resist impulsive behaviors and to postpone gratification, the ability to set goals, and the capacity to reflect upon, verbalize, and learn from past experiences. Clients who believe they have power in shaping their own destinies have a far greater likelihood of overcoming their homosexuality than do those who submit to a fatalistic attitude or who see life as happening to them. The ability to be honest with oneself and others is significant to treatment success, as is the ability to identify what one is feeling. An appreciation for the value of gender differences also does much to support the treatment plan.

Those men who have been less sexually active have better prognoses. Considering the habit-forming nature of sexual behavior, the more homosexually active the client is, the more difficult the course of treatment.

For this reason, gay-affirmative counseling services situated on high school campuses can be detrimental, because they actively support early homosexual behavior. If that same adolescent desires to grow into heterosexuality in adulthood, he will then have to face not only the burden of breaking a sexual-habit pattern, but also the gay self-identification that his behavioral patterns have fostered.

Two final qualities that are of the utmost value—second only to motivation to change—are *patience* with oneself and an *acceptance* of the ongoing nature of the struggle.

Age Factors

The average age for a homosexual client entering reparative therapy is early twenties to early thirties. Many other therapists have made the observation that this is the age group most receptive to treatment (Bieber 1962, Mayerson and Lief 1965, Rubenstein 1958). This is the time of young adulthood, when friends are getting married and family is exerting pressure to do likewise. There is a line from *The Boys in the Band* that after age 30, you can no longer introduce your lover as a roommate.

Social pressure, however, is not the only impetus. This is a time when the natural desire to enter into an exclusive relationship is most intensely felt and when the choice must be made for either Isolation or Adult Intimacy (Erickson 1958). One must now make a lifelong relational commitment, and one must know what gender that partner will be.

Treatment before the early twenties has its particular difficulties. The teenager is experiencing his sexual drive at its most intense, and after years of secrecy, isolation, and alienation, most young men find the gay world powerfully alluring, with its romantic, sensual, outrageous, and embracing qualities. At the same time that libidinal drive is at its highest, personal identity is at its most fragile. At this time the adolescent wants to experience. Although he may later have a change of heart, to propose a treatment requiring self-reflection, conviction, and self-denial is almost more than he can bear. My only successful treatment with an adolescent was a 17-year-old whose outstanding advantage was an enthusiastically supportive family and social network, with every significant person in his life committed to helping him change his life direction.

Prognosis is also poorer with older men over 35. For too many, their deeply ingrained sexual patterns have made them cynical about change. However, there is evidence of positive outcomes with highly motivated older men, especially those who have only been sporadically sexually active.

CURE

Growth through reparative therapy is in one way like the gay model of coming out of the closet. That is, it is an ongoing process. Usually some homosexual desires will persist or recur during certain times in the life cycle.

Therefore, rather than "cure," we refer to the goal of "change," a meaning shift beginning with a change in identification of self. As one married ex-gay man described it: "For many years I thought I was gay. I finally realized I was not a homosexual, but really a heterosexual man with a homosexual problem."

Within that essential change in view of self are new ways of understanding the nature of homosexual behavior and its motivational basis in unmet early love needs. One client who had been in reparative therapy for about a year described his feelings as follows:

What my homosexual feelings used to be, they aren't now. They're still around, they're still there, but they're not as upsetting. The improvement is in how they affect me emotionally, how much they shake me up, affect my self-esteem—how compulsive they are, how much I am preoccupied by them.

Another man, a former female impersonator, now married with three teenage sons, commented, "Now those homosexual fantasies are more like a gnat buzzing around my ear." Another man explained: "A problem that used to have a capital 'H' now has a small 'h.'"

While some therapies focus directly on heterosexual conversion, reparative therapy takes a wider view of the homosexual condition as it affects issues of personal power, gender identity, and self-image. Reparative therapy views change as a long-term process, and one that is in fact most probably lifelong. One 25-year-old client explained his process of change in the following letter:

I've been in group therapy now for 13 months, and I can say this time has been the most revealing, growthful, and important period in my life.

My love for my Catholic faith originally led me to seek help for my homosexuality, as I felt guilty and unhappy. However, today I continue to come to therapy because I am motivated by my own progress and the progress of the other men in the group.

The therapy has helped me understand a lot about myself, my past, and the things that have contributed to my situation. For example, my father left my mother when I was 3 years old, and I grew up never having a close male figure to identify or bond with. Consequently I never felt a true sense of maleness about myself, and as I grew up, I never really felt like one of the guys. This eventually led to an exclusive attraction to males, which I remember started around age six.

Therapy has broken down most of the fantasy world I had built up around other males. My self-esteem and sense of masculinity have improved, and this is reflected in my success at work and my newly established male friendships. I have even started dating, and now I definitely see marriage and children in my future. While my relationship with my father is still not so good, I have made him aware of my situation and he has shown compassion.

The attraction to other men has still not gone away completely, but it has certainly diminished. Other men who used to both intimidate and attract me are much less threatening today. While I do not think that my same-sex attraction will disappear 100 percent, I do think I will reach a point where my attraction to the opposite sex prevails, and I will be able to move on with my life. All of this growth comes about, I have found, through the wholesome male friendships which I have learned how to develop through therapy, a prayer life, and the sacraments of my church.

If our use of the word *change* rather than *cure* sounds pessimistic, one should consider the use of the word *cure* as it applies to other psychiatric conditions. Indeed, except for the most elementary behavior-modification programs such as smoking-cessation and treatment of certain phobias, no psychological treatment can be conceptualized in terms of absolute cure. The alcoholic is never fully cured of his desire to drink, but successful treatment does offer him an effective way of dealing with his lifelong condition. The client with low self-esteem is never fully freed of his doubts and insecurities, but he grows in self-assurance. And are the issues of Adult Children of Alcoholics (ACAs) ever no longer their issues? So rather than "cure" of homosexuality, we should think in terms of growth, by laying the right foundation of healthy nonerotic male relationships. Then for some, celibacy will be the solution; for others, heterosexual marriage is the hoped-for goal.

The validity of any therapy—no matter what the treatment method or goal—is found in its overall effect on the life of the client. Good therapy must do more than alleviate a specific symptom. If the treatment is right for the person, then the freedom and well-being it brings will radiate throughout all aspects of the personality. Most important, the move to health will bring a growing awareness of personal power.

15

The Therapeutic Relationship

TRANSFERENCE

The most critical and often the most painful dimension of psychotherapy is looking honestly at those feelings the client has transferred onto the therapist from previous relationships. During the course of treatment a broad spectrum of unresolved and unconscious conflicts, defenses, and desires from previous significant relationships are transferred onto the therapist. The client sees the therapist through the eyes of the child he once was. Transferred feelings include fear, anger, aggressive-defensive reactions, and sexual desires.

The two outstanding characteristics of transference reactions are their repetitiveness and inappropriateness. Although these reactions are not appropriate to the therapeutic relationship, they do of course accurately fit the client's experience of a previous significant relationship.

While transferential reactions can occur in any relationship, the therapist–client relationship stimulates particularly strong transference reactions because of its dependent, intense, and intimate nature. The therapist must not react to the transference out of his own unresolved feelings, nor should he prematurely cut off the expression of a transference reaction in order to avoid discomfort. It is through the therapist's gentle and tolerant interpretation of the transference that the client will begin to separate himself from his past perceptual and behavioral patterns.

While all transference is ambivalent in nature, there is the useful distinction between positive and negative transference. Positive feelings for the therapist that facilitate the working alliance and can move the client forward are trust, affection, concern, respect, and admiration. Negative transference reactions include resentment, hostility, distrust, and grievance-collecting; these too can move the client forward if they are interpreted correctly.

Transference Issues in Reparative Therapy

The homosexual client enters treatment with great hope in conflict with fear and deep-seated distrust. He still has a longing for paternal love and acceptance. Attributing unrealistically positive characteristics to the therapist, he is excited at the possibility of an intense relationship with a man who, he hopes, will fully understand him. However, there may also be "an intense readiness for a negative transference" (Wallace 1969, p. 356), and he will often interpret the therapist as being critical when it was not intended. These ambivalent feelings are usually a reenactment of his frustration with father.

The homosexual client has difficulty maintaining equality in his significant male relationships and will often either devalue or idealize the other. This is particularly true in his relationship to the therapist. Lateness, broken appointments, and forgetting to pay are passive forms of hostility. At the other extreme are direct outbursts and protests. He may project onto the therapist the omnipotent male who has the ability to devastate him, or he may devalue him as phony, money-making, or hypocritical.

On the other hand, he may not feel worthy of the therapist's attention, and this may take the form of being reluctant to ask for a needed fee reduction or an appointment time-change. More subtly, his sense of unworthiness may surface as simply not knowing what to say because he feels that he is wasting the therapist's time.

There is a common tendency to alternately idealize and degrade the therapist. The client alternates between overvaluing and undervaluing him, the latter perhaps by questioning his masculinity or heterosexuality. Or he will overvalue him by seeing him as ideally strong, self-assured, confident, and so on. Oftentimes a client develops a romantic attraction to the therapist. Needless to say, the therapist should be empathic but unresponsive to this erotic dimension. He needs to remind the client gently but firmly that his desire for same-sex intimacy is legitimate, but these needs cannot be legitimately satisfied through a sexual relationship.

Fear and hostility are the other sides of the eroticized transference. There is often a fear of the therapist's criticism—which he anticipates as being devastating—and he may protect himself from his feelings for the therapist by hiding behind a mask of teasing and sarcastic comments.

The Value of a Negative Transference

Negative transference reactions can provide a valuable therapeutic opportunity if they are correctly interpreted and understood. A 35-year-old man with a very strong positive transference drove a 3-hour round-trip for his appointment with me every Friday. He still held on to deep hurt and rage toward his father, who had severely neglected and emotionally abused him. One night I needed to cancel my evening appointments, but through a secretarial error, this client was not reached before he had left for my office. Because he had driven such a distance only to find my office closed, he was naturally very hurt and angry. In restitution, I offered him the next session without charge. He demanded—and received—three more free sessions. These too I agreed to in an effort to absorb his deep anger. His sense of having been abused continued, however, and his continuing expectations of restitution finally reached the level of complete unfairness to our relationship. He eventually came to see that he had transferred intensely negative feelings onto me from his relationship with his father.

Negative transference may also take the form of degrading the therapist's own masculinity. The client may ask, "Is your masculinity for real . . . or is it just a phony presentation?"

One 46-year-old man in treatment had a very positive transference toward me, felt very good about coming, and in fact believed that I would finally provide the solution to his lifelong problem. After 5 months of weekly sessions, he suddenly became disillusioned. Many of his sessions had been taken up by outrageous, very amusing stories of his weekly misadventures in pick-up places and his encounters with "tricks," in which he described in detail his comically desperate attempts to achieve orgasm. Although I tried several times to interpret for him why he was telling me these stories, he continued to do so. Clearly he was overvaluing me, and entertaining me was his way of justifying his relationship with me.

He missed one week's session for what appeared to be a valid reason. The next week he arrived in a less animated mood and his attitude toward me was cool. He began by questioning if I could really do him any good. All these nice theories sounded really good, he said, but would they really do anything? His doubts shifted from the treatment program to me. He questioned whether I was his type, and if he could develop his masculine identity from me. He wondered if we shouldn't end the therapy, saying he might feel more comfortable with a therapist who was more masculine. Finally, he said he suspected I too was homosexual.

When he was through talking, I told him that as far as I was concerned, our productive work together had just begun. He had given up the old role of entertainer and at last was expressing real feelings toward me. Now, his chal-

lenge was to maintain mutuality in our relationship—
neither to undervalue nor to overvalue me. Now it was he
and I together in a very real way—without the fantasy he
had held onto that I had the power to cure him. There were
two sessions at this new level of dialogue and interpretation. The following was said during one of those sessions:

In threatening to quit, I was going to do to you what I've
done to every other man . . . trash 'em. If you really were
a faggot . . . you could, I fear, reduce me to all the fuckin'
shit that all the other queers brought me down to, which is
zero.

If I've hated you, it's because I've hated my father. I
castrated you as my father castrated me. My father refused
to share his manhood with me. He'd reduce me to power-
lessness. Will you neglect me like my father?

I see myself repeat this pattern with every man. I
"thing-ize" other men. During the last few weeks I've found
I need to push you out of consciousness. I didn't want to
have any positive feelings about you.

If therapy is to be fruitful, it is essential to work
through such negative transferences, however painful.
They can be an important opportunity for progress if
understood correctly. It is working through and interpreting the transference that is the most important vehicle
for resolving past blocks to growth. There should never be
a termination until the negative transference has been
understood.

From my experience, the more hostile and traumatic
early relationships with father produce the most intense
repressed rage in psychotherapy. As a boy, the client could

not deal with the father. He gained no satisfaction and could not win with him no matter what he did.

Overt hostility toward the therapist is seen more in group than individual sessions, where the client feels support in the presence of the other members. This is where the therapist is most likely to be directly criticized or attacked. Again we see the therapeutic opportunities of the group, where negative transference can be productively used rather than viewed as a problem. At such times it must be remembered that a negative transference is usually a defense against an underlying positive transference.

Even in a positive transference, the client is sometimes unconsciously working against his own progress. As a way of weakening the therapist's effectiveness, he may attempt to become too friendly. He may suggest meeting on the outside, saying "If you weren't my therapist, I know we could be great friends." He may be flirtatious, humorous, entertaining, and he may act out a false image in the presence of the therapist.

There is an anxiety about revealing his true self, yet a desire to be accepted for who he really is. Sometimes this anxiety will take the form of constant compulsive talking; some clients cannot get the words out fast enough. This is a way of not feeling. Running away from himself, afraid of being authentic and being known, the client is slowly brought back by the therapist to himself and his authentic feelings.

Many clients have reported frustrating and ultimately unproductive therapy with aloof therapists (which is standard technique in classical psychoanalysis). This is precisely what the homosexual client *cannot* tolerate. He experienced hurt from a too-distant father, and he now desires and requires authentic personal contact. The therapist must never be austere, aloof, or authoritarian. With such a therapist, the client will leave the therapy if not in anger, then at least in severe disappointment.

The client is powerfully drawn to the therapist who possesses the qualities of the salient father – a balance of nurturance and dominance. This is the type of counselor from whom he will most benefit. The therapist should also be secure in his masculinity. He must be authentic and ready to admit error, and he must be willing to let the client point out that error. He must be committed to being transparent and nondefensive, while at the same time not burdening the client with an excessive confession of his own shortcomings.

Resistance

There are several different forms of resistance seen in reparative therapy.

A number of clients will continually question the therapy, never being quite convinced that it will help them. They may also question the therapist's motivations. Over and over the therapist will be called on to reassure, being set up to prove time and again that he really does care about the client. The therapist's need to be viewed as the good guy – to feel adequate as a helper – is perpetually undermined by this type of client. There may also be an indifference and an unwillingness to connect personally with the therapist, along with a disregard of the therapist's interventions as if he were unimportant.

Particularly deep resistance is often seen immediately

following a significant session in which there was a major breakthrough. In group the client may suddenly begin to make excuses as to why he does not belong with the others, for instance, "no one understands me." This is a reenactment of the old problem of feeling different from his male peers.

Lack of trust is at the heart of most resistance. Trust is a prerequisite to the positive transference that will give the client courage to risk insight and new behaviors. Trust is the foundation for identification—that is, feeling fully a part of the other. The client is remanding a great deal of personal power to the therapist, a man he must trust to lead him into a new way of living.

One source of resistance is the expectation to surrender sexual pleasures. Although he may fully agree with the necessity for giving them up, there remains a part of him that wants to hold onto the secret aspect of himself that was so pleasurable and exciting. Along with that is the requirement to suppress the "wild, naughty boy" that he has longed to express since he took on the false "good little boy" as a child. As one man said, "I want to change . . . but not yet. I want one last summer."

Another, perhaps greater, source of resistance is the requirement to give up the quest for that one special soul mate. Ackerley (1968) describes his search for that ever-elusive "Ideal Friend":

The Ideal Friend was always somewhere else and might have been found if only I had turned a different way. The buses that passed my own bus seemed always to contain those charming boys who were absent from mine; the

ascending escalators in the Tubes fiendishly carried them
past me as I sank helplessly into hell. [p. 132]

For many years the client may have nurtured the
dream of meeting that one man who would be his friend,
lover, confidante, and soul mate, the man who would
answer his deepest need for love and understanding.

Refusal to Identify

Originally, the groundwork was laid for homosexuality
when the young boy rejected the father and the masculinity
he represented. Later in psychotherapy this form of unconscious resistance surfaces again as a "refusal to identify."

Refusal to identify is seen most often at the very start
of therapy, or during some particularly critical phase of
treatment. A childlike type of resistance, it has been recognized in the psychoanalytic literature as an indiscriminate,
total rejection of another person, with an unwillingness to
recognize or connect with any favorable aspects of that
person. The most common form of refusal to identify is the
rationalization of some particular issue into a barrier that
blocks the relationship. Often a point of disagreement or
difference of opinion will give the client the conviction that
he cannot continue in individual or group psychotherapy.
In group, he will find reason to disengage from the others,
believing that he is too young, too old, of a different
educational or sociological background, too long in the gay
life-style, or never in the gay life-style. There follows an
abrupt and total rejection of the therapist and the therapy
group. While still committed to change, the client is led by

his refusal to identify to reject the therapist and other group members in favor of solving his problem alone.

Refusal to identify originates from the boy's self-protective maneuver against the possibility of hurt. For both the prehomosexual boy and the homosexual adult, it is used as a defense against fear of rejection. It is also the client's primary defense against the frustration of giving up homosexual behavior.

Role of the Female Therapist

Most homosexual men tend to anticipate nonacceptance from men and therefore feel more relaxed and comfortable with women. For this reason, many choose a female therapist when first beginning to deal with their problem. However the healing of homosexuality through reparative therapy comes out of work with men. A female therapist may help in general ways, but only a male can stimulate reenactment of the conflictual feelings experienced with males, particularly problems with trust and the need for male acceptance. Only through men can masculine identity be found.

As a framework, we should recall the developmental model of the boy's gender-identity formation. The boy's first and primary identification is with mother, from whom he must later disidentify in order to develop an emotional bonding with the father; then he must move on to male peer relationships. Reparative therapy is a reenactment of this developmental sequence.

The female therapist can set the emotional groundwork for the task that lies ahead. She teaches the client about self-esteem, identification and expression of feelings, and trust in therapeutic relationships. Within the framework of reparative therapy, her role will be to act as a bridge to surrender the client to a male therapist.

Transfer to the male therapist may be facilitated by agreement to conduct overlapping sessions, during which time the client sees each therapist alternately. In such an arrangement, the client is free to express to the female counselor his fears, criticisms, and doubts about the male therapist, and she can help him work through these trust issues. In any event, timetables need to be clearly understood by all three parties. This transfer can be difficult, and it requires close communication between the therapists and mutual understanding of the issues. Both must believe in the treatment's worth and anticipate the client's resistance. Resistance may appear in the form of the client's attempt to ally himself with the female therapist while criticizing the male. This resistance often comes up as a "misunderstanding," specifically, the client's sense that some aspect of himself is not being accepted. He unconsciously anticipates the critical father.

As the "good mother," however, the female therapist will need to actively facilitate the transfer. She should support but not push, being sensitive to his apprehensions but neither rejecting him nor fostering his dependence. Most importantly, she must believe in the importance of the male therapist and the reparenting process.

Childhood patterns will often repeat themselves during the transfer to a male therapist. At the first instance of misunderstanding, the homosexual client often feels unjustly used and betrayed, and reexperiences the feeling he is likely to have had with his father, which is, "I can't win with this man." His inclination is to reject this father figure, manifest indirect aggression toward him by proving him incompetent, and get mother to take his side.

If the female therapist trusts the treatment process, then as a good mother she should bolster, support, and clarify the client's position in response to father's apparent injustice, encouraging him to move out from her sphere to deal with the man directly. To best serve the client's needs, she must resist her own maternal instinct to let him retreat to her.

The primary challenge in working with homosexual clients is always trust of men—trust to continue the dialogue with mutuality in the face of an apparent injustice.

COUNTERTRANSFERENCE

Countertransference—the therapist's own unresolved conflicts projected onto the relationship with the client—can occur in two particular ways in the treatment of homosexuals. One such problem occurs when the therapist wants the client to be "for" him, not permitting the natural unfolding of progress at the client's own rate. There may be a tendency to become impatient with the cycles of progress alternating with stalemate. He might have a vested interest in proving a cure rate and bringing about an example of treatment success.

Besides excessive ego-investment, the second serious challenge to the therapist is to avoid returning the client's hostility with a hostile defensiveness of his own. The therapist should be able to tolerate negativity and respond without being either defensive or patronizing. He may also be tempted to cut short the client's hostility by providing immediate interpretation. Instead, he must make himself the object of the acting-out of feelings, and he must tolerate and understand this. What is of foremost importance is that from the start the therapist foster a trusting and intimate relationship through acceptance of the client as a unique person. He must be sensitive to him as an individual and hold him in high regard because he understands the client's struggle. Some therapists feel uncomfortable with the emotional dependency and neediness of many homo-sexual clients and feel out of control or smothered. The therapist must be the "good enough" father, willing to be "for" the son. He must reach out and give of himself sincerely and compassionately. He must challenge the client in a way that is direct and honest, without manipu-lating or contaminating the relationship with his own needs.

One danger in the area of countertransference is that the therapist who has not completely outgrown his own same-sex love needs will become emotionally dependent upon the client's admiration and will manipulate him to gain it. The therapist needs to be able to hold in check an overly seductive client, who may stir up feelings in him which he fears may be sexual (whether or not, in fact, they are). If the therapist permits a sexual encounter, needless to say the consequences will be devastating to the client. After an initial period of short-term gratification and excitement, the client will lose his ability to trust and will feel used and exploited; the therapeutic relationship will be destroyed, and the client will become cynical about all psychotherapy.

The work of the therapist depends upon many inti-mate and personal processes within himself. Consequently he must be clear about his feelings and he must be contin-ually sure of his own motivations.

16

Therapeutic
Issues

REPARATIVE THERAPY AS INITIATION

Most models of psychotherapy can be placed in one of two categories: "masculine-initiatory" or "feminine-unfolding." The unfolding model reflects the feminine psyche, and views the person as having a relatively harmonious relationship to life. Assuming that a client is given an accepting setting and ample time, it trusts the natural momentum from within to carry him to his fullest identity. The humanistic schools of psychology and, in particular, the Rogerian school, typify this approach to psychotherapy. Because the consciousness of our times has become increasingly feminine, it is relatively easy for the reader to understand this unfolding model of personal development.

Whereas the feminine function is to integrate and consolidate, masculine consciousness divides, names, and individuates. Masculine consciousness is generally thought of as crude, harsh, and somehow unhumanistic, and it has fallen from favor in today's therapeutic community. Of less popularity today, therefore, is the masculine-initiatory therapeutic process. Initiatory therapy reflects the typically linear masculine mind with its one-dimensional sense of progression: "I will move from here to there." There is a tendency to conceptualize sequentially, viewing progress as consisting of a series of tasks or trials for which there is a "win" or "lose." This hierarchical achievement mentality is witnessed at men's fraternity initiations and other such rites of passage.

Initiatory treatment is designed to accommodate this special function of the masculine psyche. In therapy, men need milestones to assess their progress. They generally have difficulty talking directly about their emotional experiences and relationships, and are inclined to express themselves obliquely through events, tasks, and objects. Women tend to find such frames of reference less necessary. For them, a felt sense of progress assures that there has been improvement.

In the realm of personal development, a man's need for scorekeeping may, in the final analysis, be impractical. But though we may dismiss a man's desire for such tangible results as unsophisticated, a truly effective therapy for men will satisfy this masculine mode of personal development.

Throughout human history a boy's passage into manhood has always been marked by some sort of initiatory trial. Mircea Eliade said that every human existence consists of a series of initiatory trials or ordeals through which man created himself. When we look closely at these rites of passage, we see that they always involve some sort of decisive choice or struggle. The masculine-initiation treatment therefore requires systematic acts of will and determination, often requiring the decision to go counter to what is easiest or most pleasurable. Its philosophy is, "If we wait for it to happen, it may never happen." This philosophy finds analogy in embryology. Unless the fetus undergoes secondary hormonal changes, it remains female. This is referred to as the "Eve first, then Adam" principle (Money 1988). Similarly, if masculine-identity tasks are not completed, one remains feminine.

Reparative therapy trusts less in the spontaneous revelatory process and places more responsibility on the client, expecting him to take charge of his destiny, with the therapist as mentor. The therapist plays a particularly directive role in this type of therapy. Whereas in the unfolding model the therapist elicits change and growth through a relatively passive presence, the initiatory therapist is actively present and challenging. He assumes a more instructive role in the treatment, facilitating growth as a mentor, leader, model, and coach. On the one hand he is supportive, and on the other, confrontative, like the salient father. He conveys confidence that gender empowerment and developmental completion are attainable. Masculine-initiatory treatment is particularly suited for the problem of homosexuality, in view of one of the origins of the condition, namely, an initiatory failure.

EGO-STRENGTHENING AND SELF-ASSERTION

A fragmented or wounded identity in any aspect – especially in one so very profound as gender identity – always diminishes ego strength and personal power. Intrinsic power comes from a clear sense of "I am," the determination that "I will," and the confidence that "I can" (Horner 1989). Resolution of homosexual feelings is associated with the development of personal power. The client is well on the way to healing when he himself becomes more of the man he finds attractive in others. As stated earlier, we do not sexualize what we identify with; when we identify with someone, we are no longer sexually attracted to them. It is always to the other-than-ourselves that we are drawn.

Ask a man with a homosexual condition what he is attracted to, and he will most likely tell you confidence, self-possession, and a take-charge attitude in his life. Ask a woman what she finds attractive in a man, and she will usually say the same things as the homosexual – because she too lacks these masculine qualities. That is not to say that she does not possess power, but she possesses it in the feminine form.

Homosexual attraction occurs most intensely when the client attempts new ways of asserting his masculine power. Confronting a colleague or boss, changing careers, moving out on his own all call upon an inner strength at variance with his old patterns of passivity, compliance, and compromise. As if exercising an undeveloped muscle, he quickly feels drained and fatigued. There is often the sensation of being out of control. However much he may not want to give in to it, sexual contact with another man briefly short-circuits the stress of having to strive for his own masculine assertion. Failure of the early family environment to nurture more than the false "good little boy" image has fostered this assumption that he is weak and fragile. Unwanted sexual acting out is also often preceded by a general sense of disconnectedness with one's feelings, one's body, and one's environment. Boredom, anxiety, and depression inhibit the natural energy flow of the emotions, disconnect a man from his true self, and block his awareness of personal power. Not knowing how to renew himself, he uses the excitement of a sexual encounter to "jump start" the flow of emotions, to spark up the power. A client in group therapy said:

> I feel like an alcoholic who is sobering up. After three months in therapy I now feel more in touch with reality and I am excited about the future. Assertion is my major issue. I am almost never assertive. I have always tended to avoid confrontations, or I confront in a defensive, anxious way instead of honestly and openly. It is an exhausting pattern. I know it has had a lot to do with my destructive sexual habits and perversions.
>
> As I assert myself and remain "sober" and aware, the patterns diminish. Also my relationships become more genuine and less defensive. My self-esteem is growing. My masculinity is something I am just beginning to develop. Through forthrightness with other men, I am slowly discovering it.

Gradually the client will outgrow the old sense of being left out, unappreciated, and easily slighted. Rather than seeking out attention, he will begin to assert himself and reach out to other men. As he begins to experience himself as generous and resourceful in his relationships with other males, he will outgrow the unconscious tendency to feel less powerful and in the receiving mode. Overcoming the unconscious assumption that he is hurt and helpless requires the client to continually challenge himself with new tasks. During therapy he is encouraged to look for practical opportunities that will lead to change and growth. In so doing, he becomes alert to a sense of inner momentum. As one client said: "I've always approached challenges obliquely – now I'm learning to hit things straight on."

As our training in assertion progresses, we address a number of related issues, including the sense of victimization, compromise of self for approval of other men, and hostile dependency. Often men report a tendency to "lose" themselves to another man, followed by anger at having to compromise themselves to gain the other's acceptance.

Bonding

In recent years we have often heard the popular term *bonding*, usually in regard to male relationships. Described in 1969 by Tiger, it results from a selective process in which two individuals choose each other because of a mutual valuing of certain qualities. Bonding conveys a self-esteem to the two individuals because they have chosen each other through the selection process. Bonding relationships are characterized by familiarity, trust, and disclosure. In such a relationship the false self is dropped, permitting honest communication with another. Male bonding characteristically occurs through a shared physical activity or common task. Unlike women, who can sit face-to-face and disclose directly, men bond indirectly through a shared doing. It is this bonding that fosters male identification.

Because they probably had few male friends in childhood and adolescence, most homosexual men missed the phase of masculine initiation, when their peers gathered in groups to tell jokes and exaggerated stories about courageous exploits, conquests with girls, and so on. The bonding that results from this male camaraderie ultimately serves the purpose of reinforcing a sense of masculine identity. Having been detached from this youthful ritual, the homosexual adult still needs to find this sense of masculine connectedness. One client reports: "Being friends . . . has ignited a fire inside me. This whole feeling of confidence I attribute to my new male friends. The idea of having a best friend who you can tell things to just seems to keep moving me." Another said: "Having male friends feels like it's restarting the developmental clock—even though developmentally, some of us are much older."

These initial attempts at male bonding in adulthood sometimes stimulate fears over personal boundary and power issues. Beneath these fears is a basic issue of trust. The client is challenged to look through the confusion and misperceptions, not to be distracted by misplaced anger, nor to withdraw from the challenge through a false, compliant self. He is challenged to overcome feelings of unworthiness and self-condemnation. Gradually he will learn how to show vulnerability and ask for help, and to be transparent and receptive to the lessons other men can teach him.

THE CHALLENGE OF VERBALIZATION

Effective self-expression is often a significant issue for homosexual men. This is understandable since effective self-expression is *the* medium of interpersonal assertion. To speak up is part of the masculine character.

So frequently presented during the course of therapy are the complaints of silent, smouldering anger and lack of assertion, that they are considered predictable symptoms of the homosexual problem. The man may feel weak and incapable of speaking up for himself, sensing himself to be speechless or paralyzed; or he may express himself in a reactionary, provocative, and therefore equally self-defeating manner.

Although homosexual men have the reputation of being highly verbal, my clinical experience has shown many men to have difficulty articulating needs and wants directly and decisively. As little boys these men were not encouraged to articulate their needs and wants, and individualistic expression was not well received within the family system. Heterosexual men are said to have more difficulty expressing their feelings; however the homosexual man's difficulty seems to lie in following through with his expression of feelings into verbalization of needs and wants, thus obtaining practical results. He may do a fine job in expressing hurt, frustration, anger, injustice, loneliness, that is, complaints, but falter in making direct and decisive requests of other persons. As one client explains: "I set my questions up carefully so I can read the answer between the lines before it comes. I try to manipulate an answer so I don't get a 'no.' A clear emphatic request might get me a clear, emphatic 'no,' and I'm afraid to hear that."

The unstructured format of group therapy poses a special challenge to each member to decide how he will solicit the group's assistance. Through spoken or unspoken consensus, the group must decide who will speak, for how long, about what, and for what purpose. Responsibility is placed upon each man to determine for himself his needs and wants in relation to the other members' needs and wants. Group therapy participation also challenges clients to give up the old habit of passive listening. Passive listening is a removed, self-centered hearing that stimulates self-associations rather than placing the emphasis on the speaker's unique experience. Passive listening as a form of defensive detachment perpetuates emotional isolationism. Active listening, on the other hand, is a felt connection with the speaker in which the listener allows himself an internal, felt response to what is being said. This felt response will naturally be accompanied by a behavioral response such as advice, questions, or comments.

GROWING OUT OF THE FALSE SELF

The homosexual man often carries a false self from childhood—a presentation of the "good little boy" who compromises his true self to comply with the expectations of one or both parents. This false self can manifest itself in one of two extremes. It can be an overanimated, theatrical, exaggerated presentation of self, in which there is an excessive expenditure of energy; or it can take the form of dreaminess, passive detachment, and a blasé, above-it-all withholding of personal energy. What makes change especially hard for this client is that he has not yet discovered what will replace the old, familiar false self. He hopes but does not yet fully believe that he *can* grow into a new sense of self with peace, a mature perspective on life, self-possession, and the capacity for intimacy and trust.

To counter the tendency to get bogged down by indecision, self-doubt, and helplessness, the therapist must strike that optimal balance between pressure and support. He must continually nurture the client's awareness of his personal power, while bringing attention to new challenges. In the middle of a client's long, detailed story of complaint, I often interrupt to ask, "So, what is it that you want?" This simple intervention is a way of returning him to his inner-directedness.

COMPETITION

Ex-gay writer and counselor Colin Cook describes an impression he had one day when walking down a path leading to a lake. From behind him came four or five young men in their early twenties, who hurtled past him down the path and threw themselves into the water. Colin watched them wrestling with each other and playing roughly in the lake—diving, laughing, throwing each other under, and playing ball. Watching them, Colin knew without doubt that they were heterosexual (Cook 1990).

Since the homosexual client is usually inclined to avoid competition, therapy must involve a test of his resources. Those clients more advanced heterosexually are usually quicker to seize opportunities, to confront challenges on the job, and to speak up effectively (but not

reactively) to male authority. Competition is important—
to experience a struggle of power, to match one's strength
against an equal other. We know that "Iron sharpens iron;
so one man sharpens another" (Proverbs 27:17).

Typically, the prehomosexual boy misses the physical
contact of rough-and-tumble play with father, and later,
he does not take part in the physical competitions
characteristic of his age. While he was often looking on
from a safe distance, his peers were roughing it up and
feeling their strength against one another. Masculinity is
inherently connected with the body, and when one is out
of contact with bodily activity, it diminishes the sense of
masculinity.

Clients report that when they engage in vigorous
physical activity, especially competitive sports, they feel
more masculine. In time, most members of the group
develop some male, sports-related interests. For one person, this may mean hiking with a friend, for another, it is
playing tennis once a week with a co-worker. For yet
another, it is going to the gym, a particularly "straight" gym
where there are no distractions. One client describes the
connection between physical activity and masculinity:

> While I wrestle with a friend or play a hard game of
> racquetball I feel real masculine. I may be thirty, but
> something clicks and there's an acceleration in me, an
> energy, and I feel real masculine. I have no attraction to the
> guys I play racquetball with . . . he's male, I'm male, I'm on
> a par with that person.
>
> I played racquetball the other day, then we got the
> usual after-game drink, Gatorade. . . . That's what you're
> supposed to drink. It felt good to be sweaty. Then I looked

out and there was a newsstand and a singles magazine. There was a woman on it and I was attracted to her. I thought, "Where is that girl now that I'm ready for her?"

I remember as a kid, I must have been five, I loved wrestling, pounding those other kids. But somewhere along the line it became a "violent sport" to me and I stopped because I wasn't supposed to be violent. But I just loved the contact and I don't understand where that shut off and I began to change. I'm sort of angry at myself for stopping. A lot of times I blame myself. If I had pushed myself and not stopped—not succumbed—I feel like I might be different today.

Although gay apologists often describe the historical competitiveness among men as a source of social evil, we in fact see competition as a natural and ingrained part of the male psyche. Competition can be a barrier to male intimacy, but it is the way in which men discover their masculine strength. In fact, it may be the only way.

NONSEXUAL MALE RELATIONSHIPS

As we have seen, central to the repairing of homosexuality is the establishment of nonsexual intimate relationships with men. Same-sex friendships have shown themselves to be therapeutic in the lives of men who, without psychotherapy, discovered their own ways of dealing with homosexuality. One such man was the great linguistic philosopher, Ludwig Wittgenstein. In 1919, Wittgenstein left the family home and took up lodgings in Vienna. As his biographer explains:

Wittgenstein was now to find the third district, selected for its convenience, convenient in an unexpected way. By walking for ten minutes . . . he could quickly reach the parkland meadows of the Prater, where rough young men were ready to cater to him sexually. Once he had discovered this place, Wittgenstein found to his horror that he could scarcely keep away from it. Several nights each week he would break away from his rooms and make the quick walk to the Prater, possessed, as he put it to friends, by a demon he could barely control. [Bartley 1985, p. 40]

His solution was twofold:

Wittgenstein would seek milieux or situations satisfying two conditions: to be removed from the temptation of easy and casual sexual relationships with street youths, and such like; and to be surrounded by youths with whom he could enjoy platonic relationships that would "bring him to life." Thus a series of close friendships developed with good-looking young men of sweet and docile disposition. . . . toward whom Wittgenstein could become emotionally very much attached . . . friendships, then, he used as moral encounters; within them he became creative, intimate, even playful. [pp. 42–43]

In short, Wittgenstein dealt with his conflict by resolving "to live in a way that will make what is problematic disappear" (p. 42) – through nonerotic male friendships. As one client explained:

Having friends has been the whole problem since I was a child. It's easier for me to make friends with men that are physically smaller or less aggressive than I am. It is a challenge for me to go out and seek out men who intimidate me when they are typical stereotypes of males.

When I am able to be friends with those people that I've often been intimidated by . . . it reaffirms my own masculinity. Often that was my problem in growing up. Instead of just trying to be friends with a certain boy, I would put myself down by thinking, I *can't* be friends with him because I'm not as good as him.

Now that I'm an adult, when I am able to be friends with such a man, this sexual area just diminishes. And it reaffirms my masculinity because I know that I'm able to be close to such a person without sexualizing him.

Another example of the natural diminishing of homosexuality through male friendships is found in Green's *The Sissy Boy Syndrome* (1987). He describes a boy in whom "the sexual need for males is seen as a substitute for nonsexual attention from males." The young man says:

I think I have found the attention I need from guys through my friends . . . so the sexual or romantic interest has declined. . . . As I came to be friends with people with whom I can discuss very personal feelings, then the need to perhaps have sex with them, or think about having sex with them, disappeared. . . . I knew that I did not share many common interests with guys my age, and I had a sense that that was wrong. Now I have common interests with my friends. I no longer have a sense of the way I was, not being interested in sports or things like that, as bad, as negative. [pp. 365–366]

Green, who does not believe homosexuals can change in both fantasy and behavior, did not know what to make of this case. He simply called it "atypical of the sample studied" and did not investigate the young man further (private correspondence).

Leonardo da Vinci was also said to have suffered from a homosexual problem. He chose the opposite course, however, and isolated himself from close male friendships. This may have contributed to his years of reputed loneliness and depression.

Freud (1911) believed homosexuals who redirected their sexual energy into social service were among those who contributed the most to society. He described "those who set themselves against an indulgence in sensual acts" through the sublimation of erotic interests as "distinguished by taking a particularly active share in the general interests of humanity" (p. 61).

The perennial dream of finding the ideal male friendship with qualities of sexual and romantic excitement locks the gay man into an addictive and perpetually frustrating cycle. To free himself from this cycle he must learn to appreciate a relaxed friendship without sexual excitement. At first this feels for some like "making do with less," settling for the colorless ordinariness of male friendship. He is likely to be cynical about "boring, common" friendships.

Problems in Homosexual–Heterosexual Male Friendships

It has been observed that girls put relationships first and group activities second, whereas boys do exactly the opposite (Sanford and Lough 1988). This difference in priorities also tends to distinguish homosexual men from heterosexuals. Many homosexuals express difficulty in developing friendships with heterosexual men. Although homosexual men may desire to "share feelings," straight guys are more likely to want to relate through shared activities. The homosexual man is often ill prepared to relate through sports or tasks. One client, expressing this frustration, said:

> Straight men talk about sports, because it's safe. But that's a real trap for us because of our need. We want a greater amount of disclosure, but when we go for that it only makes matters worse because all they want to do is talk about sports. It feels like a real catch-22; you have to talk about something really uninteresting to you in order to make the connection. You've got to talk sports before you can get to the guy's feelings.

Another client agreed: "It's got to be, like—'What are your true feelings about the Rams?'"

Sometimes this attitude leads the homosexual to the belief that he is superior to the common man. As a consequence of his sexual orientation, he is supposedly more sensitive, artistic, cultured—somehow more elite—than the ordinary straight man. We see this elitism not only in individuals, but as a characteristic of some gay groups as well.

Categories of Male Friendships

Let us consider four categories of male friendships for the homosexual in increasing order of their reparative value:

Gay friendships create the possibility of erotic attraction and a mutually exploitative sexual agenda. Honest friendship is contaminated by flirtation and vague innuendoes, with each looking for cues of sexual receptivity from

the other. Mutual game-playing and manipulation undermine efforts at establishing equality and mutuality, and
diminish the value of this type of relationship.

Celibate homosexual friendships with other non-gay homosexuals offer an empathy and special understanding.
However they are limited in their potential to break down
the male mystique, which is usually reserved for the straight
man. Challenges to these relationships include mutually
reactive defensive detachment and same-sex ambivalence.
These friendships are preparation for the more challenging
relationship with the heterosexual male, who is usually less
understanding of the homosexual's challenge.

Heterosexual, nonsexually attractive friendships have
somewhat more value. Life circumstances often put the
client into contact with such men, but he feels no motivation to establish a friendship. When the man seems ordinary, and the old familiar sexual attraction is missing, there
is often a contempt for him, and he typically seems unin-
teresting or boring. However, such friendships can offer the
opportunity for male bonding. Of particular therapeutic
value, though, is the client's disclosure of his homosexual
struggle to the straight friend. A very risky and anxiety-
producing challenge, this disclosure should be a prudent,
calculated gamble. However if it is met with understanding,
a very healing experience will result. The exchange will
bring the friendship to a new depth of honesty and intimacy, and it will break down yet another rationalization
that perpetuates defensive detachment ("If he really knew
me, he would never accept me").

Heterosexual, sexually attractive male friendships with
men for whom the client feels an erotic attraction offer the
greatest opportunity for healing. Only through such asso-

ciations can there be the transformation from erotic attraction to true friendship—that is, the demystifying of the distant male. While aesthetic appreciation for the man's good looks and masculine qualities may always be present, it will become increasingly evident that sexual fantasies do not fit within the mutually respectful friendship. As the client experiences increasing acceptance and familiarity, over time this grows into identification, and the original sexual feelings naturally diminish. This transformational shift from *sexual to fraternal* (i.e., eros to philia) is the essential healing experience of male homosexuality.

THE TRANSFORMATION

A perceptual meaning transformation occurs in the course of treatment as the client becomes increasingly aware of his true motivations. He realizes what he has always suspected—that an identification deficit lies behind his homoerotic attractions. Insight and self-awareness unavoidably alter the erotic illusion. Like a theatre patron who witnesses a prop fall during a scene in a play, he can never see the scene in the same illusional way.

This meaning transformation is described by a client in one of his sessions:

Client: In the past weeks I've noticed a difference in my attraction to guys I see on the streets. Sure there's an attraction there, but I'm getting bored with the whole thing. Before, not a half hour would pass after a sexual encounter, before I'd want to be back out cruising again. But now I feel the futility of it ahead of time. It used to be I'd feel the futility of it afterward, but now I feel it ahead of time.

Therapist: That's an essential part of the cure. . . . just seeing through to the end and that futility.

Client: Yes . . . (*laugh*) but now I want to get to the place where I don't even have the attraction . . . just the futility, that's all.

Therapist: Well, that's going to happen. As you progress, the experience of attraction and futility will occur closer together in time.

Client: Sometimes I find myself pushing away the futility by embellishing the attraction with sexual fantasy. Whereas the fantasy used to take over on its own, now I see myself trying to push the energy into fantasizing in order to postpone the inevitable futility. In some ways I'm trying to hang onto the old familiar feelings.

Another client described a sexual experience as follows:

> In the middle of it all, I suddenly felt like a kid. All of a sudden I thought, "I'm just a kid playing 'touch me' games to see what the other guy is like." Like two little kids discovering sexuality games for the first time. Like, "Well, do you have the same thing I have?"
>
> There was the feeling that I was just making up for something I missed in childhood. Touching him felt juvenile and stupid, like there was nothing real beyond this.

RELATIONSHIPS WITH WOMEN

When a young man who is homosexual encounters an attractive woman, his defensive maneuver is to stay on the level of friendship. Being friends with a woman is very easy, and he can talk for hours in a comfortable, familiar way. This kind of relationship is so familiar because it is much of what he did in childhood with mother, sisters, and their female friends. The task to accomplish here is to move beyond the interactional role of the "good little boy" that he learned to play in childhood. The good-little-boy role—a distorted creation of the unhealthy feminine—may have been fostered by mother to gratify her frustrations in an unhappy marriage.

Expecting such a man to move beyond platonic friendships with women is to set him up for almost certain failure. One main cause for past psychoanalytic treatment failures was the premature encouragement of heterosexual relations. Prior theory—which emphasized the overpossessive mother—viewed the homosexual as fearful of women (heterophobic). Ironically, it is actually his fear of *men* that leaves the homosexual developmentally unready to approach a woman sexually. Although it might be very easy for the client to become friends with a woman, it may be impossible for him to sexualize the friendship. On the other hand, the sexual attraction to men will be immediate, but he will have to work on the friendship.

Romantic relationships with women have actually little or no value in therapy until the latter stages. When I encouraged clients to develop these relationships before they were ready, they came back reporting that they felt uncomfortable, artificial, and dishonest. They saw themselves as having used the woman in an experiment. Because their feelings could not match their behavior, they believed the relationship was exploitative, and universally they returned with a sense of failure. Not only did these clinical attempts to encourage dating prove fruitless and frustrating, but the pressure they created eroded my relationship with the client. These men invariably talked about male relationships as more significant, more intense, more satisfying, and more relevant.

THERAPEUTIC DREAM WORK

Sometimes dreams have a healing wisdom to reveal, and when a particularly intense or disturbing dream erupts spontaneously into consciousness, it should be addressed in therapy.

Through progress in therapy, a 26-year-old client had begun to see his homosexuality more clearly. An aspiring actor, he described a dream he had had on three occasions:

> I'm in bed with a man, and I'm kissing him. I don't have an erection because I'm not turned on. I have a towel over my waist to cover up the fact I don't have an erection, because the other guy does. But I'm thinking, "Why am I kissing him, caressing him? I don't enjoy this. Why am I here?"
>
> Then my mind moves back to take a wide angle shot — and it turns out to be a set. And they say "Great! Cut! Good work!" And I realize I've just been doing a job.

Some emotionally repressed clients can get back in touch with their inner vitality through an exploration of dreams. However it should be cautioned that regular expenditure of energy on dreams may foster a regressive tendency that works against extroversion, which is the emphasis of reparative therapy. Clients may risk becoming too engrossed in inner images when they should be focusing instead on practical external challenges.

BIBLIOTHERAPY

Reparative therapy is strongly supported by bibliotherapy—the therapeutic utilization of books and other reading material. Availability of audio tapes, video cassettes, periodicals from ex-gay groups, and other educational sources outside the therapy setting offers support for the often lonely personal struggle. There are many outreach groups such as Exodus International, Courage, Homosexuals Anonymous, Regeneration, and Love in Action, which offset the demoralizing confusion created by gay propaganda and the popular media of our culture.

17

Group
Psychotherapy

Every client is cautious, even fearful, at the first group meeting. There is the dreaded thought, "God forbid I should meet someone I know!" Most non-gay homosexual men have never sat and spoken openly before with other men who share their struggle.

Although the first sessions are characterized by an intense curiosity about one another, there is a great fear of disclosing personal details to someone who may turn out to be connected with their everyday lives. This concern for confidentiality has a realistic base when we consider that these men do not feel proud of their condition. Their sexual feelings and internal principles have long been in discord.

PROCESS

Once a part of the group, each man discovers that this is a place to feel safe, understood, and accepted. The format is unstructured and open-ended. Each man is expected to accept responsibility when he feels ready to speak up, making a place for himself in the flow of conversation. Within the group the men share common problems, experiences, hard-won insights from their own struggles, and inspiration. Most important, they share a common challenge: the desire to resolve the internal sense of weakness and hurt in order to claim full masculine identity.

One client explained:

For me, the group has been like putting on a pair of glasses when you're nearsighted. Before, I could only see vague images and patterns.

Another said:

I figured out that I suffered this male deficit before I came here. I came here because I knew I needed help in figuring out what to do about it. The reason I never made much progress before was that I was working in a vacuum, was all alone, and wasn't talking to anybody about it. As soon as I found some camaraderie here with guys that felt the same

way and had the same troubles, then I could start dis-
cussing solutions.

Before we look at the specific dynamics that apply to
the homosexual group, we should understand a basic
model of group process, which is divided into three levels of
communication.

All interactions in group psychotherapy can be placed
into one of three categories from least to most therapeutic:

Level 1: Without
Level 2: Within
Level 3: Between

Level 1: "Without," is typical of the first part of the
group session. Both in group and individual therapy, Level
1 serves as safe warm-up talk. It typically involves conversation about what has happened during the week. It is a
reporting of external events with no consideration of interior motivations.

Level 2: "Within," is when two or more people begin to
investigate and clarify a member's internal process, that is,
the motivation behind the events he reports. There is a
shared attempt to understand how he participated in
causing the events to happen.

Level 3: "Between," is the most therapeutic level, the
most personally challenging, and that which risks the most
but offers the greatest opportunity for building trust. It
occurs when at least two members of the group talk about
their relationship with each other in the present time, while
it is happening. Timing is central to the third level, and
members must speak in the present. When expressing their

positive and negative feelings for each other in the moment, they describe what they are experiencing, while it is actually happening.

Considerable time may be required to break through to Level 3 and direct dialogue. Group members may be easily hurt at this level and there is a great deal of approach–avoidance and fault-finding. When a member is hurt, he often makes veiled references to his doubts about whether the group can really be of benefit to him. For all groups, Level 3 is the most rewarding. It affords the opportunity to experience mutuality, with its balance of challenge ("kick in the pants") and support ("pat on the back"). Group sessions should not be used as a substitute for individual counseling, but as an adjunct for the ongoing work in individual therapy.

MUTUALITY

In the beginning sessions of our groups there is an initial phase of "blemish-finding." There is resistance to identifying with the group: they're not my type, they're too old, too young, too promiscuous, too naive, and so on. This is a first manifestation of each man's defensive detachment. This defensive detachment causes the homosexual to be locked into the frustrating pattern of creating two kinds of men from all significant male relationships: he either devaluates, minimizes, dismisses, and delegates other men to an inferior position—or he elevates, admires, and places them on a pedestal.

Placement on the scale is determined by "type," the

symbolic representation of a valued masculine attribute he unconsciously feels he lacks, and which the other person supposedly possesses. These qualities with which he is fascinated usually have little to do with the character of the person, and once a realistic familiarity develops, the person as a whole usually loses his sexual attractiveness. This emotionally crippling pattern of scaled relationship is reenacted in the group process. Obsession with type is the source of much anger and disappointment in homosexual relationships and it accounts for much of the gay relationship's characteristic volatility and instability.

Besides devaluing or overvaluing other men, there is a third possible response mode—mutuality. A relationship characterized by mutuality has the qualities of honesty, disclosure, and equality. Even where there is an imbalance of age, status, or education, deep sharing with one another serves as an equalizer. Mutuality in relationships is the goal of group psychotherapy, for it is on this level of same-sex interaction that healing occurs. Mutuality creates the opening through which passes masculine identification; it is the passage through which each man enters into healing. Explained one young seminarian, who had had difficulty keeping his vow of chastity:

> For a long time there have been needs that I have been suppressing. After this year in group therapy, I have come to hold more hope for my future. Now I am less likely to sexualize affection and hugs from other men, and I am able to relate to them without sexual feelings getting in the way.

A second young man said:

> If I came to therapy with the thought that I just had to abstain from sex without any positive new direction toward

intimacy with other men, I don't think I would be hopeful for real change. Now I have accepted my need for real intimacy, not the sexual expression of it.

One group member described the group experience as follows:

My group is the masculine energy I need every day. It has been a powerful, intense, and enriching experience. Our group has become the father we all need and missed in our early years. There is a power, a presence among us that keeps us giving, healing, and caring.

Although ostensibly the subject matter of these groups is homosexuality, the underlying process, in fact, is the universal one of initiation, growth, and change. While our specific concern here is the cessation of a certain behavior, these groups are committed to the common human task of growing toward wholeness. The men see that we are all challenged to move forward into fullest adulthood, and each one of us has his own personal obstacles to overcome, based upon past developmental failures. The distinctly human abilities to self-reflect, to evaluate oneself, and to choose positive change are true miracles of human nature.

DEFENSIVE DETACHMENT AMONG GROUP MEMBERS

All psychological treatments must overcome some form of resistance against growth. We may say very simply that the treatment of homosexuality is the undoing of the resistance of defensive detachment from males. Group therapy is a powerful opportunity to identify and work through defensive detachment.

At times, it seems as if all our group-therapy members are negatively charged magnets repelling each other. While there is a sensitivity and genuine concern for each other, there is also a guardedness and criticalness that can paralyze the entire group process.

Defensive detachment is the blocking mechanism that prevents male bonding and identification. Originally a protection against childhood hurt from males, it is now a barrier to honest intimacy and mutuality with men in adulthood. The homosexual is caught between the natural desire to fulfill his masculine development through identification with men, and his defensive detachment, which creates fear and anger in male relationships. Manifestations of defensive detachment appear as hostility, competitiveness, distrust, and anxiety about acceptance. Group members are sensitive to issues of betrayal and deception because as children they felt tricked and betrayed. We see fearfulness, vulnerability and defensiveness, fragility of relationships, and slow and tentative trust easily shattered by the slightest misunderstanding.

The most common resistance to bonding with other men in group psychotherapy is silence. Silence is an expression, if a mute one. It says, "I'm not interested, not involved; I'm not affected by what you say." Some clients have difficulty identifying their feelings and thus finding something to say; others have difficulty asserting themselves by expressing what they feel.

Because it manifests itself so frequently in communication among homosexuals, sarcasm also becomes an important therapeutic issue. Sarcasm is veiled aggression; it doesn't feel good, but the person who receives a humorous barb cannot directly address its implied hostility. Sarcasm is a common weapon with which homosexual men diminish both others and themselves.

The power of sarcasm lies in its style—either humorous, innocent, or offhanded—which is difficult to respond to directly. If the person should address the hurt, then the one who leveled the sarcasm can claim innocence of responsibility for its content. As a form of covert hostility, sarcasm is the opposite of the direct, honest confrontational style among men that we hope to engender. Consequently, sarcasm is pointed out immediately—particularly in group therapy, where it is most likely to be utilized.

It is interesting to note that Gay Affirmative Therapy (GAT) encounters the very same difficulties in establishing trust among group members. Their descriptions of suspicion, distrust, and resistance are strikingly similar to ours. That the very same interpersonal difficulties should be encountered by a therapy that encourages gay identity reinforces our supposition that there is an intrapsychic dynamic (defensive detachment) that is characteristic of the homosexual condition. Each model of therapy defines this intrapsychic dynamic differently. For us it is defensive detachment; for GAT, it is seen as socially induced "homophobia."

ORDINARY VERSUS MYSTERIOUS MALES

In our group process we frequently return to the distinction made between two kinds of males by our clients: ordinary and mysterious. Mysterious men are those who possess enigmatic masculine qualities that both perplex and allure the client. Such men are overvalued and even idealized, for they are the embodiment of qualities that the client wishes he had attained for himself.

There is a resistance to developing friendships with familiar, nonmysterious males—those who do not possess these qualities. Ordinary men are devalued, sometimes contemptuously dismissed. As a result, most clients have had few or no male relationships characterized by mutuality. By placing other men in one of these two categories, he justifies his detachment. He either feels too inferior or too superior to establish the mutuality necessary for friendship. This resistance to making friendships with nonmysterious males is one reason why, after an initial interest and excitement about meeting other group members, feelings often turn to disillusionment. The client sees the other members in the group as "just as weak as I am," and he becomes contemptuous of them. He may be particularly disgusted by the "weaker" group members, those more effeminate, more emotional, who display personality traits of vulnerability. It is important that this resistance be dealt with in individual therapy.

The therapist's task is to confront this defense and to convey to the client that indeed these group members do have something to offer. He can show him how helping a weaker member can be directly instrumental in his own development. It may be necessary to remind the client that we learn a lesson better when we teach it to others. In helping weaker group members along, he will deepen his own sense of masculine security.

The essential therapeutic experience is the demystification of men from sex object to real person. Sorting out his experience of these two distinct perceptions, one 28-year-old client said:

> Immediately after every homosexual experience, it feels like something is missing. The closeness I wanted with another man just didn't happen. I'm left with the feeling that sex is just not what I wanted.
>
> This is in contrast to my relationship with my straight friend, Bob. . . . I don't feel the need to be sexual with him. To be so close to him, getting everything I want from our friendship, but not even thinking about sex . . . when I allow myself to really be in those friendships, that's very empowering.

TRANSFERENCE REACTIONS IN GROUP PSYCHOTHERAPY

Just as unresolved feelings from the past are reenacted in individual sessions, so too do we see them in group therapy. Of the various negative transference reactions seen in group sessions, the most common is defensive detachment—the self-protective emotional distancing of one member from another. Sometimes we see factions with two or three members splitting off against the others, but more often one individual detaches himself, claiming the other men are unfair or do not understand him. This solo split is a reenactment from early childhood. Emotional investment in a group of men reactivates many old uncertainties about belonging in the company of males. If the client is honest with himself he will recognize that he created excuses for not belonging, for another man's differentness is not justification for disassociation from him.

It is often obvious that a departed group member feels ambivalent, for he may continue to see other members outside the meetings. He desires to maintain a connection and a sense of belonging with the group, but feels too threatened to participate in a therapeutic process requiring accountability for his behavior and honest disclosure of his motivations. Detaching himself offers him the secondary narcissistic gratification of making him feel somehow special. All too often he represses his anxieties by hiding behind this fantasy that he is different and special, even if this so-called specialness alienates and isolates him. A question central to the healing of his homosexuality will be "How do I develop my individuality while deepening my identification with the common man?"

Our most difficult group sessions were when two or more group members needed to express negative feelings for each other (Level 3 of the communications process). An argument and resulting hurt feelings would sometimes lead one of the men to threaten to leave. At such times, other members felt disillusionment with the group process. They interpret such conflicts as proof that the group cannot work and their decision to take part was mistaken.

PROBLEMS IN THE EXPRESSION OF ANGER

Problems with anger inevitably show themselves in the course of group therapy. As boys, many clients were made to feel bad for any show of anger; their homes did not tolerate the expression of hostility. If anger was ever expressed it was on the parents' part and it emotionally devastated the entire family. When father (often an otherwise withdrawn man) did get angry, there was little or no emotional support in the relationship to cushion the hurt. Furthermore, the boy was not permitted to show his own anger in defense but was left to retreat and sulk. Consequently the following boyhood lessons were deeply ingrained: (1) Anger directed at me equals rejection of me, and (2) I am not entitled to express my anger—it is unworthy of expression.

The influence of these two lessons (I cannot give or take anger) becomes manifest in group when members encounter a relational difficulty. Expression of anger is challenging for both the giver and the receiver. The man who is expressing the anger may truly need this new opportunity to have his anger heard and respected. On the other hand, the recipient may find it hard to avoid feeling assaulted and rejected as a person. He may have great difficulty regaining his self-possession and trusting that the other man will still be there for him in friendship. Trust in the group process is the essential issue here. The men have not yet learned that there is an innate sense of fairness in such a group that comes together in benevolence. They have not yet learned to trust the resiliency and resourcefulness of men to reconcile their individual differences. In their hypersensitivity, their vulnerability and defensiveness, they may forget they share a common struggle.

As a boy, each of these men chose defensive detachment as a solution to what felt at the time to be the overwhelming challenge of male relationships. But he never imagined the price he would pay for this decision in the future. Now as an adult each man is faced with another choice—either to continue to hold tenaciously to that childhood decision, or to open himself up to a trusting relationship in the faith that healing is possible.

DESPAIR AND HOPE

The question "Why me?" is often asked by the homosexual client, especially at times of defeat and discouragement. Psychodynamically, we have answered this question in previous chapters. But the existential "Why me?" is much more difficult to respond to. This is a spiritual question for which there are no easy answers. The man who suffers in order to be reborn into fullness of life is a part of the larger cycle of birth and death, joy and pain, and birth again. The homosexual dilemma is a powerful manifestation of this age-old drama of alienation and reconciliation, death and resurrection, and intensely felt conflict. The homosexual problem offers a *via dolorosa*, a way of growing toward wholeness.

The homosexual struggle finds a strong analogy in the person who commits his life to a moral ideal. The person has a transformational insight into the truth of his life, and while not always living that life perfectly, he nevertheless directs it toward that chosen commitment.

The struggle toward wholeness requires a choice to let go and to make a leap of faith into the unknown. There is a nakedness, a yielding of control and an offering of that control to a greater power.

In the midst of the most despairing of times I attempt to make each man conscious of the new life that lies beneath his loneliness, his frustration, and his discouragement. At such times I try to support the man in going through the pain—not to run away or avoid or project or to lash out in anger or blame, but to sit with the pain and to penetrate it, trusting that there is new life on the other side of suffering.

The acquisition of masculine identity may be a lifetime process. Yet no matter what a man's earlier deprivations, opportunities remain available throughout life to grow toward wholeness.

18

The Initial
Interview

INTRODUCTION

It is usually possible to predict in the first session or two
if reparative therapy will be of help to the client. He will
usually know immediately whether or not he is in accord
with its premises. Those men who are clearly distressed
by their homosexuality and committed to working toward change typically find reparative therapy to be
exactly what they were seeking. If the first session lapses
into a debate about the merits of reparative therapy or
the ethical implications of the gay life-style alternative,

this is an indication that the client is not ready for this therapy.

With some clients, it is necessary to explore further the motivations behind their guilt. Guilt is an emotional reaction that signals danger to the conscience — and the client who is genuinely motivated to overcome his homosexuality can offer convincing reasons to justify his guilt. If his depth of commitment is strong, and he can clarify the reasons for his guilt about homosexual behavior, then he is likely to do well in therapy.

Some clients agree with the premises of reparative therapy but do not have the ego strength to see it through. Such men usually drop out within the first few months in spite of their apparent commitment. Lack of ego-strength leaves a client vulnerable to the attractions of the gay life-style. I have found a higher proportion of homosexual men with moderate to severe borderline features. While these men may value the supportive structure of individual and group sessions, their overwhelming social-adjustment concerns usually overshadow their sexual-orientation problems. Overall these men do poorly in diminishing homosexual behavior. Other clients who do poorly are those men who were brought in by parents or a spouse. Unless they are self-motivated, they usually stay a few sessions to satisfy their loved ones or to hear what I have to say about the problem. But eventually they drop out.

Another type of client who does poorly is the one who does not fit the syndrome described in this book. Many such men show pronounced narcissistic features — inflated self-regard and feelings of entitlement, with a charming exterior but little empathy for others. In their great need to be admired by others, they choose a same-sex love object, often with physical features similar to their own. However, their idealization of this other self can quickly turn to depreciation and contempt. This type of client usually has no particular difficulties with male friendships or self-assertion, shows no evidence of male gender-identity deficit, and has a family history that does not fit our pattern. The treatment issues we address are not relevant to his issues. He usually does not seek therapy on his own, but is pressured into coming in by parents or a wife who cannot tolerate his gay affairs.

Many clients have "slips" but continue to work toward change. Clients do not drop out of therapy because of the inability to control ongoing, unwanted homosexual behavior. Rather, those who drop out do so because of a loss of commitment to their goal. Then some have a change of heart and return months or even years later. In fact, some men return years later for problems other than homosexuality; their homosexuality sometimes has diminished without psychotherapy.

Some clients have never been in therapy before and never even spoken about their problems to anyone else. These men feel strongly about their dissatisfaction with homosexuality and often find this therapy to be exactly what they were looking for.

Many of the clients have been in therapy before. Their previous treatment may have been aimed at supporting their sexual-orientation change, but their therapists were usually ineffectual because they had little knowledge of the treatment issues. Very often these therapists were fondly remembered, but they had little effect in promoting any kind of behavioral change.

A number of these clients were previously in gay

affirmative therapy. After a few sessions, it became clear that this was not their type of treatment. In some cases, clients had continued in this therapy for quite a while. They reported the explicit impression that their therapist was trying to indoctrinate them against their true feelings, and they often felt this was because the therapist himself was gay-identified.

Men who seek out reparative therapy typically find their homosexual attractions distressing and embarrassing. These desires are usually in violation of their conventional value systems, their religious backgrounds, and most importantly, who they believe themselves to be.

The following intake session involves a client who is fairly typical.

INITIAL SESSION

(*Olin is 26 years old—tall, thin, well mannered, soft-spoken, and nicely dressed. He looks somewhat young for his age.*)

Therapist: Well, what can I do for you? What brings you here?

Client: I heard you work with my particular kind of problem and I called and found out that you had an office here. A friend of mine recommended that I see you. I guess my biggest worry—is why I want to see you. . . . I guess a lot of it deals with sexuality and I guess I'm trying to figure out, to understand what it comes from . . . whatever, you know. So . . .

Therapist: What exactly are you trying to figure out?

Client: Ah, my sexual orientation, but at times I don't think that I'm gay, um . . .

Therapist: Why do you think you're not gay?

Client: Well, because the whole . . . I'll tell you how. . . . I don't want to live with men. I don't think that I want to have a relationship with a man.

Therapist: Have you ever had a relationship with a man?

Client: Once.

Therapist: Do you think about having sex with men?

Client: I think about, you know, gay masturbating, you know, and all these thoughts about sexuality are male sexuality. And it scares me. And then I play out in my mind, what it would be like down the road, and I think, do you want to do this for the rest of your life?

Therapist: Do you want to have sex with men?

Client: No. I want to try to fight it. Basically I feel like maybe I'm bisexual, and that's what's been bothering me for many years.

Therapist: How old are you now?

Client: Twenty-six. And . . . (*pause*)

Therapist: So you say you don't want to be bisexual.

Client: No, I don't. I would love to be heterosexual, totally. I'd love to have a family and that's what's tearing me apart a lot.

Therapist: So you want to be attracted to women. Do you have some attraction to women?

Client: I guess, some. I have a lot of women friends.

Therapist: Why don't you want to be gay?

Client: Well, one main reason is that I really do want to get married and have kids. I know the gay life-style leads to loneliness. I know a lot of people that are like that and are very unhappy, that are alone late in life.

Therapist: You want security in a relationship that will last. Have you been in psychotherapy before?

Client: Yeah. I saw one psychologist for about four months. He kept saying that I probably wasn't gay, he thought it was all in my head. Finally I just said, "Listen, I really think I *am*. I'm really having problems with this. I don't like it. I want to change or whatever I have to do. . . ." He had this whole idea of bringing up all your past, you know . . . and that's the whole problem I had with him. I mean basically he said, "Well, yeah, this is the reason you have these feelings, this, this, this." And I say, "Okay. What's the next step?" Then he says he'll probably help you figure it all out. I got really frustrated with him before I left. Then I went to a guy after that and basically he said that there's nothing really that can be done. There's nothing really that can be changed. The best thing that you could possibly do if you don't want to be gay is just stay celibate, he says, for the rest of your life, just stay celibate.

Therapist: (*Laugh*) So one said no, you're not, and the other said yes, you are, so stay celibate.

Client: Yeah.

(*The responses of previous therapists to his complaints have been frustrating. In this first session I want to demonstrate clearly how reparative therapy is different so he can experience some hope.*)

Therapist: Do you feel masculine enough?
Client: Um—probably not.
Therapist: Have you ever thought about that before?
Client: Not really.

Therapist: Thinking about this is essential to your therapy. A lack of complete identification with masculinity can make a man sexually interested in other males. You don't look feminine, there's nothing about your looks that *says* you don't feel masculine . . . but on the inside you say you have doubts. Did you have problems finding male friends when you were growing up?

Client: Uh—really I don't know. It seemed to turn out like that. We moved a lot and it seemed like every neighborhood I was in, there wasn't any guy my age on the block. It's strange, I remember looking back and there were always so many girls. And if there were any boys they were my brother's age and he's eight years younger than I am, so there was no one really there for me. In school I had a couple of guy friends but the problem with that was—with most of the guys I hung around with when I was little, it always ended up kind of sexual.

Therapist: When you were having a sexual relationship with the boys, I think you were really trying to get close to them emotionally, trying to bond to them. I think you were short-circuiting your need for male identification and intimacy by having sexual contact. What kind of relationship did you have with your father?

Client: Uh—It's been pretty bad.

Therapist: In what way?

Client: Well, my real father died when I was a baby. So I never had a relationship with him. But I have a stepfather who raised me since I was about four. We're so different. He's . . .

Therapist: How old were you when your father died?

Client: I was just a baby, just born. I think I was two months.

Therapist: Oh really. And then this man came in when you were four . . .

Client: I was about four.

Therapist: And he was all right?

Client: Well, growing up I guess I just didn't know any difference. I don't know *when* they told me he wasn't my father. But he's so different than me. He's very quiet, kind of unemotional . . . although he's good to us, you know, in many ways.

Therapist: Who's us?

Client: My sister and my younger brother.

Therapist: Tell me more about your stepfather.

Client: He's a kind of a big macho guy, you know. He was raised on a farm . . . he's a big husky kind of guy. Very quiet—I'm more outspoken. I think more of my emotions show . . . I guess I'm more emotional. . . . I need to see emotions and feel emotions. One time I saw a tear from my stepfather. That's it. You know, I was shocked to see it. I think it surprised him. It's like . . . I've never seen this before.

Therapist: So you had no father between the time you were a few months old and when your mother remarried when you were four.

Client: Correct.

(*This client represents the often-seen developmental pattern of lack of a father figure during the critical gender-identity phase of about 2 years old. Still, we want to explore the extent to which he is identified with his stepfather.*)

Therapist: Do you ever have the desire to be closer to your father?

Client: My stepfather? Um . . . at times . . . and as I get older, yes. It gets easier now because I understand him more. For a long time I was kind of . . . not scared of him, but awkward, awkward around him. Ever since I was a boy, I would get up in the morning and find out he was already up and we would be in the kitchen together, and I wouldn't know what to say to him. It was real awkward. He can be very content to be by himself without talking at all. That's not the way I am. And I think he felt awkward around me, too, sometimes. My mother would come downstairs and say, "It's swell to see the two of you, the two of you together." I think he likes to talk to me when I talk to him. Sometimes he would just come in and just start talking to me, but I was always surprised at that.

Therapist: It would have to be more on your part.

Client: Yeah because, well . . . he's just not that way.

Therapist: Yet it sounds like the real distance is on your part because he is willing to talk to you.

Client: Yeah, but I think it goes both ways.

Therapist: Tell me about your relationship with your mother. How do you get along with her?

Client: I feel like I have two relationships with my mother. One is I love her and it's really great. In another way we just clash. . . . She's very, very stubborn, kind of overbearing.

Therapist: Overbearing?

Client: Yes . . . the way she acts.

Therapist: Did you have problems in relationships with your male peers? Did you feel comfortable with the other boys?

Client: Yeah. (*pause*) I felt uncomfortable a little bit.

Therapist: Why did you feel uncomfortable?

Client: Because for some reason I wanted to . . . I wanted intimate contact with them.

Therapist: Was it sexual contact?

Client: Sometimes.

Therapist: What I think you were trying to do, was to get that sense of masculine identification. You were trying to bond with the masculine. And that need was expressed sexually.

Client: (*Pause*) But I also rejected it.

Therapist: What did you reject?

Client: That it was sexual. I was ashamed. . . . It was strange but at the same time I gratified it, there was a real shame there. . . . (*pause*)

Even in junior high school, I was young-looking for my age and I'd have these older guys look at me, follow me around the mall and I'd wonder, "What the hell am I doing to get these guys' attention?" For me I think I got involved in it because I just needed to be close to somebody and this was always there. Someone was always coming on to me and sometimes I just let it happen.

Therapist: I'm interested in asking these questions of you because so many homosexual men have answered them similarly. . . . I asked you, "What kind of relationship did you have with your father?" You said, "Poor." "What kind of relationship did you have with male peers?" You said, "Poor." Study after study shows that homosexuals as little boys tend to have poor relationships with their fathers. Sometimes they also had problems in relation with their mothers, and they often did not have male buddies. When you were having a sexual relationship with the boys, I think you were really trying to get close to them emotionally, trying to bond to them. That's exactly what the male homosexual adult is often doing—he short-circuits his need for male identification and intimacy by having sexual contact. So the basic treatment in such a case would be to learn to develop close, intimate relationships with men without sexualizing them. What about friendships during your high school years?

Client: During the times of my high school years I was shy and at that time I had so social friends that were homosexuals at all. I had a sort of girlfriend. She was very involved in the church and we would go out. She had a lot of gay friends. The first time I was exposed to them it seemed that they had something that I was looking for . . . it was the sociability. They were so outgoing. Like, "Oh, wow, they're gay!" So I just started going out to the night-clubs.

Therapist: What's your impressions of all the night-clubs?

Client: Now? Then?

Therapist: Then and now.

Client: Well I always liked going out and dancing and just having fun. That's one of the reasons, the social aspect of it. . . .

Therapist: What kind of guys were you trying to meet?

Client: Back then? I think . . . just somebody basically who would like to go out and have fun and talk and all that.

Therapist: So tell me about the relationship you had.

Client: It was about two years ago . . . I was with this guy Jack and I felt uncomfortable in the relationship. I felt he was better than me. He had a real job, and I didn't have one.

Therapist: How long did the relationship last?

Client: About six or seven months. I felt I was being

taken care of, being protected. What happened is that he moved on and I felt really hurt. I felt like he had left me. Then I realized I wasn't doing anything about my life. Here I was, stuck, having to look at my own life.

Therapist: How did you and Jack meet?

Client: I met Jack in a gay bar. . . . I felt like I needed to be with a man. I needed that closeness, that feeling close and being loved. So we went home to my house and we went back and forth, "Can't we just be friends?" Back and forth until we just felt like having sex. We had sex for three hours.

Therapist: Three hours!

Client: (*Laughter*)

Therapist: You say that like you broke the world's record! Such pride. (*laughter*)

Client: I'm saying, as a matter of fact, three hours, yeah, and it was the basis of our friendship, our relationship for a long time and only until about a year ago when I got him out of my system.

Therapist: You got over him?

Client: Yeah. And I tried to break it off first, then he'd get a "poor little boy" look and stuff. When he finally got a job I realized, "Oh, my God"—I would have to get a job with him.

Therapist: Why did you feel you needed to get a job?

Client: Because I was older than him and I felt I should get a job. He gets this job at the Beverly Hills Hotel. My biggest fears were coming to life. Everything is collapsing. He was becoming something! He started wearing these suits and everything.

Therapist: And what was going on?

Client: My biggest fear was happening—he was realizing he was worth something. Before that, I was always the one to tell him he was worth something. So then he left me. And then I did a lot of thinking over the next year, and I realized . . . (*pause*) . . . it wasn't good for me . . . I'd been unhappy. I'd been stuck.

Therapist: You realized that you had to get free of the frustration that had kept you bound to him. (*pause*) Tell me . . . do you feel assertive enough in your life?

Client: I guess I probably don't have a solid base to start asserting myself from. I feel like I'm just on shaky ground, you know?

Therapist: What made you change your mind about finding a gay relationship? Do you still have these homosexual feelings?

Client: I think I should tell you about my attitude toward these feelings. I'm really pissed off. (*angrily*) It's ruined a lot of my life and I don't like it.

Therapist: I like that anger because anger is an energy that can help push you out of the condition. It's a lot more helpful than self-pity or depression. But we have to be careful not to direct the anger at yourself but rather at the homosexuality.

Client: Like I said, I was in therapy before. There were a lot of reasons which brought me to therapy but after going through a lot of them the bottom line has been the sexual issue. But there have always been other issues too — career decisions, relationship problems, feelings about myself — but the sexual problem always crept back in. I kept changing different things in my life but each time it got to the point that the change wasn't working anymore, then I didn't care anymore and I just gave up and got depressed. I'm not as depressed as before but this has been a core issue.

There are other issues, the father thing, which will take time, but I've always had this feeling. I've never felt I could trust anybody. I never felt there was anyone I could tell.

Therapist: Sure.

Client: Lately I've been feeling down in the dumps—it comes out sexually, lots of fantasies, lots of crap.

Therapist: Acting out?

Client: No, not anymore. You know, masturbation and pornography. I used to go into restrooms and you know, look at guys, but not lately. It's something I'm ashamed of.

Therapist: Does it make sense to you, what I've been explaining to you? (*Trying to return to some concepts for him to find encouragement in.*)

Client: Yeah.

Therapist: Have you ever had relationships with guys that weren't homosexual?

Client: Sure. Although I must admit, I wish I felt more comfortable about making friends.

Therapist: Male relationships are very important. Do you ever notice—let's see if this is true for you—some guys say it's true. When they are feeling bad or weak about themselves, or having had a failure or disappointment, that's when they seem to sexualize other guys more. When they are feeling good and secure and confident about themselves and they have their life in order and things are going well, the sexual preoccupations diminish. They can look at a nice-looking guy but not have sexually compelling feelings for them. Does that describe your feelings?

Client: Yeah. I guess that's actually true.

Therapist: Are you very sensitive to other men; you

seek their approval, you want their approval . . . but you're very sensitive to any blaming?

Client: Yeah . . . I've noticed that when I'm sitting around the table and some guy says just a slight little thing that he probably doesn't even think about, I take that really deep and personal. . . .

(*He seems to have done much reflection on his feelings of inferiority in male relationships. I thought this would be a good place to explain some transference issues.*)

Therapist: You get depressed.

Client: Yeah.

Therapist: That may happen in our relationship. I mean, if you decide to continue and we develop a therapeutic relationship you may feel like I'm slighting you or something. Talk to me about it. Put it right out, this is the place for it. . . . This is a very important point.

Client: Okay.

Therapist: And when you are depressed . . . you were saying you sometimes get depressed when another man slights you? How do you get out of your depression?

Client: I'm not sure. I get down on myself.

Therapist: Sexual fantasy?

Client: Yes.

Therapist: So when you feel down in relationships with other men, you get into sexual fantasy. And how do you feel afterwards?

Client: Terrible. It pretty much puts me in a downward slide.

Therapist: Sure. Look at what we're saying here. You

sit around with a group of guys, straight guys, and one guy says, "Fuck you," and instead of saying, "Fuck you, too," like this . . . you go, "Oh," and get crushed and instead of putting that aggression directly out to other men, you sexualize it. You look for sexual release to temporarily pull you out of your depression. . . . Am I right? I'm just hoping in this meeting that what I'm saying to you makes sense.

Client: Oh, yeah. It makes perfect sense.

Therapist: It has to ring true to you.

Client: (*Pause*) Yeah, it makes a lot of sense.

Therapist: In reparative therapy you should begin to feel better about yourself. You should feel more confident, personally stronger. Your sexual fantasies and masturbation should diminish when you begin to understand where the sexual feelings come from. When you were at home with Mom or out playing with the little girls in your neighborhood, the other guys were out in the street bumming around or roughing it up, and they were getting that male bonding, while you were detached, you were into a lonely defensive detachment. So now you have to do that work of bonding.

Client: How long does that take?

Therapist: Everybody is different, but it's gradual. It's not just a case of nothing, nothing, nothing—boom! I'm straight, I'm heterosexual.

Client: Yeah.

Therapist: You should start to experience benefits early on. There will be times when you're depressed, there will be times when you have no hope, when your sexual thoughts and feelings and behaviors are out of control . . . but there should be a gradual overall diminishing of homosexual behavior. There's going to be a time when you're going to look at a guy and say, he's a good-looking guy but I don't have a problem with sexual attraction for him. If you decide to continue here, we're going to work slowly—I don't care about the speed. I'll accept you at your rate. You need to know that. Now—what else do you think I should know about you?

Client: Well—I feel that I really want to change and I just want to get on the best I can. I'm tired of all this. . . .

Therapist: I can understand that. Are you into any sports?

Client: Yeah. Golf and swimming and tennis.

Therapist: Good. I encourage you to be more physical. First, it will help with your depression. Secondly, it will give you a stronger, more solid sense of yourself. When we exercise and we feel stronger, we feel better about ourselves. The third thing is that physical exercise is important as a way of connecting with other guys. It develops a bond. The father's relationship with his son is through *doing*. He doesn't sit and have coffee with his son like mothers and daughters might do. You would benefit from going to a gym. Have you ever been to a gym?

Client: No.

Therapist: Well, you might consider it. At the beginning of this session, you complained that your last therapist didn't give you specific direction. I think you'll find me to be different.

Client: I can see that.

Therapist: Do you think you could feel comfortable with me and this therapy?

Client: Yeah. At least, I'd like to try.

This client continued with individual sessions and later entered group therapy. He is currently doing well, having made good progress toward the first and most important goal of treatment—developing healthy, nonerotic, egalitarian male friendships.

Clients not likely to continue after the initial session are typically those who have been brought in by parents or a spouse. Even though they may be distressed by their homosexuality, they remain identified with it, accepting that "this is who I am." They are open to receiving help for distressing aspects of the gay life-style, but they are in fundamental disagreement with the premises of reparative therapy.

19

The Issues of Individual Psychotherapy

THE FALSE SELF

Case 1

(*This client, Harry, is a 52-year-old divorced man and the owner of an accounting firm. His case demonstrates the clinical feature of the false self that is often seen in homosexuals — in this case, he grew up as the "good little boy."*)

Client: Once I told my mother she should leave my dad. I told her, "Mom, I wouldn't put up with his bullshit."

Therapist: How many times have homosexual sons told their mothers to leave Dad!

Client: But why?

Therapist: Because you left Dad a long time ago. Now you want Mom to do the same. You identified with her against him.

Client: (*Laugh*) Yeah. Maybe so, but what I said was still good advice.

Therapist: Your Mom got from you the emotional goodies she did not get from her husband.

Client: But why me? I always felt I had to keep Mama happy.

Therapist: Somehow you got picked.

Client: I was a cute kid. I have a picture when I was six in this nice little outfit, curly blond hair and all this shit. I had a personality. I used to sing, entertain everybody, I was . . .

Therapist: . . . You were special.

Client: Yeah . . . I was special. . . . But I don't feel comfortable talking about this. (*long pause*)

Therapist: Why should you not feel comfortable talking about how special you were treated as a child?

Client: (*Pause*) . . . (*with some anger*) Because I don't think I was treated so special.

(*The client is confronting the contradiction of being special but not really special. This is the common paradox of the used child. At the same his parents recognized certain special talents, they failed to acknowledge his needs or reflect his true identity.*)

Therapist: How were you *not* yourself as a child? You

sang, you got all this great attention. . . . You were cute . . . with the pictures . . . what?

Client: I was trying to please everybody. I've always spent my life pleasing other people. I started by playing executive assistant to my mother and I've been doing it ever since. I was executive assistant to my wife for fifteen years. I've never been number one in my whole life. That's been my role. I was my mother's handmaiden. A long time ago a friend said to me, "Harry, you're afraid of success."

Therapist: You've never been in charge of your life. That's what this whole homosexual thing is about. Taking charge of your life. I'd like to get back to why you're afraid of your power . . . where did that come from?

Client: Well . . . where did the fear of my power originate from?

Therapist: Yes.

Client: I just fear it. My father did not allow anybody to be a star.

Therapist: But I thought you *were* the star! Were you ever allowed to show your assertion, your individual power?

Client: There was a little song I would play on the piano as a kid, and when I used to be angry I'd go over to the piano and pound out this song called "Heart and Soul," and they knew I was angry and they would laugh at me. (*angrily*) There was a lot of laughing at me . . . which is weird! There was a lot of laughing at me.

Therapist: You were not taken seriously.

Client: Uh, uh . . . Oh, no!

Therapist: So when you played this song it meant you were angry. How did the family deal with your anger?

Client: They'd laugh.

Therapist: No one ever said, "Why are you angry? What's wrong?"

Client: Nope.

Therapist: You were ignored for your protest. This is how the child loses his power. He is ignored or punished. In your case, laughter was a punishment.

Client: But I was always angry.

Therapist: Always angry?

Client: Inside.

Therapist: Tell me about that.

Client: Like I'd go to the store for my mother—I'm talking young, 9 or 10—I was doing all this shopping with a list. I'd walk into the store and hear the druggist or grocer say, "Your mother just called and she wanted you to bring this or that home."

Therapist: And how were you feeling?

Client: I don't know. (*long pause*)

Therapist: Come on. Put yourself in that little boy's place. How was he feeling?

Client: I don't know. (*long pause*)

Therapist: What would he have rather been doing instead?

Client: Playing with the other boys.

Therapist: Isn't that what all 9- or 10-year-old boys want to do? Do little boys want to go shopping for their mothers?

Client: I hated shopping. I hate shopping to this day.

Therapist: Did you ever try to express how you felt about shopping to your mother?

Client: (*Emphatically*) That I never remember.

Client: There was another incident. . . . I would have

been about 7, and my mother used to take a nap . . . and my mother . . . I would stand by her bed and fan her. (*long pause*) There's such a dichotomy inside of me. I can be a strong guy but there's a part of me that's so . . . weak. Why the hell did I want to do that as a kid? That had to be the most stupid thing. On a bright sunny day—inside, fanning my mother, rather than being out playing with the kids!

Therapist: Do you understand why you did those things? If you don't understand why, then you'll think you were just a dumb little kid, which isn't going to empower you. This is a mistake gay men make. They think that's what they *chose* as little boys.

Client: I needed the attention.

Therapist: This is not just a matter of seeking attention—you were fulfilling an identity: "This is who you are, son. This is your role in this family. This is what you are about, kid." It's identity.

Client: I feel my siblings contributed to this.

Therapist: How?

Client: They went along with this.

Therapist: Tell me how.

Client: They laughed at it. They all reinforced it. It was a whole family thing. My three older brothers were never kind to me. I was always aware of that. I always wanted a younger brother that I could be an older brother to. I had a make-believe younger brother I used to play with.

Therapist: A reparative fantasy. (*The therapist takes the opportunity to comment about a theoretical connection.*)

Client: I could have been a kid with him, a boy with him, climbing trees. Somewhere everybody contributed.

Therapist: Unless you understand why you did those

behaviors, you may all too easily believe, "Oh, that's just the way I was." But the repressed anger tells you another story. Prehomosexual boys are many times such good little boys, denying they're being used. If you want to move forward in your life you need to understand how you got tricked out of your power, your gender. Otherwise you're going to believe that's just who you are, and displace your anger elsewhere.

Client: But while you're talking, I feel the fright.

Therapist: Yes, always that fright of claiming your power. What is the fear?

Client: What is my fear? The fear that I have . . . I'll tell you exactly. In the last week I've met more women. The fear that I have is, what if the woman is a real female, a sexual woman, a woman who really enjoys sex? This frightens me.

Therapist: What are the qualities you do not feel strong enough in, that she might expect from you? (*The therapist tries to isolate the source of his fear.*)

Client: Well . . . it's like what I'm attracted to in other men.

Therapist: You're closing one door but you haven't yet opened the other door. Ironically, this is a sign of progress. You have had strong, positive feelings about our working together. So much so, that a part of you is afraid that you will change too quickly. There is a feeling here of being out of control and you want to go back to what is familiar. You've felt encouraged by our work — perhaps too encouraged.

Client: I felt like an idiot. Acting out like I did, last week. (*The client met a stranger in a bathhouse and had sex.*)

Therapist: Maybe you needed to feel like an idiot one

more time. You are becoming disidentified with the homosexual behavior and more identified with the task of outgrowing it.

Client: Yeah. I wasn't at all interested in that guy I met
there. In fact he said, "I'll be calling you." You know, it felt
like a threat, like blackmail. That would normally scare me,
but this time I felt I didn't care. Because I know this person
that goes to bathhouses isn't really me.

(Three Weeks Later)

*(This session draws our attention to how mother contributes to
the false "good little boy" role. Sexuality and aggression charac-
terize the masculine identity, and mother has systematically
avoided acknowledging these traits. Usually it is mother who has
fostered this false role, for father is typically a negligible influence in the boy's life.)*

Client: I can remember going for that walk with my
mother, and now I'm 30, 31, and hearing my mother say to
me, "Harry, you can do it. You can do it, Harry. Whatever
you make up your mind to do, you can do it." But never
feeling that she had heard what I'd been telling her.

Therapist: So you were walking with your mother at
30, and your mother said, "You can do it, Harry, you can
do it, Harry." And you feel like she never really understood
your feelings?

Client: That's right.

Therapist: Like she just threw out some kind of cliché?

Client: And she says, "You've got a wonderful life."
And she took it upon herself to talk, my mother was like
that, she would tell me to—

Therapist: Go after it, pursue it—

Client: Pursue it, much unlike my father. . . . And this goes back, Joe, to the time I was knee-high to a grasshopper. You know, I can see that throughout life, I always took care of my mom. I always took care of everything related to my mom's emotions. When I was a child, my mother had a great devotion to Our Lady of Guadalupe, and every Sunday she would make me go with her to the mission to offer our devotions to this statue. I was the only one that went. Do you understand what I'm saying about my mother?

Therapist: Yes. And I think you should talk to your mother . . . talk to her directly as if she were here in this room with us.

Client: I'm afraid of looking at it, but if I don't, I know I'm not going to get to the bottom of this. Mom played a big part in all this, but I'm not sure how.

Remember, Joe, I did not start therapy until she died. I thought it was coincidence, but I think I understand that I could not have attended to the funeral arrangements if I had started therapy. There were a lot of angry feelings about Mom that I didn't want to face until after she died. I did a beautiful job with her funeral arrangements, flowers and everything. It was all well done, very tasteful. I don't want to be "heady," just stay in my head while I'm talking to you . . . but I'm afraid if we do a Gestalt thing I just might get into some feelings that I don't want to look at about Mom. (*long pause*) And yet, you're going to just let me hang, aren't ya? (*laugh*)

Therapist: As we say, it's your time, your money, your life.

Client: (*Long pause*) Well, I don't think I'm going to get anyplace talking to you, Joe, if I'm going to just keep in my head . . . so I suppose I should attempt to talk to Mom.

Therapist: Let's put Mom here in this room. Imagine her right here. Over there. She's sitting on the couch. (*Therapist props up pillows to simulate "Mom" and sits behind client. Client attempts to begin.*)

Client: Well . . . Mom, I want to talk to you about something very important. Basically, I want to talk to you about a sexual problem. (*long pause*)

Therapist: What's happening?

Client: (*To therapist*) I hardly have a word out of my mouth when she's answering me. She's having a difficult time with the word "sex." You know, Joe, she never used the word "sex." She's having a hard time. The way she's choosing her words. I want to tell her it's a homosexual problem.

Therapist: Well, tell her about it. Face her and tell her. (*Many clients report coming from particularly repressed, puritanical homes, where sex was never discussed. Mothers were typically instrumental in setting the tone that sex was dirty or sinful.*)

Client: (*Long pause*)

Therapist: Does she cut you off? How does she stop you?

Client: I couldn't even talk to my dad. She would always cover up for Dad. "Oh, don't bother Dad, he's too busy or too tired. Dad had a hard day at the office." So there was never any dialogue with Dad. He was always in a bad mood.

Therapist: How did she control you?

Client: Tears, for one. It's getting painful recalling all this. Just talking about it, I feel a lot of pain and a lot of sadness. That's all they knew. They didn't set out to do it to me, what they did deliberately. (*pause*) I don't want to be accusatory, Mom . . . but . . . it's difficult to talk about homosexuality, even utter the word, but I want to tell you I'm in therapy right now about my homosexuality. (*pause*)

Therapist: Is she saying anything to you?

Client: No. I don't know if she's hearing me. I don't think she cares, either.

Therapist: Oh? Tell her. Tell her.

Client: (*Long pause—client seems stuck*)

Therapist: Harry, what do you want to tell your mother? What do you want her to know about you? Tell her.

Client: Well, I want you to know, Mom . . . (*pause*) It's hard for me to tell you exactly, and even if I did, that wouldn't do much good.

Therapist: What's Mom feeling right now? What's she feeling?

Client: She's saying, "Why don't we pray about it?" Mom, right now that's not what I want to do. I've done a lot of praying but it hasn't really paid off for me. (*pause*) She's saying, "Everything's going to be okay." But the fact of the matter is, it's not okay.

Therapist: I can't see your mother like you can, so you're going to have to tell me what she's saying. What is her expression, like that. I can't see her.

Client: She's sitting there very prim and proper, dressed like she always is with her jewelry, not a hair out of place, perfect. She's sitting there, very passively, as if this is just going to pass, like, let Harold talk, let Harold get it out of his system. It's just going to pass and we'll go on like normal. (*more loudly*) Mom, pay attention to what I'm saying! Hear me! Don't think this is just going to go away. . . . (*long pause*) She's still just sitting there. . . . I'm getting no reaction. (*loudly, painfully*) Ah!

Therapist: Tell her what you'd like from her. Give her a clue.

Client: I'm just finding it so difficult to talk to you. I thought all these years you and I had such a great communication. We were great conversationalists together. I thought . . . (*softly*) . . . yeah. God. What a fucking game we played. (*loudly, angrily*) You know what I feel like doing right now? I'm going to be totally honest. I feel like jacking off right now. I don't believe this. (*tearfully*) I can't believe it! (*crying quietly, buries head in hands, long pause*)

Therapist: (*Softly*) Harry, keep expressing. What's happening?

Client: (*Long pause*)

Therapist: Tell your mother why you feel like jacking off.

Client: I guess it's because . . . yeah, I suppose because I want her to know I have a fucking prick! That I'm a sexual human being! (*pause*) This is the first time I've ever had a sexual thought in her presence! (*laugh*) And a strong one!

Therapist: Do you see how your masturbation impulse is an assertion?

Client: Yeah. I really feel that. She was so castrating, I want to jerk off in front of her. I'm really feeling it in my body. (*long pause*)

Therapist: Do you think if you did that, it would affect her? Make an impression on her?

Client: No, not really. I'm just feeling sorry for her right now. I'm pitying her. . . . I'm seeing how protective I've been of her all these years. (*to Mother*) I've even created fantasies about you, the way I put you on a pedestal. You will always be Virgin Mary. What a way to live! (*Because the client is beginning to experience authentic feelings now, he is starting to perceive his mother more realistically.*)

I took care of her in her final years. (*to Mother*) While you were in the nursing home, you were still controlling all us kids, especially me. I'm the one who took care of you. The image of you in the nursing home. She lost control of her body. (*fearfully*) She did not die easily at all. She died the way she lived, resistantly and stubbornly. She hung on for so long. When she was about to die, she would not surrender. She kept gasping and gasping and would not take that final breath. Mom died the way she lived. She refused to surrender to death!

I'm trying to make some sense of all of this right now. . . . She won't talk to me. I could take a fucking dart and throw it at her and get no reaction.

Therapist: That's exactly the dynamic between you and mother.

Client: I want her to see me, my power, my masculinity, and she refuses to see, to acknowledge that side of me. That stubborn tenacious denial. I'm trying to understand how to get through to her. She met all my needs, she was a good mother, gave me money—financially she was good but her Harry was not fully a person.

Therapist: Not fully masculine?

Client: I'm a man, Mom. That's how I feel. I'm a man with what all that means. I'm not your little boy, Mom, which I've been and I'm continuing to be. (*pause, continues tearfully*) I have such a strong desire to let her know. . . . I'm sexual, that I have a penis, that it's good, it's powerful, but it's good. (*long pause*) God, I need my family to understand me.

Therapist: Understanding has to begin with yourself. Then you can let others know about it.

Client: Yeah. But before I reached puberty, they had a responsibility.

Therapist: Absolutely.

Client: I'll take the blame for what's going on now, but (*crying*) they've got to take the blame for the fact that I didn't create that situation! I continued it but they created it.

Therapist: Absolutely. They did not equip you. Right.

Client: I didn't feel Mother understood a thing, Joe.

Therapist: Right.

Client: I feel anger about all these years spent thinking things were different, that she understood me. She never really knew me, my needs, who I really was as a man.

Therapist: Your realization that she did not truly understand you feels sad. You believed it was different, and that belief was supported by the false self. There's a grieving for having lived in that belief system. A grieving over the false self, a grieving over the illusion that Mother saw you completely.

Client: And I feel that.

Therapist: That belief system allowed you to belong in the family.

Client: The relationship that never was. It was my illusion. But I need to go on. She was my mother and I loved her for what she was. She did give me life and so many things she did give me, and I want to be grateful. There's been so much control in my life. Right now throughout my whole body, I feel so much vibration from her. I guess I've had more illusions about my mother than about my Dad.

Therapist: Oh, absolutely! There was no illusion about Dad. You rejected him. He was nonexistent, a nonperson. The false self comes out of the mother–son relationship. Her projections onto you. The problem with Dad is that he did not exist.

Client: Everyone just loved mother but this woman was not real. It was all illusion. She was so well orchestrated. I never saw my mother angry.

Therapist: That was *her* false role.

Client: Oh, absolutely. I don't recall my mother ever hugging me, either as a child or as an adult. I'm just trying to figure out who my mother really was. *(laughs)*

Therapist: Your search for the real woman.

Client: I could never have proceeded with the funeral arrangements.

Therapist: Oh, absolutely. There are certain things that just need to be very well carried out.

Client: I really visualize her sitting there. She is so controlled in her own way. I'm shocked that I said what I said to her, but it's what I needed to say. I feel good about it. It's sexual . . . but it's more powerful.

Therapist: To the little boy, the penis separates him from the mother. If he doesn't have a penis, he is attached to the mother, like the girl is. Your masturbation fantasy is an attempt to individuate yourself from her. It is what makes you autonomous and independent from her. As an adult, you approach women intimately, but with a penis.

It's the penis that prevents the man from being reengulfed by the woman. Being different from the woman is one dimension of the problem, but the other, deeper issue is the false self, not being real in relationship to anyone.

THE EXPRESSION OF ANGER

Many homosexuals have grown up as "good little boys," living from a false, compliant self. Parents cultivate this false self in their sons by sabotaging their attempts at individuation and masculine power. In order for the false, compliant self to survive, the boy must deny his anger. Anger would be incompatible because it would serve as a breakthrough to the true masculine self. As a result, many homosexual adults have great difficulty allowing themselves to feel, constructively express, and even receive, anger. They either repress it or explode in a reactionary outburst. Either form of anger is unproductive and self-defeating.

To be constructively expressed, anger need not be explosive, outrageous, or destructive. It should not be used for the manipulation or control of others, but to fulfill the strongly felt need for self-expression.

Many clients remember attempts in the past during which they tried to express their anger. Anger is overtly expressed during two phases: the toddler years and adolescence. Both are separation–individuation phases. For some, overt anger was surrendered in adolescence in favor of sexual rebellion.

Case 1

(Matt, a 32-year-old man, feels intensely that he has been living a false role for many years. He was manipulated into being the compliant, passive, accommodating, nonaggressive, nonmasculine "good boy." He had a poor relationship with both parents and felt particularly controlled by his father. To regain the

personal power he lost through his parents' manipulation, he is trying to throw off the false role ascribed in him. Here we see the intense ambivalence and fear of his own anger.)

Client: The last couple of weeks I've felt like I've been at the breaking point. It feels like there's an intense out-burst just under the surface, of anger or crying. About the time I see exactly what I need to do to let it out, I pass on the opportunity. I shut down and don't allow myself to express it. I've never been one for those big emotional outbursts and stuff, but in some cases it would have done me good.

Therapist: So you felt the anger or the sadness come up and you let it go down?

Client: Oh yeah. But I didn't *let* it go down. I *pushed* it down.

Therapist: You pushed it down.

Client: Yes, it was a choice. It used to be automatic—now I reinforce it with a choice.

Therapist: It was automatic for years.

Client: I feel so disappointed in myself. I've done this for so long. It could have been just what I needed—a radical departure from the way I deal with things.

Therapist: You realize that a breakthrough to the anger will put you into a different place, a different level of feeling about yourself.

Client: Yes, I know that.

Therapist: But you were not taught how to express the anger. (*Here the therapist perhaps would have better helped by staying with the client's present struggle. Instead, he goes back to the past.*)

Therapist: Let's consider the development of this anger problem. You were not born with knowing how to suppress your anger. You were taught by your father. You've internalized your family's unacceptance of your anger and so for years you've automatically suppressed it. Now you've arrived at a certain place in your own therapy, and you realize you need to get it out, get in touch with it.

Client: I look at the pattern of my life over the past years and I can feel it build up, and then I suppress it. Now I see the anger coming up more often. It's like a roller coaster. Anger rises, then it goes down to depression. Instead of letting myself get angry, I say, "I'll go take a nap," but then I'm lying there thinking, "This is ridiculous, I've had more than enough sleep." I guess I've always known what I need to do with that anger. Now, at least, I'm feeling more comfortable talking about it.

Therapist: Do you see that as an improvement? (*The therapist is trying to show some encouraging progress, but the client turns anger on himself by denying that he is getting better.*)

Client: (*Hesitantly*) Yes. But still, I'm talking about letting it out, and I'm not doing it.

Therapist: Is there any feeling associated with expressing it?

Client: There's a real feeling of . . . (*long pause*) . . . a real feeling of frustration.

Therapist: Do you realize that when the anger comes up, you direct it toward yourself, as, "It's not coming up fast enough or well enough!"

Client: Speaking about it is doing me no good.

Therapist: Because you did not *feel* the words. You're speaking *about* anger, rather than *from* it.

Client: I know. For years I've done this. I thought talking about it would make the change.

Therapist: You'd rather just talk about your predica-

ment of not being able to express the anger. This is your
frustration.

Client: Yes. And I just can't express it. In fact it's
hitting very hard right now.

Therapist: What's hitting you?

Client: I'm actually feeling the fear for the first time
. . . even in my voice right now. (*obviously very emotional*)

Therapist: Don't run away. Stay with the fear.

Client: It's hard—because I automatically run away.
(*very softly*) For the first time, I'm actually feeling—as you're
talking . . . no, it's gone already!

Therapist: Do you want to go back to it?

Client: Yes.

Therapist: Do you really want to?

Client: Yes . . . I'm trying. (*long pause*)

Therapist: Stay.

Client: (*Long pause*) See, I can't do it. All I can do is
describe it. I'm afraid of feeling the hurt, the sadness of that
little boy who was punished.

Therapist: You've been operating from that hurt.
You've lived as if you've been hurt for a long time.

Client: Now I want to look at it. (*very softly*) Because it
hurts. I just feel an intense sadness. (*nervous laughter*) It's
scary for me because I've never felt this emotional. I've
never felt this emotional talking about anything in my life.

Therapist: I can see what you're feeling. I can *feel* what
you're feeling.

Client: And . . . this is very hard. (*softly and sadly*) I
look back and a lot of unhappy moments are just coming up
in my mind. Even right now I don't so much feel anger, as
an overwhelming sadness. I also see myself shutting off. I
just don't want to go any further.

Therapist: Can you feel the rightness? Uncovering your sadness is empowering. The empowerment will come from the fact that this is a true part of you coming forward.

(The client's perfectionistic image makes him afraid of showing the vulnerability of his true emotions, especially in front of another man. He believes these true feelings indicate weakness.)

Client: I consciously really want to make progress but I just can't do it for more than a couple of seconds. The deliberate choice to shut it off is so much of a habit.

(At this point the therapist begins to suspect that this client will not have a cathartic breakthrough, but will probably slowly release through an alternating cycle.)

Therapist: See, Matt, for you, this will come slowly. Not a big dramatic bang. I see you going to the feelings, then you move back. Just pay attention to the times in the day when you stop the deep feelings. You've done it for so long without awareness.

Client: I'd like to get everything over and done with in one fell swoop, and that angers me more than anything else.

Therapist: See how critical you are of your own style? This is not how Matt works. One big bang is not Matt's style.

Client: It's got to be done cause I just can't go on like this any longer. I can't play games any longer.

Therapist: Playing games is no longer an option. It's a matter of time until you break through.

Client: I have this feeling of revulsion at this "nice

guy." If this is how I'm going to be for the rest of my life—
these periods of suppressing a tantrum, then depression—I
mean I see these olds queens who are manic-depressive, and
I don't want to be that way.

Therapist: You can't go back. You know too much.

Client: Yeah. But . . . something is happening and it is
very uncomfortable. I feel very silly. (*He begins to giggle and
seems almost hysterical.*)

Therapist: What's silly?

Client: This is really embarrassing for me.

Therapist: What's silly and embarrassing?

Client: (*Long pause, laughter*) This is embarrassing.
(*still giggling*)

Therapist: This sadness and anger makes you feel very
vulnerable. You know, you have been more in touch with
your feelings in the last few weeks. But right now, your
defense is to step outside and become concerned about how
you appear, like an actor—rather than staying with the
movement from the inside. Every time you get into the
feeling self, you jump away and go back to the observing
self.

Client: I'm feeling the gap between them. That's the
frustration. Even now as I'm talking.

Therapist: You come to the feeling, then move away
from that. You approach the true self, then run away from
it. You were able to survive in your home by abandoning
your true, assertive, masculine self for a compliant self.
Somehow you felt you were being used but you did not
know how. This is the gap. The gap between talking about
it, and actually allowing yourself to feel it. Being real, or
being in a role and observing yourself.

Client: I'm seeing exactly what I'm doing.

Therapist: You were intimidated into being false. Right now you are externally directed—there is a self-consciousness, a theatrical sense.

Client: That's why I'm so afraid of it, because I know it's not really me. It's someone else, and that's what's frightening.

Case 2

(This gentle, soft-spoken 27-year-old man is an illustrator for a greeting-card company. He comes from a morally rigid family in which father was distant and aloof, and mother was manipulative and controlling. As a boy, he was very passive and compliant. Then he grew into a rebellious adolescent who used and sold drugs on his high school campus. By the time he entered therapy, however, he was caught up again in the "good boy" role and unable to feel anger.)

Therapist: In your adolescence, you had a lot of anger, yet today you have such difficulty getting in touch with it. What happened?

Client: I can remember a point where I became so afraid of it, that I made a little personal pact that I would never allow it to erupt again.

Therapist: Why?

Client: Maybe because I was afraid of what damage I could do.

Therapist: What damage?

Client: I saw it hurting my mother. I didn't give a damn if it hurt my father. He always made me feel like I was a failure anyway. (*long pause*) Whenever I came to him very excitedly with school projects, he would always show me how they weren't going to work. He'd show me the negative side—that my ideas were stupid. I just gave up caring about hurting my father. But I saw it was hurting my mother . . . and maybe I saw it hurting me because I saw it isolating me from the rest of the family.

Therapist: Uh-huh.

Client: I see that in the long run, this kept peace and harmony on the surface—but now I'm no more comfortable with my family after all.

Therapist: Twice you abandoned the protest. The first time was when you reached out to father enthusiastically, excitedly, and innocently. You expected father's acceptance. Somehow you felt, "He's a neat guy. He's somehow like me. I want that." Father rejected you, you got hurt, but before you gave up on father entirely, there was an intervening stage of protest. Like all other 2-year-olds, you protested at the frustration, you made a fuss, you demanded his attention. You were frustrated and you wanted gratification.

In a normal household, the parents address the protest. "What's wrong? Why is he fussing? Oh, he wants Daddy's attention!" There is the opportunity to repair the failure. "Oh, he wants Daddy to play with him, of course!" So father wakes up in response to the boy's protest. Now, in the dysfunctional family structure, they ignore the boy's protest. Maybe they don't want him to be a spoiled brat. They want him to realize he can't get attention this way. Or maybe he should just stay where they think a child belongs, close to mother. Maybe mother wants him with her, and Daddy's too busy working, anyway.

In a dysfunctional family system, parents will respond to the protest in one of three ways: they will either ignore the protest, punish him for it, or distract him with some form of indulgence.

Client: So what happens?

Therapist: They put a lid on the frustration, without really gratifying it. The boy is demanding Daddy's attention, so mother soothes him by giving him a dish of ice cream with a cookie. I don't think this is what happened in your case. You weren't indulged, you got punished.

(*Some clients' fathers are emotionally absent and uninvolved, while others are more overtly hostile. Either way, the boy is deprived of a supportive role model of male power. The only way to survive the family system is through self-defeating, nonproductive behavior.*)

Therapist: Can you imagine what happens when the boy protests and nobody pays attention?

Client: He protests louder.

Therapist: And if they still don't respond to him?

Client: Well, I suppose he has to give up eventually.

Therapist: Right. And what are the feelings when he gives up?

Client: Well, frustration.

Therapist: The internalized frustration which cannot be expressed turns into depression – anger turned inward – and helplessness. The boy learns, "It doesn't pay to show my power." Every homosexual from this type of developmental line feels weak, feels hurt. There is the hurt, weak little boy inside everyone.

Client: I can hear my parents saying, "You're such a big baby." When I think of myself getting angry I think of a little girl who sobs with her shoulders heaving. Any kind of expression of my anger feels like that, just a dramatic performance.

Therapist: But that's not a man's anger. That image of the little girl is pitiful, pathetic.

Client: But I don't see it that way. I was told that getting angry only made me a baby.

Therapist: Your parents never respected your anger.

Client: Now it seems like I'm always struggling inside with anger. (*long pause*) I'll tell you what I feel angry about. I still feel angry about sex. I feel angry that nobody told me about sex. In fact, I thought of coming in here tonight and saying to you, "Would you do me a favor? Would you tell me about sex?" and I would close my eyes, lie on the sofa, and have you tell me about sex.

Therapist: Well, ask me, I'll tell you.

Client: (*Demanding tone*) I just want you to tell me about sex. That's it. I want to know where babies come from and all that stuff. And what's this rock that grows in my pants? I just want to know.

Therapist: Ask me questions and I'll answer you.

Client: I just did, and you didn't answer me.

(*Therapist is not sure what this is all about, but rather than question it, he goes with it. He somehow senses that this is a regressive need, which should be indulged before it is interpreted. He then proceeds to explain the basic facts of life as if talking to a child. The client closes his eyes and listens.*)

Client: (*Very quietly, sadly*) I just want to cry.

Therapist: Why?

Client: I don't know. I just seem to feel hurt and angry.

Therapist: You're angry that you were not told.

Client: (*Very softly*) Uh-huh.

Therapist: Anger is essential to this therapy. Anger is the link to the true self.

Client: This is why I want to learn to express my anger. I realize I am just so angry that I was never told about sex. Just listening to what you told me just now, I had about ten more questions. Why did no one ever give me the information?

Therapist: Your anger is not about a lack of information, but that something about you was denied. Your essential identity as a sexual person was ignored. That's what the anger is about. They treated you like a sexless human being. They raised you like you were a neuter. They created a hole in your identity.

Client: (*Softly*) That's the whole story.

Therapist: Many parents never discuss sex with their kids. But the implicit masculinity given to a boy equips him to learn sexual facts later. Your parents did not prepare you for finding out about sex.

Client: I'm really having such a hard time . . . asking myself, am I really a guy or am I a girl? I've said so many times, I'm a nonsexual being. People ask, "Well, are you heterosexual or homosexual?" And I think I'm nonsexual, asexual, maybe at best bisexual.

Therapist: Many homoesexuals will say they're bisexual because they don't know what they are.

Client: I have sexual feelings but I don't know what to do with them, how to direct them.

Therapist: You don't know how to integrate your sexual feelings into your identity.

Client: And it really makes me angry. I feel like I've been cheated.

Therapist: It's okay to get into that anger!

Client: Yeah, but it's hard. Whenever I got angry at home, it was "totally inappropriate behavior."

Therapist: Absolutely. Sex and power—those are the two big identity issues and they cut you out of both. So many of you guys have had just that experience.

Client: (*Laughs*) I hate when you say that. I've always thought I was unique.

Therapist: Sorry. But it *is* a common issue—it's an expression of masculine power.

Client: Money. They did give me money.

Therapist: Okay. So how did money form your identification?

Client: (*Slowly, softly*) It was a payoff.

Therapist: You're right. It was a payoff. And that gave you a feeling of entitlement—which didn't help either.

Client: I know.

Therapist: The anger is a link to your true identity.

Client: Well, that link—is getting ready—to break off!

Therapist: Well, don't let it snap. Hold onto it, let it pull you.

Client: Oh, I'm so tired of it all. I want to let go. I'd like to get bottles of booze and smash them all over the room. I want to get violent. I want—but no, that's not "appropriate." Oh, I don't care any more, I want to get out of this, I want to quit this whole struggle!

Therapist: (*Softly*) No.

Client: I want out. I want to run away.

Therapist: No. No.

Client: I don't want to let out my anger. It's work.

Therapist: It's not work. It's release. The work is in repressing the anger.

Client: I know. That's why I'm always exhausted.

Therapist: Because you don't know how to trust the

anger. It's a power you were cut off from so long ago. What's stopping you now is your own self-consciousness.

Client: I've strived so hard to be a good person. And . . . I'm afraid. Yes, I'm afraid, I'm afraid! I'm afraid that people are going to get the wrong idea and say, "This guy's really off the handle!" I'm really afraid of stuff like that. I'm afraid people will think I'm not good. And I am good.

Therapist: You are good. You really are good. Now, it's okay to get angry. (*long pause*) You're stuck between your anger and your fear of your anger. You were taught to be afraid of your anger, not to believe in your anger.

Client: I know.

Therapist: The message was, "Your anger has nothing to do with anything. It's nothing. It means nothing."

Client: You're right. You're absolutely right. They laughed at me when I got angry. That's what they would do. They would laugh. Until eventually, I would start laughing too. Even today, when I get angry, I start laughing and it's sick.

Therapist: They manipulated you into surrendering the protest and sliding into the nice, compliant, good boy they wanted you to be. You bought it.

Client: Uh-huh.

Therapist: Lock, stock, and barrel.

Client: I feel like I've lived as a total wimp.

Therapist: You weren't taught how to claim it, to be carried by the power of it. Anger has a power that is not just destructive. It can be constructive . . . expressive . . . protective. But you were taught to disidentify from it, to sell out, to deny it. Your role was to be the nice boy in the house. But you went through a rebellious phase in adolescence. You were into drugs and the punk scene. Then—

Client: (*Interrupting*) I gave up.

Therapist: You gave up.

Client: It was so exhausting to get my parents' attention. *(long pause, emotional)* I often told my father I hated
him . . . many, many times whenever I dared to tell him
exactly what I thought. He would get ready to wash my
mouth out with soap. He'd say, "Do you still hate me?"
"Yes." "You're not supposed to hate people, you know. Do
you still hate me?" "Yes." He'd drag me into the bathroom
and get the soap. "Do you still hate me?" "Yes." "Do you
still?" "No matter what you do, I still hate you." Then he
would take the soap and wash my mouth. He'd put the bar
in my mouth until my mother, crying, would make him
stop. Anger got me nowhere. I just gave up.

FATHERS

Case 1

> *(This client is married and has four children. He came to therapy
> as a result of being arrested for soliciting sex in a public
> restroom.)*

Client: I left our session last week and I was thinking
about how emotionally I sort of gloss over my feelings, my
upheavals. I look at my life and what's happened, and I
want to deal with this, not just gloss it over. Like the time
I got arrested and my wife and my father rescued me.

Therapist: What's that?

Client: When I got arrested, I thank God that I have a
wife who understands and a father who was so generous

with me. But sometimes I think I set it up. I set myself to get into an emotional state where I'm forced to feel real feelings.

Therapist: Are you saying you create crises so that you can get in touch with feelings?

Client: Yeah. Also . . . so that I get in touch with my father . . . in a way.

Therapist: Tell me more.

Client: That . . . since he knows about my problem— I hate that he knows about the problem but at the same time . . . that's one moment when we really do connect and he's helping me with the problem. I'm the bad boy and I'm sorrowful and he forgives me.

Therapist: That's one time when he's there for you. He's there to protect you.

Client: But then I thought . . . geez . . . wouldn't it be nice to connect with my father on a whole new level where I didn't have to be . . . weak.

Therapist: Weak.

Client: "Father forgive me . . ."

Therapist: Exactly.

Client: And that was my realization of the past few days.

Therapist: That's a very important realization because you want acceptance and nurturance from your father, but it's hard to receive it as an equal, man-to-man. In your mind, to get close to a man means you have to lower yourself.

Client: Uh-huh.

Therapist: So much of your sexual behavior is about that, isn't it?

Client: That's true.

Therapist: You don't know how to get close to a man

as an equal. This is a very important aspect of your therapy. You need to experience equality in a male friendship. You need to take in the good stuff such a friendship can offer you.

Client: Yeah. But what have I been doing lately? The old, negative life patterns are still there. Like, where has that vision gone?

Therapist: (*Introducing an unexpected challenge in an attempt to upset the complacency*) Would you like to have a session with your father?

Client: (*Laughs*) . . . (*pause*) . . . (*burst of laughter*)

Therapist: What do you feel when I say that?

Client: . . . Well, yeah, I think I would.

Therapist: What's the feeling?

Client: Well, it's just that I never thought of it before.

Therapist: What's the feeling?

Client: . . . I don't know.

Therapist: Positive or negative?

Client: It's sort of positive.

Therapist: Give me a better word than positive.

Client: (*Pause*) Exhilarating!

Therapist: Good! I saw you gasp.

Client: Yes. (*laughter*)

Therapist: Is there a negative side to this question?

Client: Well, yeah . . . well, I start thinking of him here and actually . . . talking . . . (*laughter*)

Therapist: And what's the feeling?

Client: That he wouldn't get it. That he would be doing the talking.

Therapist: And what would happen to you as he did the talking?

Client: . . . (*Long pause*) . . . Sort of . . . I would be silent.

Therapist: So, let's get back to the picture. How do you want that session to go, that would feel best for you?

Client: (*Long pause – client seems stuck*)

Therapist: Come on, give me a picture.

Client: Um . . . I want to be able to talk to him about this. To talk to him in a way that says, "See, this is what I am. This is what I've been going through."

Therapist: Okay. Let's tell the chair. (*points to a chair across the room*) When you tell your father what you want, tell him instead of telling me.

Client: (*Long pause, hesitantly*)

Therapist: Look at him and tell him.

Client: (*Softly*) I love . . . you . . . and I know that you love me. I know you've done your best. Sometimes I know that you feel guilty about the things that I do . . . the homosexual behavior. I don't know what it was that made this . . . this antipathy I have. In the present, what I want from you now is to take me seriously as a man . . . to listen to the things I have to say. You can disagree with them, but at least listen. Don't make a face or roll your eyes. (*laugh*) Just listen. Let me be a friend to you, an equal. . . . That's it.

Therapist: That's it?

Client: That's right.

Therapist: Is there anything else? Are you holding back?

Client: (*Thoughtfully*) In a way there might be, because I'm not crying.

Therapist: What would the crying be about? What does it say?

Client: (*Pause*) Childhood was terrifying for me. But I don't know if it was about my father. School was terrifying. Other people were terrifying, especially boys.

Therapist: Right . . . You would be silent. Now, more importantly, what would you be feeling while you are sitting there silently listening to your father?

Client: (Laughter) . . . The first feeling was exhilaration that he could be here and that we could talk, but the second feeling was that he wouldn't understand, he wouldn't change.

Therapist: Okay. These are all ideas. Let's get back to the feelings. So what you visualize is that your father is talking and you're listening. That's probably an accurate predictor since you know your relationship so well.

Client: Well, I see it as developing into a conversation between you and him.

Therapist: About you?

Client: About me.

Therapist: As if you're the phenomenon called, "The son, the client, Jack."

Client: That's right.

Therapist: As you sit and merely listen.

Client: That's right. *(laughter)*

Therapist: How would you feel if that were to happen?

Client: Um . . . Shut out, belittled . . . not taken seriously . . . childish.

Therapist: Good. Okay, very important. Now, take a breath. How would you like it to be different?

Client: (Long pause) In a way I would want that all to fall apart.

Therapist: Tell me about that.

Client: What you say to me is about *me*, but my father talks in abstract. It's not . . . personal . . . it's not . . . *me*.

Therapist: What does it not do for you?

Client: It does not let me tell him what I'm feeling.

Therapist: Was your father terrifying? (*Here is where the stereotype of the cruel father does not fit. Father's failure is more subtle, eluding the client's understanding.*)

Client: Not really. He could definitely be very angry, but no— it's not that.

Therapist: You say your childhood was scary. Yet I hear you saying your father was not the source of the terror. Then why bring up this terrifying childhood with him? How does it connect?

Client: Sometimes I was forced to do things.

Therapist: By your father?

Client: Well, actually by my mother. I remember in the sixth grade in a school play I was forced to be like a fairy, a sort of angel. And I had to wear these silver tights on stage. I did not want to do that more than anything in the world. But my teacher and my mother made me do it and I remember just dying of embarrassment. I thought, "This is what they think of me anyway. . . ."

Therapist: . . . Which is what?

Client: (*Pause*) Sissy.

Therapist: And how does your father fit into this?

Client: He could have stopped them . . . stopped it from happening. Treated me differently so that maybe I would have felt I could have stood up to them and said no. Maybe he could have made my mother treat me differently, protected me from what she made me do.

DEFENSIVE DETACHMENT

One of the most important therapeutic goals is to teach the client the concept of defensive detachment from males.

While most clients are quick to understand and personally identify with this tendency, they need to identify exactly when and how they detach from other men.

Case 1

(This client is a brother in a religious community, and one important person in his life is his superior, Father Frank, who is a very benevolent and supportive man. The client is beginning to identify his defensive attachment maneuvers and is attempting to work against them.)

Client: Lately I've become more aware of when I detach myself. For a long time I wasn't aware I was doing it. Now I'm trying to take a different attitude with Father Frank.

Therapist: What is your attitude when you're defensive with Father Frank?

Client: When I'm defensive, I'm . . . I have very little contact. I keep it down to a quick interaction . . . minimal involvement. I don't feel I'm connecting, really. That's what it is. I'm not really connecting.

Therapist: You don't feel you're connecting?

Client: I don't trust him. I feel he's going to hurt me. I know that's not true, but I send out signals that say, "Stay away." I won't sit down in his office. I have to go against that tendency toward detaching myself.

Therapist: And how do you do that?

Client: By just relaxing and trusting . . . just being present to him in a simple way. In a poverty of spirit. By just . . . coming in without a suit of armor on.

Therapist: I like that, "a poverty of spirit," a sort of vulnerability. A simplicity, an attitude of openness.

Client: When I'm with him, I say to myself, "This is it – be empty, be empty." But I'm not consistent, I'm still on the short side. I'm still a bit hesitant. Sometimes I'm at a loss for words.

Therapist: Since words are what connect us, one form of detachment is just simply to run out of words.

Client: I don't know sometimes what to say.

Therapist: Well, how do you feel with him?

Client: I don't feel anything, just a nothing.

Therapist: You see that's really the source of the defensive detachment from others. Detachment from our own feelings.

Case 2

This is a typical explanation of defensive detachment.

Therapist: How are you feeling right now?

Client: Umm . . . towards the beginning of the session, I had butterflies in my stomach . . . but as you got into explaining about me I felt this energetic bubbliness . . . like, oh, we're going somewhere! This is meaningful! There were several times throughout the conversation when I'd feel the butterflies, then you'd say something and I'd get that energetic feeling, and I'd smile or laugh to cover it up. When I say something and you explain what it means, it makes me feel good. It makes me feel there's hope. It makes sense to somebody! He understands what's happening to me! Like, he's talking about me, he's telling me about me and it makes me feel . . . sort of like when people compliment me, give me recognition.

Therapist: Your fear is to be seen by men. This is defensive detachment. When I see you and comment on you, it both excites you and scares you.

Client: Uh-huh.

Therapist: When I comment about you, you know that I see you clearly for who you are right now, and that scares you a little bit but that also excites you because that's exactly what you want—a man to truly see you. The opposite of defensive detachment is talking to someone and seeing them accurately. That breaks through the defensive detachment. "Here's a guy who is talking about me, right now, about who I am. I can't escape. He's seeing the real me, which is frightening."

Client: And yet it's what I want. I get mad because I want men to see me, and I get mad when a friend doesn't ask me how I am, how I am doing. There is something penetrating in the way a man can see you.

REPARATIVE DRIVE

In these examples, we see reparative drive taking the form of eroticization of a relationship with a man who is successful with women. Seducing a straight man is an often-found theme in gay literature. Straight men are viewed ambivalently as contemptible, yet attractive (*The Advocate*, 1989).

Case 1

(*Twenty-four-year-old Will is sexually involved with a married man, Tom. What intrigued Will was that his friend could be sexually involved with both men and women. His married friend became a symbolic "transitional object"—that is, a link to the intimacy with women, which he desired but feared. Thus, Will gained the chance to vicariously approach the role he wished he could have for himself.)*

Client: Tom intrigues me because he's married. I wanted to find out—how does he do this? You know . . . try to pick up a man and still be married. How does he juggle it?

Therapist: He has one foot in the gay world, and one foot out in married life.

Client: Yeah. And I see Tom as a hopeful way out. A way out of the problems I'm dealing with. He's living the type of life that actually I'm afraid of, which is being married and starting a family.

Therapist: Tell me the qualities of Tom, that you are attracted to.

Client: Well . . . he's outgoing, in control . . . that type of thing.

Therapist: Can you see that as masculine strength? A level of masculine achievement that represents an ideal to you? Can you see how you sexualized that?

Client: Yeah. Because I was reaching toward something that I do not possess, that I realize that I want for myself. In fact I was mainly attracted, in the beginning, to the fact that he was married. Sounds weird, but I wanted to know about his sexual relations with his wife. I wanted to know when and how often. Part of me didn't want to know, didn't want to ask because of my own jealousy. I didn't want to hear it and yet I did want to.

Therapist: So what actually happened—did you ask him?

Client: When I had asked before, kind of indirectly,

he would never say anything. But then I got more direct. It kind of turned me on to think he had sex with his wife.

Therapist: How do you mean, "turned you on"?

Client: Well, when I first met him, I sort of looked up to him as this good-looking guy who is married and yet he likes guys—and how can he do all this so successfully? How could he do all this stuff? I liked guys and wanted to like girls, but I didn't know how to, so here's Tom, who has no problem with women. I had to admit to him that it sort of turned me on to hear about it.

Therapist: So here you are, you're not feeling quite capable of performing sexually with women. So Tom, for you, is a transitional object—an object linking you to the feared woman. You feel close to Tom, so if Tom can be successful with women, then maybe through association, you can be successful with women too. Through identity with Tom, you might gain that male power. Through him, you have one foot in that other world you seek.

Client: A foot which connects me to it . . .

Therapist: Yeah, which connects you to married life. It's like a child who's afraid of dogs, so the father says, "I'll hold your hand and I'll touch the dog and I'll bring the two of you closer together." The problem is that you got sexually turned on by Tom. You sexualized him rather than identified with him. This is a mistake, a regression. Sexual gratification confounds the identification process.

Client: So by having sex with him, I felt like I was actually getting those things.

Therapist: Right. But you were only vicariously in that other world.

Client: My attraction to him reminds me of how my friends and I used to admire guys who looked like us—we liked guys who were as much like us as possible, because we were getting a reinforcement of ourselves.

Therapist: Exactly.

Client: He looks like me. Everyone says we look alike. . . . You know it's the relationship he has, that I wanted. Like, how does he do that regularly? I mean, I've had sex with a woman, but I haven't been able to follow through with the relationship.

Therapist: He has an emotional relationship with a woman, which is expressed sexually. That's what you haven't been able to accomplish.

Client: Yeah. Which is what I feel shaky about.

Therapist: Sex is easy but the felt stuff for a woman is scary.

Case 2

(*Elliott is a 26-year-old client who has been in therapy for one year for homosexual conflicts. During the past two years he has maintained an intense, obsessively dependent relationship with his straight roommate, Sam. Sam's easy, self-confident success with women is particularly appealing. Although Elliott's dependency on Sam feels sexual, he is determined to continue to cultivate his heterosexuality. Elliott was born and raised in on a secluded farm in the Midwest. His family life was strict, dogmatically religious, and emotionally deprived. He left the farm and settled in Los Angeles, where he met Sam, an aspiring actor. He was immediately attracted to Sam's good looks, charm, and outgoing style—all of which were qualities that he himself lacked. Sam however, apparently used Elliott to feed his narcissistic needs for attention and admiration, with some sexual teasing. In spite of his success with women, Sam himself seems*

to have some narcissistic needs for male attention. This homo-
sexual component only confuses Elliott all the more. Elliott still
holds on to the fantasy that Sam will help him relate to women,
but Sam consistently undermines his roommate's fledgling ef-
forts.

We see here the common imbalance of power and depen-
dency in same-sex attractions. We also hear about the sponta-
neous longing for the good father Elliott did not have, and
fantasies of being adopted by the therapist.)

Client: I've always needed a boost. Sam gives me that
. . . it's like going in and talking to your dad. Telling him
what's bothering you and your dad patting you on the
back.

Therapist: Except your dad didn't pat you on the
back, he swatted you on the rear.

Client: Yeah. Actually he hit me across the shoulders
because it was more painful. But I wanted to talk to Sam
about what I was facing. I wanted a shoulder, you know,
like, "Geez Sam, I'm seeing this girl and I'm kind of nervous.
I'm afraid I can't get it up and she might get disappointed."
I just wanted to express my doubts to someone, not just
anybody, but to somebody like Sam.

Therapist: Why would you want to talk to Sam? In the
past he's always discouraged you.

Client: I know, but I was looking for someone who
would be a friend, a good friend who could pump me up,
bolster me, give me some pointers about how to handle her.
"Don't worry, you'll be fine," and so on. Someone who
knew I was homosexual, where I wouldn't lose his friendship. He wouldn't think any less of me.

Therapist: Let me ask you this question. Do any of

those feelings, a warm shoulder to lean on, do any of those feelings for this ideal friend feel sexual?

Client: Probably if I let them, I guess.

Therapist: Tell me about that.

Client: Well, you kind of think, "Well, you'd want a hug." Somebody patting me on the back . . . and I guess, because of the closeness it would feel kinda sexual.

Therapist: It sort of slips from admiration to affection to sexual.

Client: Oh, yeah, I see it. But I got to stop it right there. I can picture him giving me a hug, "Oh, it's okay," and holding me 'cause I'm scared. It's kinda like I'd put him on a pedestal—"Oh, he's a great guy. Nothing happens to him. . . . He has no confidence problem"—and if you're not careful, you start sexually fantasizing him. I wish my dad could have been that boost for me.

Therapist: This is the work. Getting what you didn't get from your father.

Client: Did you ever think of adopting?

Therapist: Who, adopting you?

Client: (*Laughs*)

Therapist: You want me to take you home with me?

Client: I think it would be neat if my family could have met you.

THE NEED FOR A MENTOR

(*This 53-year-old client, the divorced father of an 11-year-old boy, came into therapy for help in controlling compulsive sexual behavior. Although his life was orderly and successful on the outside, he had a compulsion to frequent gay bathhouses and solicit male prostitutes.*)

Client: You know, I've really been a psychological orphan. I've never really had a dad.

Therapist: I know.

Client: And . . . I say to myself, well, where am I going to find a father? What am I looking for right now to heal myself? Am I looking for a father? Am I looking for a—

Therapist: You're looking for a mentor. You're looking for a male image to help you. You're looking to find your masculinity. To come out of this neutered self. That's what you've been looking for, but you've sexualized that search.

Client: But when you talk about this relationship I should have with this man, I wonder, what am I going to give him in our friendship?

Therapist: This is a very important question. What you will be giving him in fact, is yourself. You see, there is not only a need for the man to find a mentor . . . but there's also a need for man to be a mentor to someone. You have a boy at home. You're doing a great thing for your son. But you also have a need to be a father. I have a need to be a therapist. You have a need to help other people in your work as a medical technician. So by your participation in the relationship, you're giving the mentor something. You're allowing him to actualize his mentor-nature. Do you understand? That's enough in itself.

Client: I understand that, but I've always had a tough time with, ah . . . I've never wanted to use people. I've always felt uncomfortable with that.

(The search for a mentor typically raises this question of "using" another person. This doubt is particularly strong because the homosexual tends to have difficulty understanding what are reasonable expectations in a male relationship.)

Therapist: Because you hear this idea of "using." That's a rationalization of your unworthiness. Just like, I don't want to get close to you or you might find out I'm a homosexual. That's a rationalization of your unworthiness.

Client: See, I'm always afraid. I've always been afraid of, of, using people. Now, I know I do use people in a sexual context . . . but I don't feel I'm *really* using them in that context.

Therapist: An important question—why are you not using them?

Client: Well, one way you can look at it, it's two people who are consenting to something, so nobody is really getting hurt. But I know there is another way to look at it. I believe that homosexuals are really seducers in that we are taking advantage of another wounded man.

Therapist: How is it that you take advantage of a wounded man?

Client: Well, if you accept the thesis that every homosexual is wounded and is lonely and is seeking for love, and you come and you're offering someone this apparent love, this freedom from loneliness, and so forth—

Therapist: This special attention.

Client: Yes. You're using them in a mutual delusion. It's a reciprocal thing, but it's still using.

Therapist: That's a good point. But mentorship is not a matter of using. It involves a relationship that is very genuine and very mutually beneficial and very personal, and that's what scares you. That's where you become concerned that you're going to use the person. In an impersonal sexual relationship you don't have to worry about using. You're both using each other, it's quick, it's over, we come out and we wash our hands. That's the vicious cycle of empty relationships that you're caught up in.

STRAIGHT FRIENDS

Case 1

This case is an example of the value of disclosure with the right kind of straight friends.

Client: New things are happening. This guy's name is Alex and we started going to the gym and working out together. The reason that's good for me is it's important to be there with another guy, not be alone there.

(*Many clients express both hopes and fears about the gym. It is one of the few all-male environments that provides both temptation and the healing sense of contact with masculinity.*)

Client: It's really good for me because it allows me to be with another guy, working on developing my body, which is what I'm there for.
Therapist: A very good opportunity.
Client: It keeps it straight. It keeps the fantasies, or at least the behavior, in check. I get less into that isolated place, looking at all the guys and stuff.
Therapist: It keeps you in a more male perspective.
Client: He's a good influence. He knows all about me, all about my sexual struggles.
Therapist: He knows all about you?
Client: Oh, his brother is bisexual, which helps because we can talk about it. But he's straighter than a doornail.
Therapist: Straighter than an arrow?

Client: (*Laughs*) Whatever is straighter. He's a good guy and a great influence in my life.

Therapist: You're very fortunate to have him.

Client: He's very supportive of my struggle and we have this sharing. He's admitted to me he has a problem with adult bookstores, you know, pornography, same as I do. And it was incredible. It's nice to talk to him about it. We opened up in detail about our sexual patterns and when I go through my temptations, I can almost laugh at how silly it is.

Therapist: You can laugh because you gained a detachment — you can look objectively at a personal problem through the sharing with a friend. Further, I think it's especially good for you to share with a straight guy that part of yourself that you feel ashamed of. You can experience his acceptance and see that straight guys also have their share of hangups.

Case 2

This is an example of a poor decision in disclosing one's homosexuality to a straight friend. The disclosure is not done for healthy reasons, but out of a fantasy that it would pull the friend closer.

Client: I feel I have nothing to offer another man in a friendship . . . it's really scary.

Therapist: It *is* scary. But that's what keeps you isolated from other men. Keeps you frustrated in male relationships.

Client: I know. There's another guy in my company,

he's a supervisor for the whole department. He asked me to do this project with him. He's sort of a masculine-type guy.

Therapist: What about that?

Client: I don't know. It makes me nervous. There's something about Barry that strikes me as real out-doorsy. *(laughs)* It's not me.

Therapist: *(Laugh)* What about that?

Client: Well, he'll think, "I'm not working with this guy after all. He's not macho. He's not into skiing and all that shit."

Therapist: What, you've got to go skiing with him to do the job? What's this?

Client: Well, maybe I'll just *go* skiing with him!

Therapist: That's not the point. He didn't ask you, anyway. *(laughs)*

Client: I just know there's going to be some barrier between us.

Therapist: Yeah. The barrier is your head.

Client: There's not going to be that bonding—

Therapist: That you want?

Client: Yeah.

Therapist: Bonding may not come in your relation-ship with him. Here, you're just doing a job together. If your emotional needs were met with other guys, you would not be looking to him. You're investing too much emotion-ally in this one man.

Client: I know.

Therapist: It's your own sense of unworthiness which blocks you. The rationalization is, if they knew I was homosexual, they would never be my friends.

Client: What is it that I think they're going to find out—that I can be intimidated? That I could get in needy situations? A couple of years back I got involved with this guy, Al. Here's a guy I figure I can be good friends with. He's straight and everything. That turns into shit.

Therapist: How does it turn into shit?

Client: Well, I find myself chasing the guy around.

Therapist: Him rejecting you? How's that?

Client: I met him in 1978—I was really uptight then. I'm going to AA meetings and he's really . . . a cute guy. (*laughs*) Anyway, we're talking. We become pretty good friends but then it just gets off-balance. I'm chasing after him!

Therapist: What goes wrong?

Client: I'm not sure.

Therapist: What I suspect goes wrong is you're not yourself, you're too self-conscious, you're not giving to the friendship. You become passive, you let him take the lead and you don't offer any ideas of your own. As long as you bask in his presence, in his "aura," and he doesn't reject you, that's good enough for you. You lose your spontaneity, you get into your complaint false self.

Client: Yeah . . . I kind of see that.

Therapist: Consequently, he sees you as boring.

Client: . . . And hanging on.

Therapist: So after a while, you are burdensome. (*pause*) It looked like it hurt when I said that.

Client: (*Laughs sarcastically*) Thanks.

Therapist: To put it frankly, the false compliant self is not appealing.

Client: (*Long pause, then softly*) I know.

Therapist: Do you know where it comes from, this sense of unwantedness, of inferiority?

Client: It's such a big issue . . . I don't know where it

comes from. I just get hung up on these guys. Sometimes I say to myself, "Just let him go. Stop thinking about him, stop falling. Fuck it, forget it. There's nothing to be had, it's just a waste of time. It's futile. It's frustrating, just stop it." The security I had hoped to find with Al, never was. He didn't need me. The more I showed him I needed him, the more he would treat me like shit. A few years back I told him about myself—my orientation. He didn't know what to do with it. I was hoping he might have had, you know, some of the same shit . . . like, "If I show him mine, he'll show me his."

Therapist: His fantasy.

Client: Right. For what it was worth, I just threw it out. This had to come out. "Al, I've just got to tell you how I really feel. I can't live with this anymore." I went through my whole story.

Therapist: How did he respond?

Client: Like nothing. Like I never said it. I can't bring up any serious issues about me. I even told him how I was doing with Alcoholics Anonymous. All he said was, "Oh, yeah?" Forget that one.

Therapist: He doesn't want to hear anything personal.

Client: He just went on about his race cars. But in a way I've been more relaxed with him than before. Back then, I was a basket case. Now there seems to be a lessening of the . . . bonding need, the . . . craving.

Therapist: Okay. Stay with it. Why should it be less? What's the change within you?

Client: Maybe it's because I realize the security I expected to find with Al, never was. I see now I've got to find it on my own. And now it's being met somewhere else. I don't have to depend on people like Al. It was a crazy relationship.

Therapist: What do you mean, you're finding it in other places?

Client: Therapy, group, other friends.

Therapist: Do you think you'll ever allow yourself to get into a dependent relationship with someone like Al again?

Client: It's too painful. It's like trying to get blood from a turnip.

Therapist: Right. Trying to get responses of love and friendship out of people who just aren't equipped to give it.

TRUST OF WOMEN

Here, we see distrust of women emerging as a major stumbling block to developing heterosexual relationships. This distrust is particularly evident in sexual matters.

Typically, homosexually oriented men avoid explicit sexual behavior when they are beginning to date women. While moral standards may play a part in this decision, this may sometimes be partly a rationalization that arises out of fear of sexual performance. For her part, the woman is often delighted to find a young man interested in her and not just her body.

Case 1

(Twenty-seven-year-old Allan came from a very puritanical household with a passive father and a manipulative mother. He

has now been in a very compatible relationship with a woman for several months.)

Client: I can't deal with sex with her right now. I'm too unsure of my motivations. Am I trying out my masculinity? Am I proving I'm straight? Am I using her as an experiment?

Therapist: I think you're wise.

Client: The more that we can be together, the more we can trust each other.

Therapist: Yes.

Client: We did sleep together and there was lots of contact.

Therapist: Were you aroused?

Client: Oh, definitely! . . . But there was something holding me back. I said to her, I must have confidentiality. I want our little inside jokes to stay with us. I don't want you to talk to your girlfriends at work about what we do in bed. I need to feel comfortable. I don't want little jokes. (*This client's concern about confidentiality and jokes comes from his fear that the feminine—originally, mother—would diminish his sexuality.*) I need to know that things that we do, she won't tell her sister jokingly, or even tell her girlfriends.

Therapist: Why is that important?

Client: Trust.

Therapist: What are you afraid of?

Client: My sexuality is an area of vulnerability.

Therapist: That goes back to your early family dynamics. You were never given confidence in your male sexuality. It was always something undermined, ignored, or shamed. What you are saying to her by way of this confidentiality issue is, "Woman, I am going to open up and trust you with my male sexuality, but don't betray me like my mother did. Don't joke with it. Don't put it down. Don't make me feel silly or stupid. I want you to respect it." You want to be sure you can trust this woman with your sexuality. It's a very vulnerable part of you and it's wise to get to know her as a friend, to trust her as a friend before you expose your male sexuality to her.

Client: I said, we will not have sex. I don't want you on the pill. No chemicals inside of you. Furthermore, I cannot walk into your parents' house knowing that we are hypocrites. So, I said, (*mockingly, haughtily*) "I want my bride to wear white!" (*laughs*)

(*It is ironic how an outrageously promiscuous homosexual man can become so conservative and moralistic with a woman. Actually, this change serves a useful purpose. Feeling ashamed of his previous life-style, he now desires to separate himself from it and start over.*)

Client: I said to her that I was promiscuous when I was your age, and now I don't want to do that anymore.

Therapist: I like your calling the terms in this relationship. You are structuring the boundaries early on and clarifying your expectations here. It's important that you not feel out of control. (*Typically I have found that when men with homosexual backgrounds enter a relationship with women, they maintain a hypervigilance in anticipation that they will lose control to the feminine.*)

Client: I'm afraid of betrayal. I don't want the girls snickering about our sexuality. Yeah, like Mom would do. (*he imitates haughty dismissive gesture*) As if such bodily things were not important.

Therapist: This has much to do with why the gay scene is so appealing. Its emphasis is on male sexuality as well-important. The penis focus and all that.

Client: Did I ever show you a picture? (*takes out picture from wallet*)

Therapist: She's very pretty. But you haven't told me how you *feel* about her.

Client: Oh, I love her. The other night I wanted to just cuddle, and it was great. I'm really happy. We need to know and trust each other. I said, we need to share our past and what I'm about to say is not to hurt you . . . but I feel I need to say this . . . I told her a few times I worked as a male prostitute. She started crying and I started crying because I saw that she was hurt, and she said, "We all do things" . . . (*he becomes tearful*) . . . this is why she's a special girl. "We all do things," she said, "and back then you were a different person."

Therapist: As times goes on, slowly, you'll need to let her know more about your sexual past and how you're trying to change it. She deserves to know.

Client: I realize that. In time. I didn't think I would ever tell a girl that I jacked people off for money!

Therapist: Right.

Client: I felt the time was right, now. I know I can trust her with this. She won't betray me with this.

Therapist: You're afraid she might dismiss or downplay you. You want her to trust *all* of what you're about.

Client: More and more I am doubting myself less because I see she won't mock me like my mother. I get aroused when there's a trust. (*Not many men reach this point in their treatment and it is not clear why some men can and others do not.*)

Therapist: You're saying, "I'm sharing my sexuality with you . . . I want you to see this is a very important part of myself, denied for so long. This is a dynamic, vital part of me!"

Client: Last week I told her . . . I told her that I masturbated after I saw her.

Therapist: You told her. What were your motivations?

Client: (*Long pause*) "This is another test to see if I can trust you. I'm sharing my sexuality with you—for now only verbally, but I'm trusting. What I'm saying sounds silly, it sounds potentially embarrassing, but here goes."

Therapist: Your mother shamed you into splitting off your male sexuality. Now you're asking another woman to help you reunite it.

Case 2

(*This 54-year-old man is on the brink of being open to intimacy with a woman. We see the barriers of avoidance, anxiety, rationalization, and flight back to homosexuality. He was married for sixteen years with no emotional intimacy and very poor sexuality.*)

Client: I've got to tell you, Joe, this thing is knocking the shit out of me.

Therapist: What thing?

Client: This . . . this whole procedure . . . this therapy.

Therapist: Yeah. I told you it would be rough, that's why it's initiatory therapy.

Client: I got no sleep last night. I went home, tried to go to sleep, but I woke up. I couldn't go back to sleep, so I got dressed and went down to a gay bar. I got this thing in my mind that I wanted to talk to gay people about this. I am so isolated and I thought, "Well, maybe I can find somebody"—but there was nobody. Then I went to another one and there was nobody. Then I went home, but I couldn't sleep. I couldn't sleep . . . so . . . three o'clock in the morning, I'm up again . . . looking . . . for somebody.

Therapist: What were you looking for?

Client: A guy to talk to—and probably have sex with. Who knows . . . what the hell.

Therapist: Right.

Client: Saturday night was the same shit all over again, only that night I had sex with a guy. I'm looking to talk to somebody. I've tried to get this whole thing out of my system.

Therapist: What are you trying to get out of your system?

Client: I'm trying to understand what's goin' on. I'm very alone on this issue. I need to talk to somebody, Joe. I did not talk with that person I had sex with.

Therapist: You were looking to talk but you had sex instead. Funny how that happens.

Client: It's painful. I'm really searching.

Therapist: I thought you were interested in a relationship with a woman. What happened?

Client: I'm scared shitless of that.

Therapist: Of course you are. So you run back to the gay bars to find that male bolstering.

Client: That's right, I agree with you. I lied to a woman, I made a date with a gal for tonight. I got scared. I turned around and called her back and lied to her.

Therapist: Do you think this has to do with all this turmoil, this upset, all this pain?

Client: I'll be honest with you, Joe. I'd like to have a good fuck with a woman, nothing more than that. I'm at the point of going to a whorehouse.

Therapist: Do you hear how intensely ambivalent you are about women? You're afraid, you're scattered, you're all over the place. You're fearful. Why go to a whorehouse, what's wrong with a nice relationship with a woman?

Client: Sex has never been a problem for me. The problem is the rest of it.

Therapist: You want a woman so you go to a gay bar? Why?

Client: I tell you, I'm scared.

Therapist: Even when you narrow it down to the correct gender, a woman, it has to be a whore. You need male support. You need male friendship. The problem is you're not getting it from male friends. You want to get it from sexual contact.

Client: What do you call this friend of mine I was with last night, who was at my house? He and I . . . he was at my house.

Therapist: Does he know what your struggle is?

Client: Oh, not at all!

Therapist: Well, that's it. Then he can't feed you. You need to tell him or any other close, straight man what your struggle is.

Client: Oooooh! (*imitation shiver*)

Therapist: Yes . . . you will experience a support, a bolstering of your masculine strength when you can disclose and have that disclosure received with respect by a straight friend.

Client: What about with a stranger . . . a straight stranger?

Therapist: If it can develop into a friendship, fine. But

otherwise it's like the whore, impersonal. It's got to be a friend!

Client: How about a friend with the same problem?

Therapist: There's the possibility of it becoming sexual.

Client: That's the risk you take.

Therapist: But why go to that risky population?

Client: Why does the alcoholic join up with other alcoholics? As you're talking, I'm fearful, I'm really afraid!

Therapist: I have no doubt of that.

Client: I was told, and everything indicated to me, that sex was dirty.

Therapist: Of course. The woman who is introduced to you is on a pedestal, the Madonna. You say you want the love of a woman, but when you get close to someone you want it to be either a guy or a whore.

Client: I was married, I had no trouble having sexual intercourse.

Therapist: You can act out sexually even with a woman but you're emotionally detached.

Client: I have no problems showing her my . . . private parts . . . or any of that stuff.

Therapist: But it's your emotions.

Client: My vulnerability, my heart. I want to run to a guy, cling to him to get the strength, the courage to have sex, to bolster.

Therapist: You're not prepared to deal intimately with a woman, that's the fear. Fill in the blank, "I'm afraid of women because they can—"

Client: —Castrate me. I've never been intimate with a woman, not even my wife, in all my life. Since my wife's death, there are all these women who want to be friends. I don't want to get involved with them! I never realized how much I don't trust women. Nobody knows about the relationship between my wife and me. Everybody on the outside thought it all looked perfectly normal. (*crying*) When she died the dream died. That's why her death was so painful. (*sobbing*) The dream that it could get better . . . that I could be close with a woman. Three weeks after my wife died I went to a whorehouse.

Therapist: A lot of homosexual men can have sex with women very easily.

Client: I think that's what's going on.

Therapist: How does this fit with all that talk last time about how women are so unsatisfying to men? Let's do a fantasy trip. I want you to close your eyes. Imagine being with a woman, your ideal woman. Picture her however you want. Here you are sitting with her on the couch in front of a fire. Maybe the two of you have a glass of wine. What's happening? Tell me about it.

Client: (*Leans back in a chair, closes his eyes, head back, takes a deep breath—long pause*) It really feels good, it really feels comfortable. I can really get turned on by her. (*long pause*)

Therapist: Go on.

Client: I can really feel a tingle, a sexual tingle. I can really imagine having sex with her. But my sexuality can hurt a woman, there's the fear of hurting. If I got down to my deepest feelings for my mother, I can probably be very angry.

Therapist: Probably? Give me a break.

Client: Well . . . I say probably because I haven't gotten in touch with the anger. I can look back on my childhood and imagine hitting. (*punches fist in palm*)

Therapist: Who?

Client: Hitting, just hitting. I don't want to hurt a woman.

Therapist: The male can only approach the woman if he has no fear of engulfment. What do you think you'll do with this girl tonight? (*The closer he gets to a woman, the more fear and anger he feels towards his mother. Trust issues toward the woman become more pronounced.*)

Client: I'll probably see her, but tell her from the beginning that I don't want to get involved.

Therapist: That's good. So you establish the boundaries. Keep the tingle.

Client: But they all want these exclusive relationships.

Therapist: Tell her, tell her up front.

Client: That's what I'm going to do. I'm going to tell her up front that I'm not ready for an exclusive relationship.

PORNOGRAPHY

Early childhood exposure to female pornography is a powerful stimulus for all children (Reisman 1990). The young boy seeing pornography will tend to see his own mother within the female figure, evoking feelings of curiosity, confusion, hurt, betrayal, and disgust. In the prehomosexual boy, early exposure to pornography may intensify barriers that are already forming against heterosexual intimacy.

(*This client exemplifies a number of men who report adverse reactions to female pornography from early boyhood. In this excerpt from a session, the client was talking about his relationship with his girlfriend, Alice, and what it might be like getting physically close to her. Suddenly he became blocked in imagining any further intimacy.)*

Therapist: Can we push ourselves through to a sexual fantasy . . . can you imagine being sexually attracted to her?

Client: (*Abruptly*) No, no, because . . . no, I don't want to see her naked. I want to see her, but not with her clothes off.

Therapist: I see.

Client: I want to look at her and feel her closeness.

Therapist: Can you imagine what she looks like naked?

Client: Yes. But she's better dressed.

Therapist: The idea of her being naked is unattractive?

Client: (*Hesitantly*) Yes.

Therapist: What's the feeling?

Client: (*Pause*) Well, I can imagine her naked but I don't like it. No.

Therapist: What's the feeling?

Client: (*Very long pause*)

Therapist: Stay with the feeling. Try to give me words to fit the feeling.

Client: (*Long pause, apparently deeply stuck*)

Therapist: Ugly? Repulsive? Cheap? Scary? Disgusting?

Client: (*Long pause*) Scary . . . no. Not scary . . . worried that I have to perform.

Therapist: What if you didn't have to perform? What if she had no expectations other than for you to undress her and to look at her, perhaps touch her? How would you feel?

Client: No. I don't like that.

Therapist: What's the feeling? The expectation is one understandable block, but beyond these expectations is another block, some negative feeling just seeing her naked. Close your eyes and try to get in touch with the feeling.

Client: Yes. I don't know what it is but, yes.

Therapist: When you were a child did you see naked women? Was it your mother? There is some block there. (*Therapist is randomly probing. Therapist himself is stuck.*)

Client: Yes . . . yes.

Therapist: There is something like that.

Client: Yes. There is something there. Yes . . . *yes!* (*sitting up straight, eyes open*). We saw magazines. I was like 6 or 7 years old and my cousin told my brothers and me about sexual acts and everything, and I remember perfectly the way he was describing . . . like, um . . . he was excited, and we saw magazines. Not Playboys, but more dirty, more graphic.

Therapist: Your brother was older? Tell me what you remember.

Client: Well . . .

Therapist: Do you remember pictures?

Client: I can remember the whole story. There was a woman—fat, not with a good body, and she was talking to a salesman and she tried to seduce him and she took off her clothes and was, how do you say, fellating the guy.

Therapist: She was what?

Client: You know, sucking the guy off, and she was blond.

Therapist: You can picture her?

Client: I remember exactly the pictures. I remember the smell (*client makes a gesture of revulsion*) of the room we were in, the basement. (*It is interesting to note the vivid details with which the pictures are remembered. The intensity of the moment is locked into the memory with its associated sensations.*)

Therapist: What was the smell? (*attempting to encourage the recall of the subtle nuances of the setting*)

Client: It was . . . when something is wet . . . when something is damp.

Therapist: Musty.

Client: Yep . . . humm . . . yeah, yeah.

Therapist: What were the pictures?

Client: Yeah, the whole story was in pictures with the words on the bottom.

Therapist: How old were you?

Client: Six or seven. I believe that did not help my image of women.

Therapist: Of course not. The little boy thinks, "This is who I have to have sex with?"

Client: It meant like, "You have to like it." Because they expect you to have to like this. My cousin who had the magazines was about thirteen. He was aroused and, you know . . . proud. And I was just shocked.

Therapist: How did you know he was aroused?

Client: Because he showed, you know, his erection in his pants. And my older brother was reading without any expression, like . . . not indifferent, but like, "I can control myself." And I was, like, "God! This is terrible!" And I was very . . . scared of what we had seen.

Therapist: Yes.

Client: We were at a party with our families. Every-body was upstairs and we had to . . . go back and . . . everybody looks the same but you feel like . . .

Therapist: You had seen something that made you different.

Client: Yeah. It's like you don't belong to that party, those people, because of what you have seen.

Therapist: Because of something you had participated in, you did not feel a part of those people having fun at the party. You felt separate from them.

Client: Yeah. And just now when I was trying to picture myself naked with Alice, it's funny how those pictures popped up in my mind so vividly.

20

The Process of Group Psychotherapy

During the group meeting presented here, several common themes came up for discussion:

1. The tendency to overvalue or undervalue other men
2. Resistance to getting close to men (defensive detachment)
3. The need to develop a support system of nonerotic male friendships
4. The problem of what is reasonable to expect from male friends, including group members
5. Self-assertion

6. The difficulty of giving up the dream of meeting that special male friend/lover, and frustration with the ongoing nature of change

This session opens with Marco describing some recent painful events that have depressed and upset him:

Marco: "The whole New Year's holiday I felt bummed out. On Friday I went to a New Year's Eve party. Nothing bums me out more than New Year's Eve. New Year's Eve is a gay curse. Nothing is more alienating.

Billy: Oh, yeah? What about Father's day? (*group laughter*)

Ethan: What about Superbowl Sunday? (*more laughter*)

Marco: I had nothing to do on New Year's Day. I get no invitations, so finally I say, "The hell with it, I'm going to a restaurant by myself." Do you know how it feels to go to a restaurant alone on a holiday? All these couples, all good-looking young people. The waiter is nice, he gives me a table in the corner, looking out the window. I guess he felt sorry for me. (*cynical laugh*)

Monday morning comes and I'm still bummed out. Then what *really* pissed me off is that Max, my boss, asked this other guy in the office, Jack, out to lunch. Max asked Jack to lunch. He doesn't ask me. Why didn't he ask me? I just get this negative paranoid feeling that Max is trying to cut me out of my work. Then Max called Jack to help him with something he was doing. "Jack, could you please help me with this?" Why isn't he talking to me? I think, "Shit is happening." You know how I'm feeling? I'm angry, despair ing, I'm depressed and self-destructive. I'm thinking suicide now. I'm even thinking how I'll get a gun. . . . (nervous laughter)

Then that night when I got home, Max calls me up and says, "What's going on? What's wrong?" This never happens to me. (disgusted laugh) When I get in these moods, nobody ever asks what's wrong. I'm always left by myself to stew these things over.

The fact that Max called and seemed concerned really helped. I tried to tell him what was going on and why I was in such a bad mood. He was concerned enough, decent enough to call, and he was not freaked out by my behavior. He didn't reject me . . . he said my work is excellent . . . nobody hates me.

(Here, Marco lapses into a lengthy discussion of his feelings for Max and what Max's phone call meant to him. We hear how deeply appreciative he is for this show of concern.)

That phone call just blew me away. Max is my supervisor, he is very good, very dynamic. (laughs) Someone I'd like to be like. Max is someone I'd like to stay associated with.

Darin: (To Marco) When you were talking about your bad mood, it kind of reminds me of what I do—I hate to use the word, but I guess I have this tendency to pout. (slight laugh) It's a way to get people to ask me what's wrong. Like this week with my roommate—it's Saturday, late afternoon, and I'm running around, and I'm getting ready for a party we are having and I'm expecting he's going to come home and help me out. Finally he comes home and

says, "I'm really tired, I'm going to take a nap." So he got
tired!

So anyway, instead of just telling him how angry I feel,
I kind of just get pissy and quiet and wait for him to come
around. I really felt stupid and embarrassed that I couldn't
speak up and tell him I thought he wasn't pulling his
weight.

Billy: What would you have liked to have said?

Darin: "Do your share, guy! I thought we both decided to do this party!" But I know where this pouting
comes from. When I was a kid, the only way to get power
was to give them the silent treatment. It finally gets me
attention. Any kind of honest confrontation never
worked, so I pouted and that always made them notice.

Therapist: But did it really work?

Darin: (*Pause*) Not really. My parents would indulge
me emotionally but never address the real reasons why I
was angry. What this comes down to is I feel like I just don't
know what I should or shouldn't expect in relationships. So
I don't ask directly for anything—I wait for them to come to
me.

(*Many clients report similar difficulties expressing anger. It is a
pattern originating in childhood where true self-expression, particularly of negative feelings, was not permissible. Pouting is a
social posture that sets people up to pay attention to the pouter
and to take responsibility for his feelings. It is a way of indirectly
showing anger, while not taking responsibility for it.*)

Therapist: You wish you could just speak up and deal
with it directly.

Darin: Uh-huh.

Therapist: Getting back to you, Marco—you told us about feeling so bummed out last week—what are the questions you have for the group?

Marco: I don't know. I just wanted to get this out. I thought, "Shit, I'm still having these feelings."

Therapist: Do you feel satisfied just reporting this experience to the group? Does it satisfy you, or do you want something else from them?

Marco: I . . . (*hesitantly*) . . . maybe I just wanted to know what you guys think. Just share and get your support.

(*Many men have difficulty deciding what are reasonable expectations of other men.*)

Brian: I want to tell you I can relate to that place. When I get depressed, I get very sensitive—especially around New Year's Eve. I feel a lot of pain at that time. But when you were talking, I also heard a lot of anger—"I'll kill myself, I'll get a gun." Sounds like, for you, the way to get rid of the anger is to get rid of yourself or throw the anger back on yourself through self-destruction. Maybe your anger goes back to a larger issue, a past anger. . . .

Marco: (*Off-handedly*) I don't think it's that. . . .

(*He then lapses back to complaining about the incident for about ten minutes. The intensity of his frustration and anger, along with his dismissal of Brian's suggestion, seems to discourage the group from interrupting him.*)

Billy: (*Taking a chance to intervene and return Marco to Brian's original point*) The way you are talking right now, I hear the same anger when you were saying earlier, "I went to this restaurant and all these other good-looking people were in couples and I was lonely." You need to admit you're not only depressed, but angry, before you can know what you're angry at.

Marco: I just asked myself that question—why am I so pissed? Sure, I was sad and lonely in the restaurant, I know that . . . but why was I *angry?*

Therapist: Truthfully, you almost always look angry.

Marco: I always feel angry at this condition. Like I thought, "Godammit, this six months of therapy investment." I know I get really angry at the struggle when there seems to be no end to it, like it's happening again, happening again. There is no end to this thing.

Joel: I know. It's the loneliness, the isolation, the inward paranoia. I'm mad at this situation too, and I wish I could walk away from it and go on with my life, but there is still this intense overflowing anger. It's my job too, my personal life, New Year's Eve . . . but at bottom, it's this homosexual problem. That's why New Year's Eve is so significant, like, "Here I am, alone again."

Darin: I can relate to that. It's the homosexuality, the worrying about it—sometimes even the *not wanting* to get rid of it! I mean, the excitement of when you see a guy, the whole fantasy—all of that, as undesirable as it is—there is still an exciting energy there.

Therapist: Sure there is an energy.

Darin: There's excitement, there's a nice drama there that I don't want to let die. If I succeed in therapy, that excitement is going to go.

Therapist: The resistance is about your not having discovered a bigger source of energy. That spark is exciting, but it's so short-lived.

Darin: Yeah, but when you're in the middle of it, you don't see what else is out there.

Therapist: But you don't have to stay in the middle of it.

Darin: But that's another thing that I'm afraid of—how long are we going to be doing this? You know, I feel like—Okay, I know that I'm making progress. I see it, but I think, in three or four years am I still going to be struggling like this?

Therapist: Every time you have these doubts, you have a choice—to either feel sorry for yourself and go down and down . . . or you can do something that is very simple. It means the next time you meet a significant male, be real with him. When you're real, especially with a man, you're awake, you're in the process of connecting. As soon as you start taking those chances, you start saying truthfully how you feel. In that state of suspended animation you can get trapped in, the only thing that seems gratifying is that spark of sexual excitement, that forbidden drama. You've got to stop getting stuck in that trend of passive, helpless, suspended-animation bullshit.

Darin: Yeah. But I hate to talk to people about my fears, my . . . (*pause*) . . . I hate that!

Therapist: Why?

Darin: I don't know. It sounds too weak, feminine. Like someone who complains, a little boy . . . yuk. Most of the gay guys do that. I don't know how complaining to another man can make you feel fine. I don't want to hear (*imitating a patronizing tone*) "Oh no, poor you!"

Therapist: It doesn't help?

Darin: No. I hate it. And of course I'm always trying to keep my . . . my image.

Therapist: I'm not saying you should be a wimp. You're just telling a friend what you're going through. It doesn't have to come across as weakness and femininity. You're sharing your experiences, you're letting him in on what's bothering you. You don't want sympathy.

Darin: No.

Therapist: You're not asking for sympathy, you're asking for understanding. I talk to my friends about what I'm dealing with . . . maybe to get me to see the problem a little differently, a little better.

Darin: (*Pause*) Yeah. I know what you mean because when somebody is talking to me like my friend Franco— Franco talks to me about everything.

Therapist: Yes. He is a good example and he is straight. You don't see him as weak or effeminate, do you?

Darin: No.

Therapist: Seeing disclosure as weak or effeminate is a way of keeping yourself away from men. It's a rationalization, an excuse to justify a deeper irrational belief. You want to keep that image. To disclose a trouble causes you to feel weak. Franco is a good example of how a man can express concerns, confusions, and disappointments and not look like a wimp.

But let's get back to why Marco was feeling so angry. Marco, a few guys here just put out some reasons why you might be angry, above and beyond the situation at work. Brian said it might be your past. Joel said maybe it's the homosexual condition itself. Do you want to explore any of their suggestions?

Marco: (*Long pause, then hesitantly*) They sound valid but what do I do with them! (*angrily*) I mean, what good is it to explore them? Maybe I should just jump up and down and just get this anger out of my system?

Ethan: You just said earlier that you didn't know why you felt upset and angry. If you don't verbalize—

Marco: (Interrupting) . . . it just was a surprise, like I know the tendency is there but all at once it just happened. Like, shit! Here it goes again. I felt so bad, I canceled my individual session with Joe. I'm saying to myself, "You feel so bad you can't even go to your therapy session? How screwed up *are* you?"

(Here we cannot help but suspect that Marco is indulging in what van den Aardweg calls self-dramatization.)

Sean: Do you see *some* progress in therapy?

Marco: There is a part of me that sees progress, but part of me does not.

Sean: Maybe it's a good idea when you are really depressed to look at some of the positive things and remember the progress you have been making, Marco.

Marco: (Responding to Sean's gentleness, he makes a shift from self-dramatization to self-reflection.) I don't know why this happens. I shouldn't get so upset just because two guys don't invite me to lunch. It's just a pattern that seems to repeat itself over and over in my life. But then to have a guy call me up in such a considerate and concerned way—*this* just *never* happened to me! I never expected him to call.

Billy: Yeah. And you said that your depression lifted after he called. But what if he hadn't called?

Marco: If he hadn't called, I would have really been depressed. Somebody cared, somebody gave a shit. Here's a guy I'm working for, he's not just some typical uptight boss. . . . I was impressed. I thought, "I owe this guy a lot. I'll always be the best possible person I can be working for him."

Therapist: I think it's really neat that Max called, but I wonder if you could have done something for yourself without being at the mercy of a phone call.

Marco: To have done something for myself? (*as if stumped by the possibility*)

Brian: In other words, was it so special because someone called you, or was there something you could have done to get the same results? I'm wondering if you could have called somebody or reached out to somebody? Like, "This is where I'm at right now. . . ."

Marco: Well, sooner or later I would have, but I just didn't want to.

Joel: One way of preventing this from happening is to avoid creating a dependency upon one person. What if he didn't call? I guess the homework for you and me and for all of us is to create a safety net for ourselves. You may not have anyone right now, but you need to develop that. What Max gave you at that moment was the feeling that somebody cared.

Marco: Yeah. I needed that just then. (*gesturing dramatically*) I mean I wanted to call Suicide Prevention! I used to work for them. I used to man the phones! (*group laughter*)

Joel: We need to remember, we all need to challenge ourselves to develop this safety net of people who care about us.

Therapist: Joel, that strong advice to Marco goes back to the principle in group therapy—the one who's most mindful of why he is in group is the one who is most helpful to the others.

Joel: Because I can see myself . . . and when you're helping someone else, you can see it clearer for yourself. By putting my struggle into his situation, I'm applying my own understanding to my problem and getting a clear sense of what gets me.

Therapist: Right. "I'm putting it out there for somebody else, but it's helping me."

Joel: That's what I did during the last few months. I'd come in and complain and people would say, "So then what are you going to do about it?" (*turns to Marco*) That's what I see you doing. Talking about it. Talking about it is great, but it doesn't give you the answers so that in six weeks you don't boil over again.

Therapist: Let's get back to the other point.

(*The therapist should have stayed with Joel's comments to Marco. It could have been a valuable opportunity for Marco to give an honest response to Joel. Instead, he moved on to what Max might symbolize.*)

I'm thinking about how important that phone call was to you. I want you to hear it in your own words. What you said was, "I really appreciate Max's calling me back. Now I'm going to treat him differently. Now I'll always be a good worker for him." It sounds like a very deep loyalty thing.

Marco: Oh, yeah.

Therapist: But listen to the investment you've put into this guy! Now he's in a different category, he's special. You are so appreciative of what he did that you are swearing your loyalty to him. From now on you are determined to do a good job, to please him. We're willing to work hard for a good father. I'm not putting you down . . . this is very natural. We want to do well for our fathers. We want our fathers to be proud of us. But do you see what kind of devotion you are investing in this one person?

Marco: Yeah. I hear that.

Therapist: It goes back to this male-attention issue. You're so needy for that special male attention that now Jack will have a special place in your life. You may be setting yourself up. I haven't heard anybody focus on the real issue yet tonight—that anger and frustration are about not getting male attention.

Marco: Well, I felt hurt, because Max is a guy I'd like to have a positive relationship with.

Therapist: How do you mean, a "positive relationship"?

Marco: Hmm . . . maybe he would like my work, like me, and want to keep me around. Be friends.

Therapist: Acceptance issues.

Marco: Yeah.

Therapist: Employment issues.

Marco: Yeah.

Therapist: But all this has to do with what? What are the larger, underlying issues?

Marco: My relationship with Max.

Therapist: More than that. Max represents an issue for you.

Billy: It's men. You feel rejected as soon as a friend turns to someone else.

Marco: Yeah . . . that's right.

Billy: Because you built up a dependency on him.

Ethan: You've also built him up in your eyes. You've described him as everything you'd like to be.

Marco: Oh, yeah.

Ethan: And any little sign of rejection, and you'll be bummed out.

Therapist: (*Looks to group*) Does this sound like a new problem for us? (*group laughter*)

We need to see the issues here, which go back to father. It's a male-rejection issue . . . here are these powerful male figures in my life, and if they don't show me full affirmation, I get depressed. These two important guys— who I've *made* important—are going out to lunch together and leaving me out, and it brings up old stuff—like feeling excluded, not being good enough. On the outside looking in. (*looking to group*) We need to pick up these underlying themes. We need to understand this first, before we can ask, as Joel asks, "What can we do about it?" Find out how you really got into it, which means recognizing the larger issues.

Just recognizing these same old issues for what they are takes away some of the sting, the pain. It gives you a perspective, a helpful detachment from which you gain a little more ego strength to deal with the problem. How can you pick up the phone and call a friend when you don't know what the problem really is?

Marco: I get caught up in the romantic illusion. I'm fascinated by the younger, more powerful, successful guy who has an attitude . . . has a way of talking—he drives a Mercedes, he's really got it made. He's got it fucking made!

Therapist: That son of a bitch! (*group laughter*)

Marco: And I compare myself very unfavorably.

Brian: I can relate to this exactly. When I'm in it, I can't remember the larger issue. When I'm not in it, I remember exactly. (*turning to therapist*) So if you were the friend who we were to call, how would you help him?

Therapist: I would ask him – if it were two *women* who were going to lunch and didn't invite you, that would not have upset you that way, am I right or wrong?

Brian: Yeah. It wouldn't affect me as much.

Therapist: (*To group*) Would it affect any of you as much?

Several group members: No.

Therapist: So we know it's about male relationships. You need to recognize that the actual situation does not in itself justify such a depressive reaction. If the friend you call for support is informed, if he is familiar with the issues of homosexuality, he will know this is an issue of male rejection. The friend on the phone needs to ask some questions. I hope your friend uncovers the real issues. Why should such an incident affect you? Is it an unconscious projection? Are you anticipating rejection?

(*The therapist could have withheld offering the answers, giving the group members time to formulate their own solutions.*)

Brian: Fine. Then what? Because he is still going to be in pain.

Billy: It's like, I understand the problem, but I'm slitting my wrists anyway! (*laughter*)

Therapist: Like, "I got the idea, but it still hurts" . . . sure. But then you say, "What can we do?" If he calls you up and you're free, you might want to meet with him. If not that moment, maybe the next night . . . whatever. It helps sometimes to know that you're going to meet someone, even if it's a day or two later.

Darin: We have forgotten the real value here of some guy being there for you when you need him.

Therapist: Excellent! That's really the point—his being there for you, irrespective of any actual advice he may give you. It will help offset the previous rejection . . . just hearing, being connected to a person. You may not be overjoyed when you get off the phone with him, but you'll probably be in a better place.

Joel: One reason we get into these positions is that we don't have anything else. We invest so heavily in these men—we make them so important.

Ethan: You've got to have something else going in your life, otherwise every male relationship can be devastating.

Therapist: The fact is, the homosexual male has a greater need for male bonding. Know that you need this. This is an area in which you have been deprived and if these needs are not met in good affirmative friendships, they'll get eroticized. If you don't develop and maintain a circle of male friendships, you're just setting yourself up for disaster.

Brian: I don't necessarily have sexual fantasies about these guys. It's more romantic illusion where I just lose myself.

Billy: Yeah, but eventually the frustration will lead to homosexual behavior.

Brian: Yeah, or at least intense preoccupation with sexual fantasies.

Therapist: Right.

Darin: Either way it's just demoralizing.

Therapist: Marco, you said in the beginning, "I don't know what I want from group. I just want to air, or express, an incident." But we pushed a bit and came up with a deeper understanding. We see there is this resistance about pushing ourselves onto other guys, not really knowing if we are becoming a nuisance, if we are expecting too much from them in relationships . . . wondering, how realistic are our expectations? We see how this manifests itself in group, where a lot of you guys will just hold back because you're not sure exactly what you deserve from other men.

Brian: From the guys here in the group, or from straight friends we have outside the group. I know I can make other men too important, too significant, where everything hinges on whether they like me or don't like me—or I just decide I'm going to reject them completely.

Billy: You know, growing up I always thought straight guys were phony. I didn't have many straight friends because I didn't think I could relate to them. When you hear a bunch of straight guys speak to each other, they say things like "Hey, bud," and "Hey, dude." (*laughs*) I used to think that sounded so stupid. But you know, now I really like being called that.

Therapist: That's exactly the ambivalence toward straight guys. It's the idea that they're not worth getting close to, they must be phony.

Billy: But I'm realizing that it's a real thing. It's not a phony thing.

Therapist: The way to protect yourself against not feeling a part of straight guys is to suspect they're phony.

Billy: Well, there *is* something phony-sounding about it. But what prompts it is real.

Therapist: Like any pet name, there's something contrived about it—but underneath it, there's a genuine feeling of brotherly affection.

These clinical vignettes show the continuing struggle for a more secure male gender-identity, which is necessary for these men to overcome the defensive detachment by which they distanced themselves from an emotionally absent or rejecting father or father figure. Exacerbating this detachment may have been an overly close relationship with the mother, producing a boy who identified with the feminine and who viewed masculine behavior as exciting but dangerous. As these boys reach puberty, their need to achieve male bonding may cause them to reach out emotionally and ultimately sexually to other men.

Although this is not the sole cause of male homosexuality, it plays a major role in the backgrounds of the men I have seen in my own clinical practice—men who have sought therapy as a means to alleviate their inner turmoil and start on the path of self-understanding, healthy assertion, nonerotic male friendships, and gratifying heterosexual relationships.

References

Aaron, W. (1972). *Straight*. New York: Bantam Books.

Abelin, E. (1971). The role of the father in the separation–individuation process. In *Separation–Individuation: Essays in Honor of Margaret S. Mahler*, ed. J. B. McDevitt and C. F. Settlage, pp. 229–252. New York: International Universities Press.

_____ (1975). Some further observations and comments on the earliest role of the father. *Journal of the American Psychoanalytic Association* 56:293–306.

Ackerly, J. R. (1968). *My Father and Myself*. New York: Poseidon Press.

Acosta, F. (1975). Etiology and treatment of homosexuality: a review. *Archives of Sexual Behavior* 4:9–29.

Adler, K. A. (1967). Life style, gender role, and the symptom of homosexuality. *Journal of Individual Psychology* 23:67–78.

Allen, C. (1962). *A Textbook of Psychosexual Disorders*. New York: Oxford University Press.

Anomaly (1948). *The Invert*. London: Bailliere, Tindall and Cox.

APA Panel (1978). The role of the father in the preoedipal years. *Journal of the American Psychoanalytic Association* 26:143–161.

Apfelberg, B., Sugar, C., and Pfeffer, A. (1944). A psychiatric study of 250 sex offenders. *American Journal of Psychiatry* 100:762–770.

Apperson, L., and McAdoo, G. (1968). Parental factors in the childhood of homosexuals. *Journal of Abnormal Psychology* 73:201–206.

Bach, G. (1946). Father-fantasies and father-typing in father-separated children. *Child Development* 17:63–80.

Badaines, J. (1976). Identification, imitation, and sex-role preference in father-present and father-absent Black and Chicano boys. *Journal of Psychology* 92:14–24.

Barnhouse, R. (1977). *Homosexuality: A Symbolic Confusion*. New York: Seabury Press.

Bartley, W. (1973). *Wittgenstein*. La Salle, IL: Open Court.

Bayer, R. V. (1981). *Homosexuality and American Psychiatry: The Politics of Diagnosis*. New York: Basic Books.

Beecher, W., and Beecher, M. (1972). *Beyond Success and Failure*. New York: Pocket Books.

Bell, A., and Weinberg, M. (1978). *Homosexualities: A Study of Diversity among Men and Women*. New York: Simon & Schuster.

Bell, A., Weinberg, M., and Hammersmith, S. (1981). *Sexual Preference: Its Development in Men and Women*. Bloomington, IN: Indiana University Press.

Bender, L., and Paster, S. (1941). Homosexual trends in children. *The American Journal of Orthopsychiatry* 11:730–743.

Bene, E. (1965). On the genesis of male homosexuality: an attempt at clarifying the role of the parents. *British Journal of Psychiatry* 3:803–813.

Bergler, E. (1951). *Neurotic Counterfeit-sex*. New York: Grune and Stratton.

_____ (1971). *Homosexuality: Disease or Way of Life?* New York: Collier Books.

Bernard, L. (1981). The multi-dimensional aspects of masculinity-feminity. *Journal of Personality and Social Psychology* 41:797–802.

Bernard, L., and Epstein, D. (1978). Androgyny scores of matched homosexual and heterosexual males. *Journal of Homosexuality* 4:169–178.

Bieber, I. (1968). Advising the homosexual. *Medical Aspects of Human Sexuality*, 2:34–39.

Bieber, I., Dain, H., Dince, P., Drellich, M., Grand, H., Gundlach, R., Kremer, M. Rifkin, A. Wilbur, C., and Bieber, T. (1962). *Homsexuality: A Psychoanalytic Study of Male Homosexuals*. New York: Basic Books.

Bieber, T. (1967). On treating male homosexuals. *Archives of General Psychiatry* 16:60–63.

Biller, H. (1968). A note on father-absence and masculine development in young lower-class negro and white boys. *Child Development* 39:1003–1006.

_____ (1969). Father absence, maternal encouragement, and sex-role development in kindergarten age boys. *Child Development* 40:539–546.

_____ (1974). Paternal deprivation, cognitive functioning, and the feminized classroom. In *Child Personality and Psychopathology*, ed. A. Davids. New York: Wiley.

Birk, L. (1974). Group psychotherapy for men who are homosexual. *Journal of Sex and Marital Therapy* 1:29–52.

Birke, L. (1981). Is homosexuality hormonally determined? *Journal of Homosexuality* 6:35–49.

Blos, P. (1986). Freud and the father commplex. *Psychoanalytic Study of the Child* 42:425–441. New Haven, CT: Yale University Press.

Bly, R. (1990). *Iron John: A Book About Men*. Reading, MA: Addison-Wesley.

Boyd, M. (1984). *Take Off the Masks*. Philadelphia, PA: New Society Publishers.

Braaten, L., and Darling, D. (1965). Overt and covert homosexual problems among male college students. *Genetic Psychology Monographs* 71:269–310.

Brim, O. (1958). Family structure and sex-role learning by children. *Sociometry* 21:1–16.

Bronfenbrenner, U. (1960). Freudian theories of identification and their derivatives. *Child Development* 31:15–40.

Bronstein, P. (1988). Father–child interaction: implications for gender-role socialization. In *Fatherhood Today – Men's Changing Role in the Family*, ed. P. Bronstein and C. Cowan. New York: Wiley.

Brown, J. H. (1963). Homosexuality as an adaptation in handling aggression. *Journal of the Louisiana State Medical Society* 115:304–311.

Buhrich, N., Armstrong, M., and McConaghy, N. (1982). Bisexual feelings and opposite sex behavior in male Malaysian medical students. *Archives of Sexual Behavior* 11:387–393.

Campbell, J. (1971). *The Hero with a Thousand Faces.* Princeton, NJ: Princeton University Press.

Capote, T. (1948). *Other Voices, Other Rooms*. New York: Random House.

Carrier, J. M. (1980). Homosexual behavior in cross-cultural perspective. In *Homosexual Behavior*, ed. J. Marmor, pp. 100–122. New York: Basic Books.

Chang, J., and Black, J. (1960). A study of identification in male homosexuals. *Journal of Consulting Psychology* 24:307–310.

Chapman, A. (1976). *Harry Stack Sullivan: His Life and His Work*. New York: G. P. Putnam's Sons.

Churchill, W. (1967). *Homosexual Behavior Among Males: A Cross-cultural and Cross-species Investigation*. New York: Hawthorne Books.

Colley, T. (1959). The nature and origins of psychological sexual identity. *Psychological Review* 66:165–177.

Comiskey, A. (1989). *Pursuing Sexual Wholeness: How Jesus Heals the Homosexual.* Lake Mary, FL: Creation House.

Cook, C. (1985). *Homosexuality: An Open Door?* Boise, ID: Pacific Press.

_____ (1990). National Courage Conference, Philadelphia, PA.

Cook, E. (1985). *Psychological Androgyne.* New York: Pergamon Press.

Dailey, D. (1979). Adjustment of heterosexual and homosexual couples in pairing relationships: an exploratory study. *Journal of Sex Research* 15:143–159.

Dallas, J. (1990). Passivity and recovery of male homosexuality. Exodus International Conference, July. San Antonio, Texas.

Dank, B. (1974). The homosexual. In *Sexual Deviance and Sexual Deviants*, ed. E. Goode and R. Troiden, pp. 174–210. New York: William Morrow and Co.

De Angelis, T. (1988). Moralism: full circle. *APA Monitor*, December, p. 5.

Dorner, G., Rohde, W., Stahl, F., Krell, L., and Masins, W. (1975). A neuroendocrine predisposition for homosexuality in men. *Archives of Sexual Behavior* 4:1–7.

Ehrhardt, A., and Meyer-Bahlburg, H. (1981). Effects of prenatal sex hormones on gender-related behavior. *Science* 211:1312–1318.

Eidelberg, L. (1956). Analysis of a case of male homosexuality. In *Perversions*, ed. S. Lorand and M. Balint. New York: Gramercy Books.

Eliade, M. (1975). *Rites and Symbols of Initiation: Mysteries of Birth and Rebirth.* New York: Harper and Row.

Ellis, A. (1956). Effectiveness of psychotherapy with individuals who have severe homosexual problems. *Journal of Consulting Psychology* 20:191–195.

Erickson, E. H. (1958). *Childhood and society.* New York: W. W. Norton.

Evans, R. (1969). Childhood parental relationships of homosexual men. *Journal of Consulting and Clinical Psychology* 33:129–135.

_____ (1971). Adjective check list scores of homosexual men. *Journal of Personality Assessment* 35:344–349.

Fagot, B. I. (1985a). Beyond the reinforcement principle: another step toward understanding sex-role development. *Developmental Psychology* 21:1097–1104.

_____ (1985b). Changes in thinking about early sex-role development. *Developmental Review* 5:83–98.

Fast, I. (1984). *Gender Identity: A Differentiation Model.* Hillsdale, NJ: Lawrence Erlbaum Associates.

Feldman, M. P., and McCulloch, M. J. (1971). *Homosexual Behavior.* Oxford: Pergamon Press.

Feldman, S. (1956). On homosexuality. In *Perversions,* ed. S. Lorand and M. Balint. New York: Gramercy Books.

Fenichel, O. (1945). *The Psychoanalytic Theory of Neurosis.* New York: W. W. Norton.

_____ (1946). On Acting. *Psychoanalytic Quarterly* 15:144–160.

_____ (1953). *The Collected Papers of Otto Fenichel: First Series.* New York: W. W. Norton.

_____ (1954). *The Collected Papers of Otto Fenichel: Second Series.* New York: W. W. Norton.

Ferenczi, S. (1914). The nosology of male homosexuality. In *Sex in Psychoanalysis.* New York: Basic Books, 1950.

Fisher, P. (1973). *The Gay Mystique.* New York: Stein and Day.

Ford, C. S., and Beach, F. A. (1951). *Patterns of Sexual Behavior.* New York: Harper Bros.

Franzoi, S. (1989). The beauty bind, by P. Calistro, *Los Angeles Times Magazine,* May 28, p. 34.

Freud, A. (1946). The ego and the mechanisms of defense. In *The Writings of Anna Freud,* vol. II. New York: International Universities Press, 1968.

_____ (1949). Some clinical remarks concerning the treatment of male homosexuality. *The International Journal of Psycho-Analysis* 30:195.

_____ (1951). Clinical observations on the treatment of manifest male homosexuality. *Psychoanalytic Quarterly* 20:337–338.

_____ (1952). Studies in passivity: notes on homosexuality. In _The Writings of Anna Freud: Indications for Child Analysis and Other Papers_, vol. 4. New York: International Universities Press, 1968.

Freud, S. (1905). Three essays on the theory of sexuality. _Standard Edition_ 7:123–246.

_____ (1910). Leonardo da Vinci and a memory of his childhood. _Standard Edition_ 11:59–138.

_____ (1911). Psychoanalytic notes upon an autobiographical account of a case of paranoia (dementia paranoia). _Standard Edition_ 12:1–84.

_____ (1914). On narcissism: an introduction. _Standard Edition_ 14:73–102.

_____ (1919). "A child is being beaten, a child is being beaten": a contribution to the study of the origins of sexual perversions. _Standard Edition_ 17:175–204.

_____ (1920). Beyond the pleasure principle. _Standard Edition_ 18:3–64.

_____ (1921). Group psychology. _Standard Edition_ 18:67–145.

_____ (1922). Some neurotic mechanisms in jealousy, paranoia and homosexuality. _Standard Edition_ 18:221–232.

_____ (1923). The infantile genital organization. _Standard Edition_ 19:41.

_____ (1929). _Civilization and Its Discontents. Standard Edition_ 21:57–146.

_____ (1937). Analysis, terminable and interminable. _Collected Papers_ 5:316–357.

_____ (1949). _An Outline of Psychoanalysis_. New York: W. W. Norton.

_____ (1951). Letter published in _American Journal of Psychiatry_ 107:786.

_____ (1959). _The Collected Papers of Sigmund Freud_, ed. E. Jones. New York: Basic Books.

_____ (1964–1966). _The Standard Edition of the Complete Psychological Works of Sigmund Freud_. London: Hogarth Press.

Freund, K. (1974). Male homosexuality: an analysis of the pattern. In *Understanding Homosexuality*, ed. J. Loraine. New York: American Elsevier.

Freund, K., and Blanchard, R. (1987). Feminine gender identity and physical aggressiveness in heterosexual and homosexual pedophiles. *Journal of Sex and Marital Therapy* 13:25–34.

Freund, K., Langevin, J., Satterberg, J., and Steiner, B. (1977). Extension of the gender identity scale for males. *Archives of Sexual Behavior* 6:507–519.

Freund, K., Nagler, E., Langevin, R., Zajac, A., and Steiner, B. (1974). Measuring feminine gender identity in homosexual males. *Archives of Sexual Behavior* 3:249–260.

Friedberg, R. (1975). Early recollections of homosexuals as indicators of their life styles. *Journal of Individual Psychology* 13:196–204.

Friedman, R. (1986). The psychoanalytic model of male homosexuality: a historical and theoretical critique. *Psychoanalytic Review* 73.

_____ (1988). *Male Homosexuality: A Contemporary Psychoanalytic Perspective.* New Haven, CT: Yale University Press.

Friedman, R., and Stern, L. (1980). Juvenile aggressivity and sissiness in homosexual and heterosexual males. *Journal of the American Academy of Psychoanalysis* 8:427–440.

Gadpaille, W. (1980). Cross-species and cross-cultural contributions to understanding homosexual activity. *Archives of General Psychiatry* 37:349–356.

Gershman, H. (1953). Considerations of some aspects of homosexuality. *American Journal of Psychoanalysis* 13:82–83.

_____ (1981). Homosexual marriages. *American Journal of Psychoanalysis* 41:149–159.

Gottlieb, D. (1977). *The Gay Tapes.* Briarcliff Manor, NY: Stein and Day Scarborough House.

Gough, H. (1966). A cross-cultural analysis of the CPI femininity scale. *Journal of Consulting Psychology* 30:136–141.

Gray, J. (1985). Growing yams and men. *Journal of Homosexuality* 11:55–68.

Green, R. (1975). Sexual identity: research strategies. *Archives of Sexual Behavior* 4:337–352.

_____ (1985). Gender identity in childhood and later sexual orientation: follow-up of 78 males. *American Journal of Psychiatry* 142:339–341.

_____ (1987). *The "Sissy Boy Syndrome" and the Development of Homosexuality.* New Haven, CT: Yale University Press.

Green, R., Roberts, C. W., Williams, K., Goodman, M., and Mixon, A. (1987). Specific cross-gender behavior in boyhood and later homosexual orientation. *British Journal of Psychiatry* 151:48.

Green, R., Williams, K., and Goodman, M. (1985). Masculine or feminine gender identity in boys: developmental differences between two diverse family groups. *Sex Roles* 12:1155–1162.

Greenacre, P. (1966). Problems of overidealization of the analyst and of analysis: their manifestations in the transference and countertransference relationship. In *Emotional Growth*, pp. 743–761. New York: International Universities Press.

Greenson, R. (1968). Disidentifying from mother: its special importance for the boy. *International Journal of Psycho-Analysis* 49:370–374.

Greenspan, S. (1982). "The second other": the role of the father in early personality formation and the dyadic–phallic phase of development. In *Father and Child*, ed. S. Cath. Boston: Little, Brown.

Gundlach, R. (1969). Childhood parental relationships and the establishment of gender roles of homosexuals. *Journal of Consulting and Clinical Psychology* 33:136–139.

Hadden, S. (1966). Group psychotherapy of male homosexuals. *Current Psychiatric Theories* 6:177–186.

Hamilton, D. (1939). Some aspects of homosexuality in relation to total personality development. *The Psychiatric Quarterly* 13:229–244.

Harry, J. (1978). Marriages between gay males. In *The Social Organization of Gay Males*, ed. J. Harry and V. Devall. New York: Praeger.

_____ (1982). *Gay Children Grown Up*. New York: Praeger.

Harvey, J. (1987). *The Homosexual Person: New Thinking in Pastoral Care*. San Fransisco, CA: Ignatius Press.

Hatterer, L. (1970). *Changing Homosexuality in the Males: Treatment for Men Troubled by Homosexuality*. New York: McGraw-Hill.

Hawkins, D., Herron, W. G., Gibson, W., Hoban, G., and Herron, M. J. (1988). Homosexual and heterosexual sex-role orientation on sex-role scales. *Perceptual and Motor Skills* 66:863–871.

Helper, M. (1955). Learning theory and the self-concept. *Journal of Abnormal Psychology* 51:184–194.

Herzog, J. (1980). Sleep disturbance and father hunger in 18–28-month-old boys: the Erlkonig syndrome. *Psychoanalytic Study of the Child* 35:219–233. New Haven, CT: Yale University Press.

_____ (1982). On father hunger: the father's role in the modulation of aggressive drive and fantasy. In *Father and Child*, ed. S. Cath. Boston, MA: Little, Brown.

Hetherington, E. (1965). A developmental study of the effects of sex of the dominant parent on sex-role preference, identification and initiation in children. *Journal of Personality and Social Psychology* 2:188–194.

_____ (1966). Effects of paternal absence on sex-typed behaviors in Negro and white preadolescent males. *Journal of Personality and Social Psychology* 4:87–91.

Higham, E. (1976). Case management of the gender incongruity syndrome in childhood and adolescence. *Journal of Homosexuality* 2:49–57.

Hirschfeld, M. (1914). *Die Homosexualitat des Mannes und das Weibes*. Berlin: Louis Marcus, 1920.

Hockenberry, S. L., and Billingham, R. C. (1987). Sexual orientation and boyhood gender conformity: development of the boyhood gender conformity scale (BGCS). *Archives of Sexual Behavior* 16:475–487.

Hodges, R. (1979). Deep fellowship: homosexuality and male

bonding in the life and fiction of Joseph Conrad. *Journal of Homosexuality* 4:379.

Hodgman, C. (1982). How to be a more effective father. *Medical Aspects of Human Sexuality* 3:32K-32FF.

Hoffman, M. (1968). *The Gay World: Male Homosexuality and the Social Creation of Evil.* New York: Basic Books.

Hooker, E. (1965). An empirical study of some relations between sexual patterns and gender identity in male homosexuals. In *Sex Research, New Developments,* ed. J. Money, pp. 24-52. New York: Holt, Rinehart and Winston.

Horner, A. J. (1984). *Object Relations and the Developing Ego in Therapy.* Northvale, NJ: Jason Aronson.

_____ (1989). *The Wish for Power and the Fear of Having It.* Northvale, NJ: Jason Aronson.

Horney, K. (1937). *The Neurotic Personality of Our Time.* New York: W. W. Norton.

_____ (1945). *Our Inner Conflicts: A Constructive Theory of Neurosis.* New York: W. W. Norton.

Hoult, T. (1984). Human sexuality in biological perspective. In *Bisexual and Homosexual Identities: Critical Theoretical Issues,* ed. J. DeCecco and M. Shiveley. New York: Haworth Press.

How to seduce a straight man (1989). *The Advocate,* March 28.

Ibrahim, A. (1976). The home situation and the homosexual. *The Journal of Sex Research* 12:263-282.

Indians (1973). Alexandria, VA: Time-Life Books.

Isay, R. (1987). Fathers and their homosexually inclined sons in childhood. *Psychoanalytic Study of the Child* 42:275-294. New Haven, CT: Yale University Press.

Jacobi, J. (1969). A case of homosexuality. *Journal of Analytical Psychology* 14:48-64.

Jonas, C. (1944). An objective approach to the personality and environment in homosexuality. *Psychiatric Quarterly* 18:626-641.

Jons, R., and Bates, J. (1978). Satisfaction in male homosexual couples. *Journal of Homosexuality* 3:217-224.

Jung, C. (1917). Archetypes of the collective unconscious. In *Collected Works*, vol. 7, trans. R. F. Hull, pp. 90–113. Princeton, NJ: Princeton University Press, 1968.

—— (1922). The love problems of the student. In *Collected Works*, vol. 10, trans. R. F. Hull, pp. 97–112. Princeton, NJ: Princeton University Press, 1968.

—— (1934). The development of personality. In *Collected Works*, vol. 17, trans. R. F. Hull, pp. 165–186. Princeton, NJ: Princeton University Press, 1968.

—— (1951). The syzygy: anima and animus. In *Collected Works*, vol. 9, trans. R. F. Hull, pp. ii–22. Princeton, NJ: Princeton University Press, 1968.

—— (1954). Concerning the archetype and the anima concept. In *Collected Works*, vol. 9, trans. R. F. Hull, pp. 54–74. Princeton, NJ: Princeton University Press, 1968.

Kaplan, E. (1967). Homosexuality: a search for the ego-ideal. *Archives of General Psychiatry* 16:355–358.

Kardiner, A. (1954). *The Flight from Masculinity in Sex and Morality*. New York: Bobbs-Merrill.

—— (1978). The social distress syndrome of our time. II. *Journal American Academy of Psychoanalysis* 6:215–230.

Karlen, A. (1971). *Sexuality and Homosexuality: A New View*. New York: W. W. Norton.

Kinsey, A.C., Pomeroy, W. B., Clyde, M. E., and Gebhard, P. H. (1953). *Sexual Behavior in the Human Female*. Philadelphia, PA: W. B. Saunders.

Kinsey, A. C., Pomeroy, W. B., and Martin, C. E. (1948). *Sexual Behavior in the Human Male*. Philadelphia, PA: W. B. Saunders.

Kohlberg, L. (1966). A cognitive-developmental analysis of children's sex-role concepts and attitudes. In *The Development of Sex Differences*, ed. E. Maccoby. Stanford, CA: Stanford University Press.

Kolb, L. (1963). Therapy of homosexuality. In *Current Psychiatric Therapies*, vol. 3, ed. Jules and Masserman, pp. 131–137. New York: Grune and Stratton.

Kolb, L., and Johnson, A. (1955). Etiology and therapy of overt homosexuality. *Psychoanalytic Quarterly* 24:506–515.

Krafft-Ebing, R. von. (1922). *Psychopathia sexualis.* Trans. R. J. Rebman. Brooklyn, New York: Physicians and Surgeons.

Kranz, S., ed. (1971). *The H persuasion: How Persons Have Permanently Changed from Homosexuality through the Study of Aesthetic Realism.* New York: Definition Press.

Kronemeyer, R. (1980). *Overcoming Homosexuality.* New York: Macmillan.

Kurdek, L. (1987). Sex-role self-schema and psychological adjustment in coupled homosexual and heterosexual men and women. *Sex Roles* 17:549–651.

Lamb, M. (1981). The development of the father–infant relationship. In *The Role of the Father in Child Development*, ed. M. Lamb. New York: Wiley.

Langevin. R. (1973). *Sexual Strands: Understanding and Treating Sexual Anomalies in Men.* Hillsdale, NJ: Lawrence Erlbaum Associates.

_____ , ed. (1985). *Erotic Preference, Gender Identity, and Aggression in Men: New Research Studies.* Hillsdale, NJ: Lawrence Erlbaum Associates.

LaTorre, R. (1979). *Sexual Identity.* Chicago, IL: Nelson-Hall.

Layland, W. (1981). In search of a loving father. *International Journal of Psycho-Analysis* 62:215–223.

Liddicoat, R. (1957). Homosexuality. *British Medical Journal* 9:1110–1111.

Litin, E., Griffin, M., and Johnson, A. (1956). Parental influences in unusual social behaviors in children. *Psychoanalytic Quarterly* 25:37–55.

Loewald, H. (1951). Ego and reality. *International Journal of Psycho-Analysis* 41:16–33.

Lunneborg, P. (1972). Dimensionality of MF. *Journal of Clinical Psychology* 28:314–317.

Lynn, D. (1961). Sex differences in identification development. *Sociometry* 24:373–383.

Lynn, D., and Sawrey, W. (1959). The effects of father-absence on Norwegian boys and girls. *Journal of Abnormal and Social Psychology* 59:258–262.

MacCoby, E., ed. (1966). *The Development of Sex Differences.* Stanford, CA: Stanford University Press.

MacCoby, E., and Jacklin, C. (1974). *The Psychiatry of Sex Differences.* Stanford, CA: Stanford University Press.

Mahler, M. (1975). Reply to Stoller's "Healthy parental influences on the earliest development of masculinity in baby boys." *Psychoanalytic Forum* 5:232–262.

Mahler, M., and Gosliner, R. (1955). On symbiotic child psychosis: genetic, dynamic and restitutive aspects. *Psychoanalytic Study of the Child* 10:195–212. New York: International Universities Press.

Mahler, M., Pine, F., and Bergman, A. (1975). *The Psychological Birth of the Human Infant.* New York: Basic Books.

Mallen, C. (1987). Sex-role stereotypes, gender identity and parental relationships in male homosexuals and heterosexuals. *Journal of Homosexuality* 9:55.

Malyon, A. (1982). Psychotherapeutic implications of internalized homophobia in gay men. *Journal of Homosexuality* 7:59–69.

Manosevitz, M. (1971). Item analysis of the M.M.P.I. scale using homosexual and heterosexual males. *Journal of Consulting and Clinical Psychology* 36:395–399.

Marmor, J. (1965). *Sexual Inversion.* New York: Basic Books.

———, ed. (1980). *Homosexual Behavior: A Modern Reappraisal.* New York: Basic Books.

Masters, W., and Johnson, V. (1979). *Homosexuality in Perspective.* Boston, MA: Little, Brown.

Masters, W., Johnson, V., and Kolodny, R. (1985). *Human Sexuality,* 2nd ed. Boston, MA: Little, Brown.

Mayerson, P., and Lief, H. (1965). Psychotherapy of homosexuals: a follow-up study. In *Sexual Inversion: The Multiple Roots of Homosexuality,* ed. J. Marmor. New York: Basic Books.

McConaghy, N., and Armstrong, M. (1983). Sexual orientation

and consistency of sexual identity. *Archives of Sexual Behavior* 12:317–327.

McConaghy, N., Armstrong, M., Birrel, P., and Buhrich, N. (1979). The incidence of bisexual feelings and opposite sex behavior in medical students. *Journal of Nervous and Mental Disease* 167:685–688.

McCord, J., McCord, W., and Thurber, E. (1962). Some effects of parental absence on male children. *Journal of Abnormal and Social Psychology* 64:361–369.

McDonald, G. (1982). Individual differences in the coming-out process for gay men. *Journal of Homosexuality* 8:47–59.

McDonald, G., and Moore, R. (1978). Sex-role self-concepts of homosexual men and their attitude toward both women and male homosexuality. *Journal of Homosexuality* 4:3–13.

McWhirter, D., and Mattison, A. (1984). *The Male Couple: How Relationships Develop*. Englewood Cliffs, NJ: Prentice-Hall.

Meyer-Bahlburg, H. (1977). Sex hormones and male homosexuality in comparative perspective. *Archives of Sexual Behavior* 6:297–325.

Milic, J., and Crowne, D. (1986). Recalled parent-child relations and need for approval of homosexual and heterosexual men. *Archives of Sexual Behavior* 15:239–246.

Miller, P. R. (1958). The effeminate, passive, obligatory homosexual. *AMA Archives of Neurology and Psychiatry* 80:612–618.

Mintz, E. (1966). Overt male homosexuals in combined group and individual treatment. *Journal of Consulting Psychology* 30:193–198.

Moberly, E. (1983). *Homosexuality: A New Christian Ethic*. Greenwood, SC: Attic Press.

Money, J. (1965). *Sex Research: New Developments*. New York: Holt, Rinehart and Winston.

——— (1980). *Love and Love Sickness: The Science of Sex, Gender Difference, and Pair-Bonding*. Baltimore, MD: John Hopkins University Press.

_____ (1986). *Venuses Penuses: Sexology, Sexosophy and Exigency Theory.* Buffalo, NY: Prometheus Books.

_____ (1987). Sin, sickness or status? Homosexual gender identity and psycho-neuroendocrinology. *American Psychologist* 42:384–399.

_____ (1988). *Gay, Straight and In Between: The Sexology of Erotic Orientation.* New York: Oxford University Press.

Money, J., and Ehrhardt, A. (1972). *Man and Woman, Boy and Girl.* Baltimore, MD: Johns Hopkins University Press.

Money, J., and Russo, A. (1979). Homosexual outcome of discordant gender identity/role in childhood: longitudinal follow-up. *Journal of Pediatric Psychology* 4:29–41.

Monroe, R. R., and Enelow, M. L. (1960). The therapeutic motivation in male homosexuality. *American Journal of Psychotherapy* 14:474–490.

Morin, S. (1977). Heterosexual bias in psychological research on lesbianism and male homosexuality. *American Psychologist* 32:629–637.

Mowrer, O. (1950). *Learning Theory and Personality Dynamics.* New York: Ronald Press.

Mussen, P., and Distler, L. (1959). Masculinity, identification and father–son relationships. *Journal of Abnormal Social Psychology* 59:350–356.

_____ (1960). Child-rearing antecedents of masculine identification in kindergarten boys. *Child Development* 31:89–100.

Mussen, P., and Rutherford, E. (1963). Parent–child relations and parental personality in relation to young children's sex-role preferences. *Child Development* 34:589–607.

Myers, W. (1989). A transference resistance in male patients with inhibition of urination in public places. *Psychoanalytic Quarterly* 58:245–250.

Nash, J., and Hayes, T. (1965). The parental relationships of male homosexuals: some theoretical issues and a pilot study. *Australian Journal of Psychology* 17:35–43.

Nunberg, H. (1938). Homosexuality, magic and aggression. *International Journal of Psycho-Analysis* 14:1–16.

O'Connor, P. (1964). Aetiological factors in homosexuality as seen in Royal Air Force practice. *British Journal of Psychiatry* 110:38–39.

Ovesey, L. (1969). *Homosexuality and Pseudohomosexuality.* New York: Science House.

Ovesey, L., and Woods, S., (1980). Pseudohomosexuality and homosexuality in men: psychodynamics as a guide to treatment. In *Homosexual Behavior: A Modern Reappraisal,* ed. J. Marmor. New York: Basic Books.

Parsons, T. (1954). The father symbol: an appraisal in the light of psychoanalytic and sociological theory. In *Symbols and Values,* ed. L. Bryson, L. Finkelstein, R. MacIver, and R. McKeon. New York: Harper and Row.

_____ (1955). Family structure and socialization of the child. In *Family, Socialization and Interaction Process,* ed. T. Parsons and R. Bales. Glencoe, IL: Free Press.

Pattison, E. M., and Pattison, M. L. (1980). "Ex-gays": religiously mediated change in homosexuals. *American Journal of Psychiatry* 137:1553–1562.

Payne, D., and Mussen, P. (1956). Parent–child relations and father identification among adolescent boys. *Journal of Abnormal and Social Psychology* 52:358–362.

Payne, L. (1981). *The Broken Image: Restoring Personal Wholeness Through Healing Prayer.* Westchester, IL: Crossway Books.

_____ (1984). *The Healing of the Homosexual.* Westchester, IL: Crossway Books.

_____ (1985). *Crisis in Masculinity.* Westchester, IL: Crossway Books.

Peplau, L. (1982). Research on homosexual couples: an overview. *Journal of Homosexuality* 8:3–7.

Perloff, W. (1965). Hormones and homosexuality. In *Sexual Inversion,* ed. J. Marmor. New York: Basic Books.

Pillard, R., and Weinrich, J. (1986). Evidence of familial nature of male homosexuality. *Archives of General Psychiatry* 43:808–812.

Poe, J. S. (1952). The successful treatment of a 45-year-old passive homosexual based upon an adaptational view of homosexual behavior. *Psychoanalytic Review* 39:23.

Pollak, M. (1985). Male homosexuality. In *Western Sexuality: Practice and Precept in Past and Present Times*, ed. P. Aries and A. Bejin, pp. 40–61. New York: Basil Blackwell.

Ponse, B. (1978). *Identities in the Lesbian World: The Social Construction of Self.* Westport, CT: Greenwood Press.

Rado, S. (1949). An adaptational view of sexual behavior. In *Psychoanalysis of Behavior: Collected Papers.* New York: Grune and Stratton, 1956.

Rechy, J. (1963). *City of Night.* New York: Grove Press.

Reisman, J. (1990). *Images of Childhood: Crimes of Violence in Playboy, Penthouse and Hustler.* Lafayette, LA: Huntington House.

Rekers, G. (1987). *The Formation of a Homosexual Orientation.* Paper presented at the Free Congress Foundation and the North American Social Science Network Conference, Hope and Homosexuality.

Richardson, D. (1984). The dilemma of essentiality in homosexual theory. *Journal of Homosexuality* 9:79–90.

——— (1987). Recent challenges to traditional assumptions about homosexuality: some implications for practice. *Journal of Homosexuality* 13:1–11.

Robertson, G. (1972). Parent–child relationships and homosexuality. *British Journal of Psychiatry* 121:525–528.

Rosen, I. (1988). Psycho-analysis and homosexuality: a critical appraisal of helpful attitudes. In *Hope for Homosexuals*, ed. P. Fagan, pp. 28–45. Washington, DC: Free Congress Research and Education Foundation.

Ross, J. (1977). Toward fatherhood: the epigenesis of paternal identity during a boy's first decade. *International Review of Psycho-Analysis* 4:327–347.

——— (1979). Fathering: a review of some psychoanalytic contributions on paternity. *International Journal of Psycho-Analysis* 60:317–320.

Ross, M., and Mendelsohn, F. (1958). Homosexuality in College. *AMA Archives of Neurological Psychiatry* 80:253–263.

Ross, M. W., Rogers, L. J., and McCulloch, H. (1978). Stigma, sex and society: a new look at gender differentiation and sexual variation. *Journal of Homosexuality* 3:315–329.

Ross, N. (1960). Rivalry with the product. *Journal of the American Psychoanalytic Association* 8:450–463.

Rubenstein, L. H. (1958). Psychotherapeutic aspects of male homosexuality. *British Journal of Medical Psychology* 31:14–18.

Saghir, M., and Robins, E. (1973). *Male and Female Homosexuality: A Comprehensive Investigation.* Baltimore, MD: Williams and Wilkins.

Sanders, R., Bain, J., and Langevin, R. (1985). Feminine gender identity in men: how common is it? In *Erotic Preference, Gender Identity, and Aggression in Men: New Research Studies,* ed. R. Langevin. Hillsdale, NJ: Lawrence Erlbaum Associates.

Sanford, J., and Lough, G. (1988). *What Men Are Like.* Mahwah, NY: Paulist Press.

Santrock, J. W. (1970). Paternal absence, sex-typing and identification. *Developmental Psychology* 2:264–272.

Schechter, D. (1978). Attachment, detachment and psychoanalytic therapy. In *Interpersonal Psychoanalysis,* ed. E. Wittenberg. New York: Gardner Press.

Schoefield M. (1965). *Sociological Aspects of Homosexuality: A Comparative Study of Three Types of Homosexuals.* London: Longmans, Green and Co.

Schwartz, M. F., and Masters, W. H. (1984). The Masters and Johnson treatment program for dissatisfied homosexual men. *American Journal of Psychiatry* 141:173–181.

Sears, R. (1953). Child-rearing factors related to the playing of sex-typed roles. *American Psychologist* 8:431.

———— (1965). Development of gender role. In *Sex and Behavior,* ed. F. A. Beach. New York: Wiley.

Sears, R., McCabe, E., and Levin, H. (1957). *Patterns of Child Rearing.* Evanston, IL: Rowe, Peterson and Co.

Shearer, M. (1966). Homosexuality and the pediatrician: early recognition and preventation counseling. *Clinical Pediatrics* 5:514–518.

Siegelman, M. (1974). Parental background of male homosexuals and heterosexuals. *Archives of Sexual Behavior* 3:3–17.

Silberner, J.(1984). Hormone markers for homosexuality. *Science News* 126:198–199.

Silverstein, C., and White, E. (1977). *The Joy of Gay Sex.* New York: Crown.

Snortum, J., Marshall, J., Gillespie, J., Mosberg, L., and McLaughlin, J. (1969). Family dynamics and homosexuality. *Psychological Reports* 24:763–770.

Socarides, C. (1968a). A provisional theory of etiology in the male homosexual: a case of pre-oedipal origin. *International Journal of Psychiatry* 49:27–37.

———— (1968b). *The Overt Homosexual.* New York: Grune and Stratton.

———— (1969). The desire for sexual transformation: a psychiatric evaluation of transsexualism. *American Journal of Psychiatry* 125:10.

———— (1973). Sexual perversion and the fear of engulfment. *International Journal of Psycho-Analytic Psychotherapy* 2:432–448.

———— (1976). Homosexuality is not just an alternative lifestyle. In *Male and Female: Christian Approaches to Sexuality,* ed. R. Barnhouse and J. Holmes, p. 145. New York: Seabury Press.

———— (1978). *Homosexuality.* New York: Jason Aronson.

Stein, T., and Cohen, C. (1986). *Contemporary Perspectives on Psychotherapy with Lesbians and Gay Men.* New York: Plenum.

Stekel, W. (1930). Is homosexuality curable? *Psychology Review* 17:443–451.

Stephan, W. G. (1973). Parental relationships and early social experiences of activist male homosexuals and male heterosexuals. *Journal of Abnormal Psychology* 82:506–513.

Stoller, R. (1965). The sense of maleness. *Psychoanalytic Quarterly* 34:207–218.

———— (1968). *Sex and Gender*. New York: Science House.

———— (1975). Healthy parental influences on the earliest development of masculinity in baby boys. *Psychoanalytic Forum* 5:232–262.

———— (1978). Boyhood gender aberrations: treatment issues. *Journal of the American Psychoanalytic Association* 26:541–558.

———— (1979). A contribution to the study of gender identity: follow-up interview. *International Journal of Psycho-Analysis* 60:433–441.

———— (1985). *Presentations of Gender*. New Haven, CT: Yale University Press.

Stoller, R., and Herdt, G. (1981). The development of masculinity: a cross-cultural contribution. *Journal of the American Psychology Association* 30:29–59.

———— (1985). Theories of origins of male homosexuality: a cross-cultural look. *Archives of General Psychiatry* 42:399–404.

Sullivan, H. S. (1953). *Conceptions of Modern Psychiatry*. New York: W. W. Norton.

Suppe, F. (1981). The Bell and Weinberg study: future priorities for research on homosexuality. *Journal of Homosexuality* 6:69–97.

Terman, L., and Miles, C. (1936). *Sex and Personality*. New York: Russell and Russell.

Thompson, C. (1947). Changing concepts of homosexuality in psychoanalysis. *Psychiatry* 10:183–189.

Thompson, N., Schwartz, D., McCandless, B., and Edwards, D. (1973). Parent–child relationships and sexual identity in male and female homosexuals and heterosexuals. *Journal of Consulting and Clinical Psychiatry* 41:120–127.

Tiger, L. (1969). *Men in Groups*. New York: Random House.

Timmons, S. (1990). *The Trouble with Harry Hay*. Boston, MA: Alyson.

Townes, B., Ferguson, W., and Gillam, S. (1976). Differences in psychological sex adjustment and familial influences among homosexual and non-homosexual populations. *Journal of Homosexuality* 1:261.

Tripp, C. (1975). *The Homosexual Matrix.* New York: McGraw-Hill.

Tuber, S., and Coates, S. (1989). Indices of psychopathology in the Rorschachs of boys with severe gender identity disorder: a comparison with normal control subjects. *Journal of Personality Assessment* 53:100–112.

Tyson, P. (1985). The role of the father in gender identity, urethral erotism and phallic narcissism. In *Father and Child: Developmental and Clinical Perspectives,* ed. S. Cath, pp. 175–187. Boston: Little, Brown.

——— (1986). Male gender identity: early developmental roots. *Psychoanalytic Review* 73:1–21.

van den Aardweg, G. (1985). *Homosexuality and Hope: A Psychologist Talks about Treatment and Change.* Ann Arbor, MI: Servant Books.

——— (1986). *On the Origins and Treatment of Homosexuality: A Psychoanalytic Reinterpretation.* Westport, CT: Praeger.

Van Wyk, F., and Geist, C. (1984). Psychosocial development of heterosexual, bisexual and homosexual behavior. *Archives of Sexual Behavior* 13:505–544.

Wallace, L. (1969). Psychotherapy of a male homosexual. *Psychoanalytic Review* 56:346–364.

Warren, C. (1974). *Identity and Community in the Gay World.* New York: Wiley & Sons.

Weinberg, G. (1972). *Society and the Healthy Homosexual.* New York: St. Martin's Press.

Weinberg, M., and Williams C. (1974). *Male Homosexuals: Their Problems and Adaptations.* New York: Oxford University Press.

Weinrich, J. (1985). Transsexuals, homosexuals, and sissy boys: on the mathematics of follow-up studies. *Journal of Sex Research* 21:322–335.

Weiss, F. (1963). *The meaning of homosexual trends in therapy: a roundtable discussion.* Irving Bieber. Paper presented before the Association for the Advancement of Psychoanalysis, New York, January.

Werner, D. (1979). A cross-cultural perspective on theory and research on male homosexuality. *Journal of Homosexuality* 4:345–361.

West, D. J. (1959). Parental figures in the genesis of male homosexuality. *International Journal of Social Psychiatry* 5:85–97.

_____ (1967). *Homosexuality.* Chicago, IL: Aldine.

_____ (1977). *Homosexuality Re-examined.* Minneapolis, MN: University of Minnesota Press.

Westwood, G. A. (1960). *A Minority Report on the Life of the Male Homosexual in Great Britain.* London: Longmans, Green & Co.

Whitam, F. L. (1977). Childhood indicators of male homosexuality. *Archives of Sexual Behavior* 6:89–96.

_____ (1980). The prehomosexual male child in three societies: the United States, Guatemala and Brazil. *Archives of Sexual Behavior* 9:87–99.

_____ (1983). Culturally invariable properties of male homosexuality: tentative conclusions from cross-cultural research. *Archives of Sexual Behavior* 12:207.

Whitam, F. L., and Zent, M. (1984). A cross-cultural assessment of early cross-gender behavior and familial factors in male homosexuality. *Archives of Sexual Behavior* 13:427–439.

Whitener, R., and Nikelly, A. (1962). Sexual deviation in college students. *American Journal of Orthopsychiatry* 34:486–492, 1964.

Winnicott, D. (1965). *The Maturational Processes and the Facilitating Environment.* New York: International Universities Press.

Wolpe, J. (1969). *The Practice of Behavior Therapy.* New York: Pergamon Press.

Yablonsky, L. (1982). *Fathers and Sons.* New York: Simon and Schuster.

Zucker, K., Doering, R., Bradley, S., and Finegan, J. (1982). Sex-typed play in gender-disturbed children: a comparison to sibling and psychiatric controls. *Archives of Sexual Behavior* 11.

Zuger, B. (1970). The role of familial factors in persistent effeminate behavior in boys. *American Journal of Psychiatry* 126:151–154.

———— (1978). Effeminate behavior present in boys from childhood: ten additional years of follow-up. *Comprehensive Psychiatry* 19:363–369.

———— (1984). Early effeminate behavior in boys: outcome and significance for homosexuality. *The Journal of Nervous and Mental Disease* 172:90–97.

———— (1987). Childhood cross-gender behavior and adult homosexuality. *Archives of Sexual Behavior* 16:85–87.

———— (1988). Is early effeminate behavior in boys early homosexuality? *Comprehensive Psychiatry* 29:509–519.

Index